WORD 2000

NO EXPERIENCE REQUIRED

WORD 2000

NO EXPERIENCE REQUIRED™

Guy Hart-Davis

SYBEX®

San Francisco • Paris • Düsseldorf • Soest • London

Associate Publisher: Amy Romanoff
Contracts and Licensing Manager: Kristine O'Callaghan
Acquisitions & Developmental Editor: Sherry Bonelli
Editor: Ed Copony
Technical Editor: Maryann Brown
Book Designer: Patrick Dintino, Catalin Dulfu, Maureen Forys
Graphic Illustrator: Tony Jonick
Electronic Publishing Specialist: Tony Jonick
Production Coordinator: Catherine Morris
Indexer: Matthew Spence
Cover Designer: Design Site
Cover Illustrator/Photographer: Jack D. Myers

Library of Congress Card Number: 99-60019
ISBN: 0-7821-2400-3
Manufactured in the United States of America

10 9 8 7 6 5 4 3 2 1

This book is dedicated to my parents.

Acknowledgments

I'd like to thank the following people for their help and support with this book: Amy Romanoff and Sherry Bonelli for getting the project going; Rhonda Holmes for revising a number of the chapters; Ed Copony for speedy and patient editing; Maryann Brown for reviewing the manuscript for technical accuracy; Tony Jonick for typesetting the book and fixing color problems with some figures; Catherine Morris for coordinating the production of the book; and Matthew Spence for creating the index.

Finally, thanks go to Robert Calvert for many great lyrics and to Ian Kilmister for unadulterated noise—neither of which I should have been listening to while working on this book. . .

Contents at a Glance

Table of Contents

Introduction

Word 2000 is the latest version of Microsoft's immensely popular word processing application. Word 2000 builds on the success of previous versions of Word and adds many new features, including the ability to save Word documents in HTML format as Web pages on Web servers, a Wizard for creating your own Web site, and exceptionally tight integration with the other Office applications.

What Will You Learn from This Book?

This book aims to teach you everything you need to know to use Word productively in your home or office.

Word has many features that you will not only never use but that you will never even need to know about. This book discusses only the features that you're likely to use the most. If you need to learn to use an esoteric feature that Word offers but that this book does not discuss, the knowledge you gain from this book will stand you in good stead for either puzzling out what each command and feature does or for determinedly ransacking the Help file in your quest for knowledge.

How Much Do You Need to Know Already?

In order to be concise, this book assumes that you know the basics of the Windows 95, Windows 98, or Windows NT 4 graphical user interface:

- How to use Windows and navigate its interface enough to start Word with either the keyboard or the mouse.

- How to use Windows applications—how to start them and how to exit them; how to use the menus and dialog boxes to make choices; and how to get help whenever you need it by pressing the F1 key or clicking any convenient Help button.

- That you click toggle buttons (such as those for boldface and italic) to select them, and that they'll appear to be pushed in when they're selected.

- That you *select* a check box by clicking in it (or clicking the text that accompanies it) to place a check mark in it, and that you *clear* a check box by clicking in it (or clicking its text) to remove the check mark.

- That you normally click the left (or primary) mouse button to choose an item or to perform an action, and that, in the Windows interface, you click the right (or secondary) mouse button to produce a *context menu* (sometimes called a *shortcut menu*) of commands related to that item.

- The basics of using the Windows Explorer or Windows NT Explorer for file management, and how to manage files within Windows' common dialog boxes by using the commands on the context menu

How to Use This Book

This book is set up so that you can go straight to the topic you want and instantly learn what you need to know to get a specific task done. The book is divided into 18 skills, each of which teaches you a set of techniques for working with Word documents. If you complete all 18 skills in the book, you'll have a good command of Word and will be able to create most any type of document commonly used in an office setting. For the ambitious, there are also two full bonus skills on advanced topics and several shorter sections on advanced features; you can download these skills and sections from the Sybex Web site as described in the next section.

Here's how the skills are arranged:

- Skill 1 shows you the basics of working with Word: What you'll see in the Word window; how to use the menus and toolbars; how to arrange the elements of the Word window to suit you; how to use the different views that Word provides; and how to get help.

- Skill 2 covers how to create simple documents in Word. In this skill, you'll learn how to create a document; how to enter text and symbols in it; and how to save the document. You'll also learn how to save Word documents in different formats (for example, for use with other word processing applications) and how to open documents created in other formats in Word.

- Skill 3 discusses how to print a document, both simply—printing the whole document at once—and with the options that Word offers. It also covers how to print envelopes and labels from Word.

- Skill 4 shows you how to format a document using some of the many different kinds of formatting that Word provides: character formatting, paragraph formatting, and language formatting. It also shows you how to use Word's page-setup options to set margins, paper size, and paper orientation; and how to add borders and shading to elements in your documents.

- Skill 5 starts by taking you deeper into Word's formatting, covering styles (collections of formatting that you can apply all at once to a word or a paragraph) and themes (color schemes for the elements in a document). From there, it discusses how to use sections to format separate parts of your documents differently; how to use automatic features such as bullets and numbering, AutoCorrect, and AutoFormat; and finally, how to add footnotes and endnotes to a document.

- Skill 6 discusses how to use Word's Find and Replace feature to maximum effect. Find and Replace is an exceptionally powerful tool, and this skill shows you how to tap as much of that power as you need.

- Skill 7 concentrates on using the tools that Word provides for improving your documents. You'll learn how to use the spell and grammar checker and the thesaurus.

- Skill 8 covers four tools that Word offers for automating information in your documents. AutoText provides a quick way of entering text and graphics; automatic captioning keeps track of your figures and tables; bookmarks let you electronically mark and move to locations in your documents; and fields enable you to insert and easily update variable information.

- Skill 9 shows you how to work with tables to lay out information in your documents in rows and columns. Beyond covering the key aspects of creating tables and arranging information in them, this skill shows you how to sort information.

- Skill 10 discusses how to use graphical elements and text boxes to enhance your documents. You'll learn how to insert everything from a picture to a chart, to import pictures into the Microsoft Clip Gallery, and to work with the drawing tools built into Word.

- Skill 11 discusses how to create headers and footers, text (and graphics if you want) that repeats at the top or bottom of all pages or selected pages in a document. It also covers how to insert watermarks in your documents by using the header and footer area.

- Skill 12 shows you how to use Word's tools for creating Web sites and Web pages—some of the most exciting improvements in this version of Word.

- Skill 13 covers all you need to know to create mail-merge documents effectively.

- Skill 14 discusses how to use Word's outlining tools, which are vital to working quickly and efficiently in long documents. It also covers master documents and subdocuments, which you can use to handle multi-part projects without creating unmanageably large files.

- Skill 15 shows you how to create key parts of complex documents: newspaper-style columns for newsletters and magazines; tables of contents and tables of figures for reports or books; tables of authorities for legal and scholarly documents; and indexes for projects of any size.

- Skill 16 covers how to customize Word so that you can work in it most efficiently. This skill shows you how to customize the menus, toolbars, context menus, and keyboard combinations to speed up your work. It also explains the many options that Word provides, and offers advice on which settings to choose.

- Skill 17 discusses some features that Word supports for integrating Word with other applications. Automation (formerly known as Object Linking and Embedding, or OLE) lets you link or embed information from another application in a Word document, while Office binders can integrate files from different applications into one seamless project.

- Skill 18 covers Word's workgroup features: Adding comments to a document; using Track Changes (formerly known as revision-marking); saving multiple versions of a document in the same file; locking and protecting documents against changes; tools for online collaboration on a document; and sending Word documents via e-mail right from the Word window.

- The Appendix shows you how to install Word on your computer, how to add and remove features as needed, and how to repair your installation of Word if files get corrupted.

NOTE NOTE NOTE NOTE NOTE NOTE NOTE NOTE NOTE NOTE NOTE NOTE NOTE NOTE NOTE

Notes, Tips, and Warnings, each identified clearly with an icon and the appropriate keyword, give you extra guidance on specific topics.

Where Are the Bonus Skills?

If you looked at the back cover of the book before you bought it, or if you read the previous section, you probably noticed that two bonus skills and some advanced sections are available for this book online.

These bonus skills are on Sybex's Web site. Point your Web browser at `http://www.sybex.com` to reach the Sybex home page, then click the Catalog button to get to the catalog page. Then enter the four-digit book number for this book—2400—in the Search box and click the Search button. That will get you to the main Web page for this book. From there, click the Downloads button. You'll see a legal notice; read this and click the Accept button if you can handle it. From there, you'll be able to download the two bonus skills in Adobe Acrobat Portable Document Format (PDF). To read them, you'll need either a Web browser that has an Acrobat reader built in or a plug-in component for your existing browser (available at `http://www.adobe.com`).

So that's where the bonus skills are. Now, *what* are they?

- The first bonus skill covers macros—sequences of commands that you can either record by using Word's Macro Recorder or create by hand in the Visual Basic Editor. The skill discusses what macros are, why you'll want to use them, and how to get started with them. It shows you how to work in the Visual Basic Editor, the application that Word uses for creating and editing macros. There are a couple of detailed examples that you may want to try.

- The second bonus skill covers creating forms for gathering and processing information. By building forms with form fields such as text boxes, drop-down lists, and check boxes, you can swiftly gather information from the user. Better yet, you can process it electronically. A quick note: You can use macros in forms, so if you download this bonus skill, you may want to download the first bonus skill as well.

Conventions Used in This Book

This book uses a number of conventions to convey more information clearly in fewer pages:

- ➤ designates choosing a command from a menu. For example, choose File ➤ Open means that you should pull down the File menu and choose the Open command from it.

- \+ signs indicate key combinations. For example, *press Ctrl+Shift+F9* means that you hold down the Ctrl and Shift keys, then press the F9 key. Some of these keyboard combinations are visually confusing, so you may need to read them carefully; for example, Ctrl++ means that you hold down Ctrl and press the + key (i.e., hold down the Ctrl key and the Shift key together and press the = key). I've spelled out some of the most confusing combinations, such as Ctrl+– (Ctrl+minus).

- ↑, ↓, ←, and → represent the arrow keys that should appear in some form on your keyboard. The important thing to note is that ← is *not* the Backspace key (which on many keyboards bears a similar arrow). The Backspace key is represented by "Backspace" or "the Backspace key."

- **Boldface** indicates items that you may want to type in letter for letter.

- *Italics* indicate either new terms being introduced or variable information (such as a drive letter that will vary from computer to computer and that you'll need to establish on your own).

Word 2000 Basics

- → **Starting Word**
- → **Setting up your screen**
- → **Using menus and toolbars**
- → **Displaying and positioning toolbars**
- → **Viewing documents**
- → **Getting Help**
- → **Exiting Word**

In this skill, you'll get started with Word. You'll start by setting up the screen so you're working comfortably and can see what you need to see. I'll discuss how to use the menus and the toolbars, and how to choose which toolbars to display on screen and how to change their shape and location. You'll start a basic document so you have something to look at. Then I'll discuss the various views that Word provides for looking at your documents and when you may want to use each of these views. After that, we'll look at how you get Help when using Word. Finally, you'll exit Word.

If you haven't installed Word yet, turn to the Appendix for instructions on installing it smoothly and swiftly.

Starting Word

You can start Word in any of several ways:

- If you have the Office Shortcut Bar displayed, click the Word button on it.

- Choose Start ➤ Programs ➤ Microsoft Word.
- If you have a shortcut to Word on the Windows Desktop, click or double-click it (depending on whether you're using the Web-style Desktop or the "Windows Classic" style).
- If you have a shortcut to Word on the Quick Launch toolbar, click it.

TIP TIP TIP TIP TIP TIP TIP TIP TIP TIP TIP TIP TIP TIP TIP TIP TIP TIP TIP TIP TIP TIP TIP TIP TIP

To create a shortcut to Word on the Desktop or the Quick Launch toolbar, choose Start ➤ Programs to display the Programs submenu. Then hold down the Ctrl key, click the Microsoft Word menu item, and drag it to the Desktop or to a position on the Quick Launch toolbar, as appropriate. Because you can keep the Quick Launch toolbar available all the time you're working in Windows, this is the easiest way to launch Word regularly.

Setting Up Your Screen

Before we get into working with documents, let's quickly look at how Word appears on the screen (see Figure 1.1).

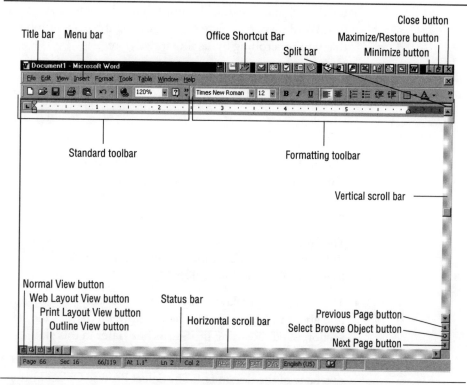

FIGURE 1.1: The elements of the Word window. The Office Shortcut Bar appears only if you have Microsoft Office installed and running on your computer.

I'll discuss most of these features in the rest of this skill. The following list discusses the features that will be familiar if you've used other Windows applications and points to the discussion of the topics treated in more depth later in this skill.

- The title bar shows the name of the document in the window, followed by *Microsoft Word*.

- The menu bar provides access to the commands on the menus.

- The toolbars provide access to assorted commands. We'll look at how to work with them a little later in this skill.

- You use the Maximize/Restore, Minimize, and Close buttons to resize or close the Word window. We'll look at working with windows next.

- Use the vertical scroll bar to move backward and forward in your document. You can click the up-arrow button and down-arrow button to scroll one line at a time. Alternatively, drag the scroll box (technically known as the *thumb*) to move quickly through the document. As you drag the scroll box, Word displays a ScreenTip showing the page number and the heading that you're scrolling by, as illustrated here.

> Page: 38
>
> Saving Private Data

- Use the horizontal scroll bar to move from side to side in your document. The horizontal scroll bar is useful in layout views when the page you're working on is too wide to fit on the screen at a readable magnification. As with the vertical scroll bar, you can either click the scroll buttons or drag the scroll box.

- The Split bar lets you split the Word window into two so that you can see different parts of a document at the same time. We'll look at this feature toward the end of this skill.

- The status bar displays information about the position of the insertion point and about the document in the window. I'll discuss the status bar in the section titled "Reading the Status Bar" later in this skill.

- The Next Page and Previous Page buttons display the next page and previous page of the document. The Select Browse Object button, which we'll look at in Skill 6, changes the behavior of the Next Page and Previous Page buttons. For example, instead of moving to the next page or previous page, you can move to the next table or previous table.

- The Normal View button, Web Layout button, Print Layout View button, and Outline View button change the view. We'll look at the three main views later in this skill. Outline view (which is more complex) is described in Skill 14.

Using the Menus

To display a menu, click it with the mouse or press the Alt key followed by the underlined letter on the menu (for example, press Alt and then F to display the

File menu). To close a menu without choosing a command, click the menu's name again, or click in the document window, or press Alt again, or press Esc.

To choose an item from a menu, click it with the mouse, or press the key for the underlined letter, or use ↓ and ↑ to move the highlight to it and press Enter.

If a menu item is shown in gray embossed letters rather than black letters, it is currently unavailable. For example, the Footnotes item on the View menu will be unavailable until you create a footnote in the document.

Word's menus are *two-stage* and *adaptive:* They appear in two stages, and they change as you use them. At first, when you display a menu, Word shows only the most-used commands on the menu to keep the menu as brief as possible. If you don't choose one of the items within a second or so, Word displays the rest of the menu. This is disconcerting at first, but you may get used to it pretty quickly. If you don't get used to it or if you don't like the effect, you can make Word display the menus normally, as you'll see in a moment.

The last item on the short version of the menu has two arrows pointing downward, indicating that further menu items are available. You can either click this item to display the rest of the menu or wait for Word to display it, as described in the previous paragraph.

The most-used items on the menu are shown in the regular medium gray of most Windows menus. The less-used items appear in a lighter gray. But the first time you use one of the lighter-gray items, Word promotes it to the regular gray and includes it in the short version of the menu from then on. Word also promotes the menu items you use most frequently toward the top of the menu, changing the order of the menu items somewhat. If you're used to regular menu behavior, this can make it harder for you to find the items you need on the menus.

BACK FROM THE FUTURE I: GETTING FULL MENUS AND NON-ADAPTIVE MENUS

If you don't like the new two-stage, adaptive menus, you can make them behave like "normal" menus in previous versions of Word (and in most other Windows applications):

1. Choose Tools ➢ Customize to display the Customize dialog box.
2. Click the Options tab to display it (if it isn't already displayed).

continued

3. In the Personalized Menus And Toolbars area, clear the Menus Show Recently Used Commands First check box. This will gray out the Show Full Menus After A Short Delay check box, and will make Word show the full menu at once.

4. Click the Close button to close the Customize dialog box.

Using Toolbars

Word comes with a variety of toolbars containing buttons that give you quick access to actions—everything from italicizing your text to running a mail merge. To see what a button represents, you can display a ScreenTip by moving the mouse pointer over a button and holding it there for a moment.

By default, Word displays the Standard and Formatting toolbars, arranging them to share the screen with their most commonly used buttons visible (depending on the screen resolution and window size you are using). But you can easily choose to display other toolbars (such as the Tables And Borders toolbar or the Drawing toolbar) if you need them. Alternatively, you can hide the Standard and Formatting toolbars to give yourself more screen real estate.

Like many Windows applications, Word can display its toolbars and the menu bar as either *docked* panels attached to one side of the screen or as free-floating (or *undocked*) panels that you can drag anywhere on your screen. At the right-hand end of the visible part of any docked toolbar (or the lower end of a vertically docked toolbar), Word displays the More Buttons button: a minimal button with a single downward-pointing arrow. When part of a toolbar is hidden by another toolbar, Word displays >> on the More Buttons button. Click the More Buttons button to display a panel containing the remaining buttons, as shown here.

Like the menus, Word's toolbars are adaptive. When you use a button that was previously on a hidden part of a toolbar, Word will promote it to the displayed part of the toolbar. If two toolbars are sharing a row across the screen, part of the toolbar that the button was not on may be removed to make space for the button you used.

BACK FROM THE FUTURE II: DISPLAYING THE FULL STANDARD TOOLBAR AND FORMATTING TOOLBAR

If you're used to using most of the buttons on the Standard toolbar and the Formatting toolbar in previous versions of Word, you may find it awkward to have them competing for space on the same line. Here's how to tell Word to display them separately:

1. Choose Tools ➤ Customize to display the Customize dialog box.
2. Click the Options tab to display it (if it isn't already displayed).
3. Clear the Standard And Formatting Toolbars Share One Row check box.
4. Click the Close button to close the Customize dialog box.

One more thing you can do in the Customize dialog box is reset your toolbars and menus to their default settings. To do so, click the Reset My Usage Data button.

Displaying and Hiding Toolbars

To display and hide toolbars:

- With the mouse, right-click anywhere in the menu bar or in a displayed toolbar to display a list of toolbars. Check marks will appear next to those currently displayed. Click next to a displayed toolbar to hide it or next to a hidden toolbar to display it.

- With the keyboard (or the mouse), choose View ➤ Toolbars to display the list of toolbars. Again, check marks will appear next to those toolbars currently displayed. Use ↓ and ↑ (or move the mouse pointer) to move the highlight to the displayed toolbar you want to hide or the hidden toolbar you want to display, then press Enter (or click the highlighted item).

TIP TIP TIP TIP TIP TIP TIP TIP TIP TIP TIP TIP TIP TIP TIP TIP TIP TIP TIP TIP TIP TIP TIP TIP

Unless you have a huge monitor or high screen resolution (or both), hide toolbars when you don't need immediate access to them so that you have more of the screen available for working in.

Moving and Reshaping Toolbars

Word can display its toolbars and the menu bar either attached to one side of the screen or as free-floating. Docked toolbars can overlap each other, which means that you can arrange them to save space on screen. Figure 1.2 shows toolbars arranged somewhat improbably on screen, demonstrating the possibilities.

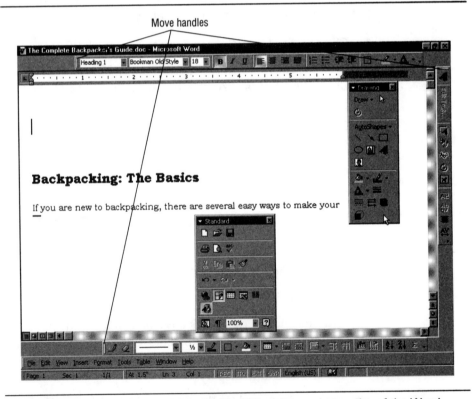

FIGURE 1.2: You can display your toolbars at any extremity of the Word screen, or you can place them plumb in the middle.

To move a toolbar or the menu bar from its current position, click the move handle at its left end (or its top end, if it's positioned vertically) or in any space in the toolbar or menu bar not occupied by a button or menu item and drag it where you want it—either to one of the edges, in which case it will snap into position, or to the middle of the screen.

To uncover more of a docked toolbar that is obscured by another docked toolbar, drag the move handle of the toolbar that is doing the obscuring.

TIP TIP TIP TIP TIP TIP TIP TIP TIP TIP TIP TIP TIP TIP TIP TIP TIP TIP TIP TIP TIP TIP TIP

You can dock a floating toolbar (or the floating menu bar) by double-clicking its title bar.

To reshape a floating toolbar or floating menu bar, move the mouse pointer over one of its borders until the pointer turns into a double-ended arrow, then click and drag to resize the toolbar. Because of the shape of their buttons or menu names, toolbars and the menu bar resize in jumps rather than smoothly like windows do.

NOTE NOTE NOTE NOTE NOTE NOTE NOTE NOTE NOTE NOTE NOTE NOTE NOTE NOTE NOTE

You can customize the toolbars (not to mention the menu bar and the shortcut menus) to suit the way you work. I'll discuss how to do this in Skill 16.

Reading the Status Bar

The status bar (see Figure 1.3) provides the following information from left to right:

- The number of the page the insertion point is currently on.

- The number of the section the insertion point is currently in. (I'll discuss sections and their use in Skill 5.)

- The current page number and the number of pages in the whole document.

- The vertical position of the insertion point from the top of the page (for example, **At 4.2"**).

- The *column number*—the number of characters between the current position of the insertion point and the left margin (for example, **Col 36**).

- Whether macro-recording mode is on (the REC indicator will be darkened if it is).

- Whether change-tracking is on (the TRK indicator will be darkened if it is). Change-tracking is also known as *revision marking;* we'll examine it in Skill 18.

- Whether extend-selection mode is on (the EXT indicator will be darkened if it is). We'll look at extend-selection mode later in this skill.

- Whether Overtype mode is on (the OVR indicator will be darkened if it is). We'll look at Overtype mode later in this skill as well.

- The language the current selection (or the text at the position of the insertion point) is formatted as—for example, **English (US)**.

- The state of spell-checking and grammar-checking in the document. While Word is checking the spelling and grammar as you work, you'll see a pen moving across the page on the icon. When Word has finished checking, you'll see a red cross on the right-hand page of the icon if there's a spelling or grammar problem, and a red check mark if Word considers all to be well.

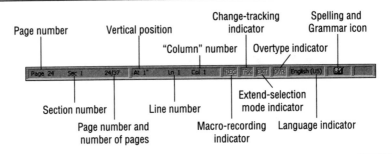

FIGURE 1.3: The status bar provides information about the position of the insertion point, the document, and what Word is currently doing.

Displaying and Hiding the Status Bar and Scroll Bars

To adjust the amount of free space you have on screen, you can hide and redisplay the status bar and scroll bars as necessary. I find the status bar and vertical scroll bar more or less indispensable, but usually get rid of the horizontal scroll bar:

1. Choose Tools ➤ Options to display the Options dialog box.

2. Click the View tab to bring it to the front of the dialog box if it's not already displayed.

3. In the Show group box, clear the Status Bar, Horizontal Scroll Bar, and Vertical Scroll Bar check boxes to hide the status bar and scroll bars. Select these check boxes to display the status bar and scroll bars.

4. Click the OK button to close the Options dialog box.

Displaying and Hiding the Rulers

To help you position your text optimally on the page, Word offers a horizontal ruler in Normal view and Web Layout view and both horizontal and vertical rulers in Print Layout view and Print Preview. The horizontal ruler displays margin stops and tab stops for the current paragraph or selected paragraphs. We'll look at how to set margins and tabs in Skill 4.

You can either display the ruler on screen all the time or keep it hidden but available. To toggle the display of the ruler on and off, choose View ➢ Ruler. To pop up the horizontal ruler momentarily, move the mouse pointer to the thin, light-gray bar at the top of the current document window:

The ruler will appear automatically so that you can view text positioning or work with tabs:

The ruler will disappear when you move the mouse pointer away from it.

To pop up the vertical ruler in Print Layout view or Print Preview, move the mouse pointer to the thin, light-gray bar at the left edge of the current document window. The vertical ruler will appear automatically, and will disappear when you move the pointer away again.

NOTE NOTE NOTE NOTE NOTE NOTE NOTE NOTE NOTE NOTE NOTE NOTE NOTE NOTE NOTE

These pop-up rulers are controlled by the Provide Feedback With Animation check box on the General tab of the Options dialog box. To prevent the rulers from popping up, select Tools ➢ Options to display the Options dialog box, click the General tab, clear the Provide Feedback With Animation check box, and choose the OK button.

Understanding and Arranging Windows

In this section, we'll look at how Word uses windows and how you work with them.

How Word Handles Windows

To work effectively in Word, you need to understand how Word handles windows when you have more than one document open. Word 2000 uses a different arrangement of windows than previous versions. Previous versions kept all document windows within one main window, the application window. Only the main application window appeared on the Taskbar, identifying itself as *Microsoft Word* and the name of the document that was currently active in it—for example, *Microsoft Word—September Report Memo*.

Now, each document appears in a separate document window, and each document window appears as a separate icon on the Taskbar, identified by the name of the document: For example, one document window might be identified as *September Report Memo*, another as *Letter to Mom*, and a third *Ode to the Bosnians*. This makes it easier to switch from one open document to another by using the Taskbar. However, not having an application window as such can make it confusing as to when you're closing a document and when you're closing Word itself. When you have only one document open, the Word menu bar grows a Close Window button at its right-hand end, as shown in Figure 1.4. By clicking this Close Window button, you can close the document rather than Word. (As soon as you open another document, the Close Window button disappears.) Clicking the Close button on the title bar of the window closes Word.

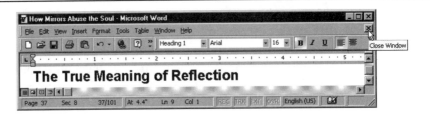

FIGURE 1.4: When only one document is open, Word displays a Close Window button at the right-hand end of the menu bar. Clicking this Close Window button closes the document; clicking the Close button on the window's title bar closes the application.

Switching from One Document Window to Another

If you have the Taskbar displayed, the easiest way to switch from one document window to another is to click the Taskbar icon for the window you want to activate. Alternatively, you can press Alt+Tab to *coolswitch* (switch quickly) through all the Word windows and other running applications. You can also use the Window menu in Word to move between document windows. The Window menu lists the first nine document windows you have open; you can activate any of these document windows by choosing its item from the menu. If you have more than nine documents open (which, under normal circumstances, you'll seldom need to), the Window menu will include a More Windows item that displays the Activate dialog box shown in Figure 1.5. Either double-click the listing for the window you want or select the listing and choose the OK button.

FIGURE 1.5: When you have more than nine documents open, Word provides the Activate dialog box as a way of moving from one document to another.

Arranging Windows

As usual in any Windows application, you can resize the Word document windows to any size that suits you by dragging the borders or corners of any window. This is the easiest way to get the windows you want to work with to a suitable size. (If a window is maximized, you need to restore it to a non-maximized state before you can resize it.) You can also arrange windows by choosing Window ➢ Arrange All. The Arrange All command *tiles* the windows on the Desktop, giving each as equal a share of space as possible. Unfortunately, Arrange All tiles two or three windows by dividing the screen horizontally rather than vertically, which typically makes them too small to do much work in.

You can also arrange Word document windows, together with any other windows of your choice, by using the Cascade Windows, Tile Windows Horizontally, and Tile Windows Vertically items on the context menu on the Windows Taskbar. (To display the context menu, right-click in an open space in the Taskbar.) These commands work on any windows that are not minimized. For example, to arrange two Word windows side by side, right-click in any open space in the Taskbar and choose Tile Windows Vertically from the context menu.

For most purposes, you'll usually do best to maximize the Word window so you have as much space as possible to work in. Unless you have a huge monitor (or need to see other applications while you work in Word), I suggest maximizing the Word window by clicking the Maximize button on the title bar. Once you've maximized the Word window, Word will replace the Maximize button with the Restore button; click the Restore button to restore the window to the size it was before it was last maximized.

You may also want to use Zoom to enlarge or shrink the display. If so, skip ahead to the section titled "Viewing the Document" later in this skill.

Viewing the Document

Word offers five main ways of viewing your documents, each of which has its strengths and weaknesses: Normal view, Web Layout view, Print Layout view, Print Preview, and Outline view. In the following sections, I'll describe each view briefly. In conjunction with the five views, there are two features that you can use: split-screen view and the Document Map. I'll discuss these as well.

Normal View

Normal view provides the easiest view of the text and other elements on screen and is probably the view you'll spend most of your time using when creating and editing documents. In Normal view, Word approximates the fonts and other formatting that you'll see when you print your document, but adapts the document so that you can see as much of it as possible on your screen. In Normal view, you don't see the margins of the paper, the headers and footers, or the footnotes and comments. Word can also wrap the text horizontally to the size of the window so that no text disappears off the side of the screen.

To switch the document to Normal view, choose View ➤ Normal or click the Normal View button at the left end of the horizontal scroll bar.

Web Layout View

Web Layout view is designed for creating and reading online documents. Web Layout view (see Figure 1.6) splits the screen vertically, displaying the Document Map (a collapsible outline of the document) in the left pane and the document itself in the right pane at an easily readable size.

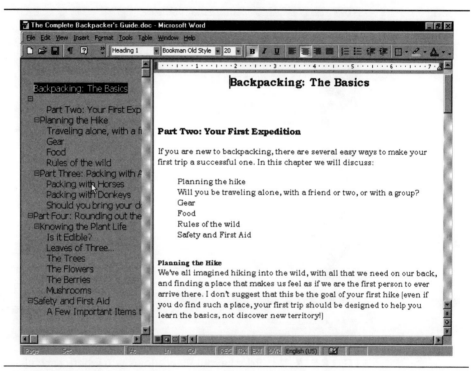

FIGURE 1.6: Web Layout view provides special features for working with online documents.

To switch to Web Layout view, choose View ➤ Web Layout or click the Web Layout View button on the horizontal scroll bar.

Print Layout View

Print Layout view is useful for getting an idea of how your documents will look when you print them. In Print Layout view, Word shows you the margins of the sheet or sheets of paper you're working on, any headers or footers, and any footnotes or comments. Word doesn't wrap text to the size of the window, as doing so would change the page from its print format.

To switch to Print Layout view, choose View ➤ Print Layout or click the Print Layout View button on the horizontal scroll bar. You'll see an approximation of the layout of your document, complete with margins (see Figure 1.7). If necessary, zoom to a more appropriate zoom percentage (see the section titled "Zooming the View" a couple of blocks south of here).

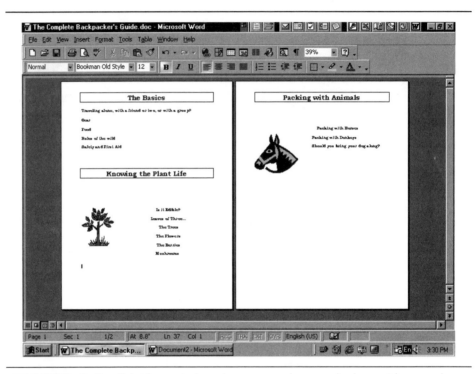

FIGURE 1.7: Print Layout view shows you where each element in your document will appear when printed.

Print Preview

Word's Print Preview provides a way for you to scan your documents on screen for formatting mistakes before you commit them to paper. Print Preview shows you, as closely as Word can, the effect you'll get when you print your document on the currently selected printer. We'll look at Print Preview in detail in Skill 3.

Outline View

Word's Outline view lets you collapse your documents to a specified number of heading levels—for example, you can choose to view only the first-level heads in your documents or the first three levels of heads. Outline view is very useful for structuring long documents and is much more complex than the other views. We'll examine it in detail in Skill 14.

Split-Screen View

Word also offers split-screen view, in which the screen is divided into two panes. You can use a different view in each pane, display a different part of the document in each pane, and zoom each pane to a different zoom percentage. Split-screen view is especially useful when you need to see two separate parts of a document (for example, the beginning and the end) on screen at the same time.

To split the screen, choose Window ➤ Split. The mouse pointer will change to a double-headed arrow pointing up and down and dragging a thick gray line. Move the line up or down the screen to where you want to split it, then click to place the line.

To reunite the split screen, choose Window ➤ Remove Split.

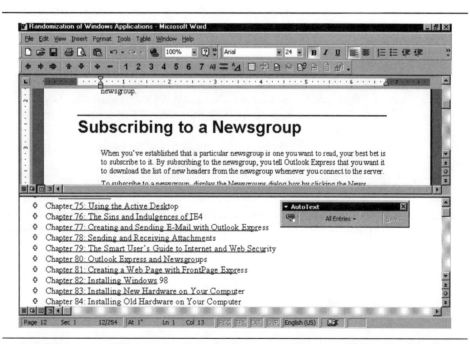

FIGURE 1.8: Choose Window ➤ Split to split the screen into two panes. You can then work in a different view or at a different zoom percentage in each pane.

TIP TIP TIP TIP TIP TIP TIP TIP TIP TIP TIP TIP TIP TIP TIP TIP TIP TIP TIP TIP TIP TIP

To split the window in half quickly, double-click the split bar—the tiny horizontal bar at the top of the vertical scroll bar. Double-click the bar dividing the screen to remove the split.

Document Map

The Document Map, shown in Figure 1.6 earlier in the skill, is a prime component of Web Layout view. You can also use the Document Map with Normal view, Print Layout view, and Outline view (though it is largely redundant for Outline view). You cannot use the Document Map with Print Preview.

The Document Map consists of an outline pane that shows the outline of the document. The outline consists of the various levels of headings in the document (you define headings by using the Heading 1 through Heading 9 styles; I'll discuss styles in Skill 5). You can collapse and expand the outline to show different levels of headings by clicking the plus sign or minus sign in the little box to the left of any heading that has subheadings. You can right-click in the Document Map to display a context menu of commands, including commands to collapse or expand the Document Map to show a specified number of levels of heading. For example, to display three levels of headings in the Document Map, right-click in it and choose Show Heading 3 from the context menu. You can click a heading in the Document Map to display that part of the document in the main pane of the Word window.

We'll look at the Document Map in more detail in Skill 12.

Zooming the View

In any of Word's views, you can use the Zoom feature to increase or decrease the size of the display. Word lets you set any zoom percentage between 10% and 500% of full size.

You can use either the Zoom box on the Standard toolbar or the Zoom dialog box to set the zoom percentage.

Zooming with the Zoom Box on the Standard Toolbar

To zoom the view with the Zoom box on the Standard toolbar:

1.   Display the Standard toolbar if it isn't visible.

2.   Click the button to the right of the Zoom box to display a drop-down list of zoom percentages.

3. Choose a zoom percentage from the drop-down list or type in a different percentage (between 10% and 500%).

Zooming with the Zoom Dialog Box

To zoom the view with the Zoom dialog box:

1. Choose View ➤ Zoom to display the Zoom dialog box (see Figure 1.9).

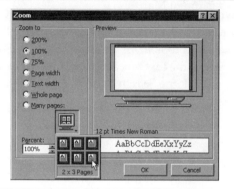

FIGURE 1.9: In the Zoom dialog box, choose the zoom percentage you want in the Zoom To box.

2. In the Zoom To box, choose the zoom percentage you want:

    - To zoom to 200%, 100%, 75%, Page Width, Text Width, or Whole Page (which is available only in Print Layout view and Print Preview), click the appropriate option button in the Zoom To box.

    - To display more than one page at a time (only in Print Layout view and Print Preview), click the monitor next to the Many Pages option button and drag through the grid it displays to indicate the configuration of pages you want to view: 2 × 2 pages, 2 × 3 pages, and so on. You'll have more display options for a document that contains many pages than a document that contains only a few.

    - To display the page or pages at a precise zoom percentage of your choosing, adjust the setting in the Percent box at the bottom-left corner of the Zoom dialog box.

3. Click the OK button to apply the zoom percentage to the document.

Getting Help

Word comes with a sophisticated Help system designed to answer questions you have about working with Word. You can get help by using the Office Assistant or by accessing the Microsoft Word Help application directly.

The Office Assistant is the default interface for the Microsoft Office Help application. The Office Assistant consists of animated characters and graphics such as Rocky, the dog seen here. Click the Office Assistant to display the prompt balloon shown in the left part of Figure 1.10. (If the Office Assistant is hiding, you can summon it by pressing the F1 key, clicking the Microsoft Word Help button on the Standard toolbar, or choosing Help ➤ Show The Office Assistant.)

Type into the text box at the bottom of the Office Assistant balloon, then press Enter or click the Search button to display the list of topics that the Office Assistant associates with that topic.

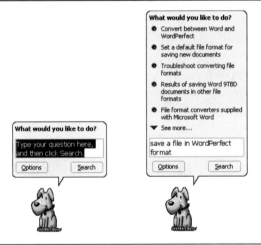

FIGURE 1.10: Use the Office Assistant to access Word's Help system.

If one of the Office Assistant's suggestions is suitable, click it to display the Microsoft Word Help window with instructions or advice for the procedure or topic you chose. If there's a See More button toward the bottom of the Office Assistant's balloon, you can click that to display further related topics.

To find further topics from the Microsoft Word Help window, click the Show button to display the left panel of the Microsoft Word Help window (see Figure 1.11):

- The Contents tab of this panel contains a list of the topics in the Word Help file. To expand any topic, click the + sign to the left of it. To collapse an expanded topic, click the – sign to the left of it.

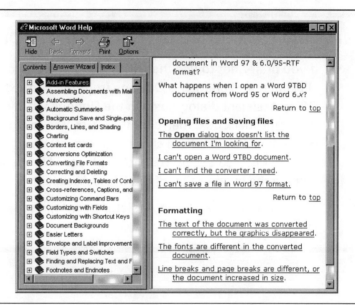

FIGURE 1.11: Use the left panel of the Microsoft Word Help application window to access further information.

- The Answer Wizard tab provides a way to search for Help topics without using the Office Assistant. Enter your question, or relevant words, in the What Would You Like To Do? text box, then click the Search button. Double-click the topic in the Select Topic To Display list box to display the topic in the main part of the Microsoft Word Help window.

- The Index tab provides an alphabetical list of the keywords in the Help file. Either type one or more keywords in the Type Keywords text box and press Enter, or click the Search button, or select a keyword in the Or Choose Keywords list box. Double-click the topic you want in the Choose A Topic list box to display it in the main part of the Microsoft Word Help window.

To move backward and forward between the Help topics you've been working with, use the Back and Forward buttons on the toolbar of the Microsoft Word Help window. The Forward button will become available only when you've used the Back button.

To close the Microsoft Word Help application, click its Close button.

DOWNSIZING YOUR OFFICE: GETTING RID OF THE OFFICE ASSISTANT

If you prefer not to use the Office Assistant, you can turn it off by right-clicking it and choosing Options from the context menu to display the Office Assistant dialog box. On the Options tab, clear the Use The Office Assistant check box, then click the OK button to close the Office Assistant dialog box. You can then click the Microsoft Word Help button or choose Help ➢ Microsoft Word Help to display the Microsoft Word Help window without the intervention of the Office Assistant.

To start using the Office Assistant again, choose Help ➢ Show The Office Assistant.

Exiting Word

When you finish working in Word, choose File ➢ Exit to exit and get back to the Windows Desktop. If you have unsaved documents, Word or the Office Assistant will prompt you to save them. For the moment, choose No, because in this skill you've been working only with a scratch document. In the next skill, we'll look at how to save a document.

Are You Experienced?

Now you can . . .

- ☑ start Word
- ☑ display and hide toolbars
- ☑ use Word's various views
- ☑ zoom the view
- ☑ get Help
- ☑ exit Word

Creating Simple Word Documents

- ➔ **Creating new documents**
- ➔ **Working with text**
- ➔ **Using Undo and Redo**
- ➔ **Inserting dates and special characters**
- ➔ **Saving a document**
- ➔ **Saving a document in a different format**
- ➔ **Closing a document**
- ➔ **Opening a document**

In this skill, we'll look at how to work with Word documents. You'll create a new Word document and save it to disk. After that, I'll discuss how to close a document you've been working on and how to reopen that document or open another document. Along the way, I'll discuss the most common things you'll want to do in documents you create: Enter text in them, undo mistakes you've made, and insert information such as dates or special characters.

Creating a New Document

As you saw in Skill 1, when you run Word, it opens a new blank document and names it Document1.

To create a new document based on the default template (Blank Document), click the New Blank Document button on the Standard toolbar or press Ctrl+N. Word will open a new document named Document*x*—Document2, Document3, and so on.

At other times, you'll probably want to create a new document based on a template that already contains some text or that provides a different look and feel than the default template. To create a new document based on a different template:

1. Choose File ➤ New. Word will display the New dialog box (see Figure 2.1).

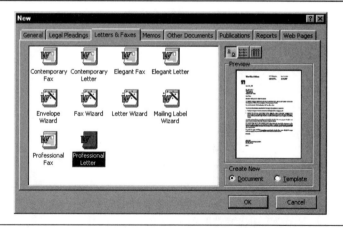

FIGURE 2.1: To create a new document based on a template other than Blank Document, choose File ➤ New and select the template in the New dialog box.

2. In the Create New group box at the lower-right corner of the New dialog box, make sure that the Document option button is selected rather than the Template option button. (You use the Template option button for creating a new template—the skeleton upon which a document is based.)

3. In the New dialog box, choose the tab that contains the type of document you want to create: General, Legal Pleadings, Letters & Faxes, Memos, Other Documents, Publications, Reports, or Web Pages.

   - If you didn't install all the templates that Word offers, you may not see all of these tabs in the New dialog box. Then again, if you or someone else has created more templates in another folder, you may see more tabs than those listed here.

   - To see a preview of a template in the tab you chose, click a template. The preview will appear in the box on the right side of the New dialog box.

NOTE NOTE NOTE NOTE NOTE NOTE NOTE NOTE NOTE NOTE NOTE NOTE NOTE NOTE NOTE

A *template* is a special type of document that you use to produce documents that share the same look or contents. Templates can contain styles, AutoText entries, toolbars, and macros, all of which we'll get to in later skills. By basing a document on a different template, you can change its styles instantly, change its look completely, and virtually typeset it differently, in seconds. (Word calls this "attaching" a template to a document.) Take a look at the Preview box as you click some of the templates offered to get an idea of the different templates available.

   - You can choose between three views of the templates available by clicking any of the three buttons above the Preview box. The leftmost button gives the Large Icons view; the second gives the List view; and the third gives the Details view.

TIP TIP TIP TIP TIP TIP TIP TIP TIP TIP TIP TIP TIP TIP TIP TIP TIP TIP TIP TIP TIP TIP TIP

Details view offers the most information of the three views, and you can sort the templates by name, size, type, or date last modified by clicking the buttons at the top of the columns.

4. To start a document based on the template you chose, double-click the icon or listing for the template, or click it once and then click the OK button.

Working with Text

As in most word-processing applications, Word's basic unit is the paragraph. These aren't paragraphs as people generally understand them: A paragraph in Word consists of a paragraph mark (made by pressing the Enter key) and any text (or graphic) between it and the previous paragraph mark (or the beginning of the document). In other words, a paragraph consists of anything (text, a graphic, space, or even nothing at all) that appears between two paragraph marks, up to and including the second paragraph mark. Strange as it seems, a paragraph mark with nothing between it and the previous paragraph mark is considered a full paragraph. You can treat each paragraph as a unit for formatting with styles (which we'll look at in Skill 5) or for moving and copying.

Each blank document you create contains one paragraph, which is located at the start of the document. You can add as many paragraphs to a document as you need.

TIP TIP TIP TIP TIP TIP TIP TIP TIP TIP TIP TIP TIP TIP TIP TIP TIP TIP TIP TIP TIP TIP TIP

If you don't see paragraph marks on your screen, click the ¶ button on the Standard toolbar. This is the Show/Hide ¶ button and it toggles the display of spaces, tabs, paragraph marks, and the like. Some people find it easier to work with these marks displayed; others find them distracting. You can also display and hide these marks by pressing Ctrl+Shift+8.

Entering Text

To enter text into your document, position the insertion point where you want the text to appear and type it in. Word will automatically wrap text as it reaches the end of a line, so you don't need to press the Enter key when you get there. Press the Enter key when you need to start a new paragraph.

NOTE NOTE NOTE NOTE NOTE NOTE NOTE NOTE NOTE NOTE NOTE NOTE NOTE NOTE NOTE

If you're working in Normal view (discussed in Skill 1), Word will adjust the display of the text to suit the screen and window size you are working with, rather than display the text as it will appear when you print it out. For precise layout, you'll need to work in Print Layout view (View ➢ Print Layout) rather than Normal view.

If you want to move to a new line without starting a new paragraph—for example, so there is no extra space between lines—press Shift+Enter to start a new line within the same paragraph.

As you reach the end of a page, Word will automatically break text onto the next page. If you want, you can start a new page at any point by inserting a page break. To do so, press Ctrl+Enter.

In Print Layout view, Web Layout view, and Print Preview, Word 2000 provides a new feature called Click and Type that enables you to double-click where you want to enter text on the page. Word automatically enters any blank paragraphs and tabs required to position the insertion point where you double-clicked, and changes the alignment of the paragraph if necessary. (If there are already superfluous blank paragraphs or tabs beyond where you double-clicked, Word removes them automatically.) For example, to create a centered heading one-third of the way down the fresh page in a new blank document, double-click one-third of the way down the page and in the middle of the line. Word will place the insertion point there, add blank paragraphs from the top of the page to the line of the heading, and apply center alignment. You can then create a right-aligned paragraph at the bottom of the page by double-clicking at the right margin toward the bottom of the page.

The mouse pointer displays the type of alignment that Click and Type will implement if you double-click in that area: centering around the horizontal middle of the page, right alignment near to the right margin, and left alignment everywhere else.

Insert and Overtype Modes

Word offers two *modes* (methods of behavior) for adding text to your documents: Insert mode and Overtype mode. In *Insert mode* (the default mode), characters you type are inserted into the text at the insertion point, pushing along any characters to the right of the insertion point. If you want to type over existing text in Insert mode, select the text using either the mouse or the keyboard (see the next section for instructions on selecting text) and type in the text you want to insert in its place. In Insert mode, the OVR indicator on the status bar is dimmed.

In *Overtype mode*, any character you type replaces the character (if any) to the immediate right of the insertion point. When Word is in Overtype mode, the OVR indicator on the status bar is active (darkened), as shown here.

To toggle between Insert mode and Overtype mode, double-click the OVR indicator on the status bar or press the Insert key. Alternatively, choose Tools ➢ Options to display the Options dialog box, click the Edit tab to display it, select the Overtype Mode check box, and click the OK button.

Moving the Insertion Point

In Word, you can move the insertion point using the mouse, the keyboard, or a combination of the two. In most situations, you can use whichever means you prefer, though you will probably find the mouse easier for some operations and the keyboard easier for others.

Using the Mouse

To position the insertion point using the mouse, simply move the insertion point to where you want it, and click.

Use the vertical scroll bar to move up and down through your document (or, if you have an IntelliMouse or other scrolling mouse, use the mouse's roller). When you scroll with the scroll bar (the thumb) in a multipage document, Word will display a small box next to the scroll bar showing which page and heading you're scrolling past. Use the horizontal scroll bar to move from side to side as necessary.

TIP TIP TIP TIP TIP TIP TIP TIP TIP TIP TIP TIP TIP TIP TIP TIP TIP TIP TIP TIP TIP TIP TIP

If you often need to scroll horizontally in Normal view to see the full width of your documents, turn on Word's Wrap To Window option, which makes the text fit into the current window size, regardless of width. To turn on Wrap To Window, choose Tools ≻ Options, click the View tab, and select the Wrap To Window check box. Click the OK button to close the Options dialog box.

Click the Next Page and Previous Page buttons at the foot of the vertical scroll bar to move to the next page and previous page. Make sure that these buttons are black, which indicates that Word is browsing by pages. If they're blue, Word is browsing by a different item, such as sections or comments; clicking the buttons while they are blue will take you to the next (or previous) section or comment in the document. To reset Word to browse by pages, click the Object Browser button between the Next and Previous buttons and choose the Browse By Page button in the Object Browser list, as shown here.

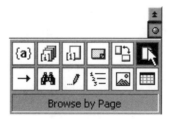

NOTE NOTE NOTE NOTE NOTE NOTE NOTE NOTE NOTE NOTE NOTE NOTE NOTE NOTE NOTE NOTE

The Object Browser is a feature introduced in Word 97 that allows you to choose which type of item you want to navigate to in the document. You can move to the previous or next field, endnote, footnote, comment, section, page, Go To item, Find item, edit, heading, graphic, or table. This provides a way of moving quickly from one instance of an item to the next or previous instance. For example, if you need to check each table in a document, choose Table from the Object Browser list and then use the Previous and Next buttons to navigate from table to table.

Using Keyboard Shortcuts

Word offers a number of keystroke combinations to move the insertion point swiftly through the document without removing your hands from the keyboard. Besides ← to move left one character, → to move right one character, ↑ to move up one line, and ↓ to move down one line, you can use the following:

Keystroke	Action
Ctrl+→	One word to the right
Ctrl+←	One word to the left
Ctrl+↑	To the beginning of the current paragraph or (if the insertion point is at the beginning of a paragraph) to the beginning of the previous paragraph
Ctrl+↓	To the beginning of the next paragraph
End	To the end of the current line
Ctrl+End	To the end of the document
Home	To the start of the current line
Ctrl+Home	To the start of the document
PageUp	Up one screen's worth of text
PageDown	Down one screen's worth of text
Ctrl+PageUp	To the first character on the current screen
Ctrl+PageDown	To the last character on the current screen

TIP TIP TIP TIP TIP TIP TIP TIP TIP TIP TIP TIP TIP TIP TIP TIP TIP TIP TIP TIP TIP TIP TIP

You can quickly move to the last three places you edited in a document by pressing Shift+F5 (Go Back) once, twice, or three times. This is especially useful when you open a document and need to return to the point at which you were last working.

Selecting Text

Word offers a number of different ways to select text: You can use the keyboard, the mouse, or the two in combination. You'll find that some ways of selecting text work better than others with certain equipment; experiment to find which are the fastest and most comfortable methods for you.

Selected text appears highlighted in reverse video—for example, if your normal text is black on a white background, selected text will be white on a black background.

Selecting Text with the Mouse

The simplest way to select text with the mouse is to position the insertion point at the beginning or end of the block you want to select, then click and drag to the end or beginning of the block.

TIP TIP TIP TIP TIP TIP TIP TIP TIP TIP TIP TIP TIP TIP TIP TIP TIP TIP TIP TIP TIP TIP TIP TIP

Word offers an automatic word-selection feature to help you select whole words more quickly with the mouse. When this feature is switched on, as soon as you drag the mouse pointer from one word to the next, Word will select the whole of the first word and the whole of the second; when the mouse pointer reaches the third, it selects that too, and so on. To temporarily override automatic word selection, hold down the Alt key before you click and drag. To turn off automatic word selection, choose Tools ➢ Options to display the Options dialog box. Click the Edit tab to bring it to the front of the dialog box, and clear the When Selecting, Automatically Select Entire Word check box. Then click the OK button. To turn automatic word selection on, select the When Selecting, Automatically Select Entire Word check box.

You can also select text with multiple clicks:

- Double-click in a word to select it.

- Triple-click in a paragraph to select it.

- Ctrl-click in a sentence to select it.

In the *selection bar* on the left side of the screen (where the insertion point turns from an I-beam to an arrow pointing up and to the right), you can click to select text as follows:

- Click once to select the line the arrow is pointing at.

- Double-click to select the paragraph the arrow is pointing at.

- Triple-click (or Ctrl-click once) to select the entire document.

Selecting Text with the Keyboard

To select text with the keyboard, hold down the Shift key and move the insertion point by using the keyboard shortcuts listed in the section titled "Using Keyboard Shortcuts" earlier in this skill.

SELECTING TEXT WITH THE EXTEND SELECTION FEATURE

You can also select text by using Word's Extend Selection feature, though for most uses it's slow and clumsy. Press the F8 key once to enter Extend Selection mode; you'll see EXT appear undimmed on the status bar. Press F8 a second time to select the current word, a third time to select the current sentence, a fourth time to select the current paragraph, and a fifth time to select the whole document. Then press the Esc key to turn off Extend Selection mode.

Extend Selection also works with other keys on the keyboard: To select a sentence, press F8 at the beginning of the sentence and then press the punctuation mark that appears at the end of the sentence. To select some text, position the insertion point at the beginning of that text, press F8, and then press the letter up to which you want to select. If there is another instance of the letter before the one you want to select, press the letter again.

To select a paragraph, place the insertion point at the start of the paragraph, press F8, and then press the Enter key.

Selecting Text with the Mouse and Keyboard

Word also offers ways to select text using the mouse and keyboard together. These techniques are well worth trying out, as you can quickly select awkward blocks of text—for example, if you want to select a few sentences from a paragraph or to select columns of characters.

To select a block of text using the mouse and the keyboard, position the insertion point at the start (or end) of a block and click. Then move the insertion point to the end (or start) of the block—scroll if necessary with the mouse roller or the scroll bar, but don't use the keyboard—hold down the Shift key, then click again.

To select columns of characters, hold down the Alt key and click and drag from one end of the block to the other (see Figure 2.2). This technique can be very useful for getting rid of extra spaces or tabs used to align text.

If·you·are·new·to·backpacking,·there·are·several·easy·ways·to·make·your·
first·trip·a·successful·one.··In·this·chapter·we·will·discuss:¶
→ The·destination¶
→ Will·you·be·traveling·alone,·with·a·friend·or·two,·or·with·a·group?¶
→ Planning·the·hike¶
→ Gear¶
→ Food¶
→ Rules·of·the·wild¶
¶
We've·all·imagined·hiking·into·the·wild,·with·all·that·we·need·on·our·

FIGURE 2.2: To select columns of characters without selecting whole lines, hold down the Alt key and drag through the block.

NOTE NOTE NOTE NOTE NOTE NOTE NOTE NOTE NOTE NOTE NOTE NOTE NOTE NOTE

Selecting text in a table works a little differently from selecting regular text, so I'll discuss that in Skill 9.

Deleting Text

Word lets you delete text swiftly and easily:

- To delete a block of text, simply select it and press the Delete key.

- To delete the character to the left of the insertion point, press the Backspace key.

- To delete the character to the right of the insertion point, press the Delete key.

- To delete the word to the right of the insertion point, press Ctrl+Delete. This actually deletes from the insertion point to the beginning of the next word (or the end of the line, if the current word is the last one in the line); so if the insertion point is in a word when you press Ctrl+Delete, you won't delete the whole word.

- To delete the word to the left of the insertion point, press Ctrl+Backspace. Again, if the insertion point isn't at the end of the word, only the part of the word to the left of the insertion point will be deleted.

TIP TIP TIP TIP TIP TIP TIP TIP TIP TIP TIP TIP TIP TIP TIP TIP TIP TIP TIP TIP TIP TIP TIP TIP TIP
You can also delete selected text by choosing Edit ➤ Clear or by right-clicking in the selection and choosing Cut from the context menu that appears. (Some context menus—which are different for the various elements of Word documents—don't have a Cut command.)

Cutting, Pasting, and Moving Text

You can easily copy and move text (and graphics) around your document either by using the Cut, Copy, and Paste commands or by using Word's drag-and-drop feature, which lets you copy or move text using your mouse.

The Office 2000 applications improve on previous versions by having their own Clipboard, which can contain up to 12 different copied or cut items, rather than relying on the Windows Clipboard, which can contain only one text item and one graphical item at a time. This new Office Clipboard is implemented as a toolbar, and its contents are available to each of the Office applications. As shown in Figure 2.3, the Office Clipboard uses icons to indicate the type of information each of the 12 storage containers holds: a Word document icon for text from a Word document, an Excel spreadsheet icon to indicate cells from a spreadsheet, an Excel chart icon to indicate a chart, a PowerPoint slide icon to indicate a slide from a presentation, and so on.

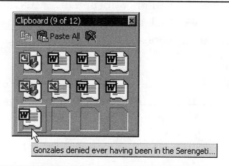

FIGURE 2.3: The new Office Clipboard can contain up to 12 items of different types. To see a simplified version of the contents of an item on the Clipboard, move the mouse pointer over it so that a ScreenTip appears.

As you cut or copy items, they are added to the Office Clipboard until it contains 12 items. When you cut or copy a thirteenth item, Word or the Office Assistant will warn you that copying this item will drop the first item from the Clipboard. Choose OK or Cancel.

You can paste any individual item from the Clipboard to the current position of the insertion point by clicking it. Alternatively, you can paste all the items from the Clipboard by clicking the Paste All button on the Clipboard's toolbar. The Paste All command is useful for gathering a number of items in sequence—for example, you might want to cull a dozen headings or paragraphs from a report to create a summary.

When the Clipboard is full, or nearing full, you can remove all the items from the Clipboard by clicking the Clear Clipboard button on the Clipboard's toolbar.

The most recent text item or graphical item on the Office Clipboard is also placed on the Windows Clipboard, so that you can transfer information to and from non-Office programs much as before. Likewise, the current text or graphical item on the Windows Clipboard is also placed on the Office Clipboard.

Cut

The Cut command removes the selected text (or graphics) from the Word document and places it on the Office Clipboard and Windows Clipboard. From there, you can paste it into another part of the document, into another document, or into another application. To cut the current selection, click the Cut button, then right-click and choose Cut from the context menu, choose Edit ➢ Cut, or press Ctrl+X.

Copy

The Copy command copies the selected text (or graphics) to the Office Clipboard and the Windows Clipboard. From there, you can paste it into another part of the document, into another document, or into another application. To copy the current selection, click the Copy button, then right-click and choose Copy from the context menu, choose Edit ➢ Copy, or press Ctrl+C.

Paste

The Paste command pastes a copy of the Windows Clipboard's contents into your Word document at the insertion point. To paste the contents of the Windows Clipboard, right-click and choose Paste from the context menu, click the Paste button, choose Edit ➢ Paste, or press Ctrl+V.

Using Undo and Redo

Word provides an Undo feature that can undo one or more of the last actions that you've taken, and a Redo feature that can redo anything that you've just chosen to undo.

To undo the last action you've taken, click the Undo button on the Standard toolbar, press Ctrl+Z, or choose Edit ➤ Undo.

To undo more than one action, click the arrow to the right of the Undo button and choose the number of actions to undo from the drop-down list, as shown here.

To redo a single action, click the Redo button on the Standard toolbar, press Ctrl+Y, or choose Edit ➤ Redo. (Often, the Redo button is on the part of the Standard toolbar that is covered by the Formatting toolbar.) To redo more than one action, click the arrow to the right of the Redo button and choose the number of actions to redo from the drop-down list.

When there is no action that can be undone, the Undo button will be dimmed and unavailable. When there is no undone action that can be redone, the Redo button will be dimmed and unavailable.

WARNING WARNING WARNING WARNING WARNING WARNING WARNING WARNING

There are a few actions that Word *can't* undo, including File ➤ Save, File ➤ Close, and a number of others. If you find yourself needing to undo an action that Word says it cannot undo, you may need to resort to closing the document without saving changes to it. You will lose all changes made since the last time you saved it—but if you've done something truly horrible to the document, this sacrifice may be worthwhile. (This is another argument for saving your documents frequently, preferably after just enough reflection to be sure you haven't ruined them.)

Inserting a Date

To insert a date in a document:

1. Position the insertion point where you want the date to appear. (If necessary, use the Click and Type feature to position the insertion point.)

2. Choose Insert ➤ Date And Time to display the Date And Time dialog box (see Figure 2.4).

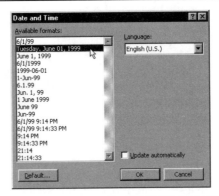

FIGURE 2.4: Use the Date And Time dialog box to quickly insert a date in a document.

3. In the Available Formats list box, choose the date format that you want to use.

   - The Language drop-down list box will show the language you're currently working in. You can choose another language—for example, *English (Australian)* instead of *English (US)*—to see the date formats available for that language.

   - If you want to make the date format in the Available Formats list box the default date format, click the Default button, and then choose the Yes button in the confirmation dialog box that appears. Word will then select that date format automatically every time you display the Date And Time dialog box.

4. If you want the date to be updated every time the document is opened, select the Update Automatically check box. This is useful for documents such as reports, which you often want to bear the date (and perhaps the time) on which they were printed, not the date on which they were created. For documents such as business letters and memos, on the other hand, you usually will want to make sure this check box is cleared, so that the date you insert remains the same no matter when you open or print the document.

5. Click the OK button to insert the date in your document.

Inserting Symbols and Special Characters

Word offers enough symbols and special characters for you to typeset almost any document. Symbols can be any character from multiplication or division signs to the fancy ➤ arrow Sybex uses to indicate menu commands. Special characters are a subset of symbols that include em dashes (—) and en dashes (–), trademark symbols (™), and the like—symbols that Microsoft thinks you might want to insert more frequently and with less effort than the symbols relegated to the Symbols tab.

To insert a symbol or special character at the insertion point or in place of the current selection:

1. Choose Insert ➤ Symbol to display the Symbol dialog box (see Figure 2.5).

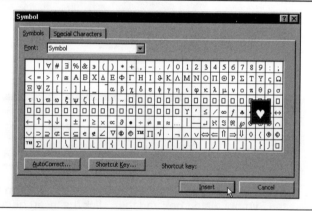

FIGURE 2.5: In the Symbol dialog box, choose the symbol or special character to insert and then click the Insert button.

2. To insert a symbol, click the Symbols tab to bring it to the front of the dialog box if it isn't already there, and then choose the symbol to insert from the box.

    *   Use the Font drop-down list to pick the font you want to see in the dialog box. For some fonts, a Subset drop-down list will appear to the right of the Font drop-down list; you can also choose a different subset of the font from this drop-down list.

    *   To enlarge a character so you can see it more clearly, click it once. An enlarged version of it will pop out at you. You can then move the zoom box around the Symbols dialog box by using →, ↗, ⊙, and ↙, or by clicking it and dragging with the mouse.

NOTE NOTE NOTE NOTE NOTE NOTE NOTE NOTE NOTE NOTE NOTE NOTE NOTE NOTE NOTE
Word will display a shortcut key for the symbol (if there is one) to the right of the Shortcut Key button. If you're often inserting a particular symbol, you can use the shortcut key instead—or you can create a shortcut key of your own, as we'll see in the next section. You can also create an AutoCorrect entry, which can be a handy way of inserting symbols in text. We'll look at how to do this in Skill 5.

3. To insert a special character, click the Special Characters tab to bring it to the front (unless it's already there). Choose the character to insert from the list box (see Figure 2.6).

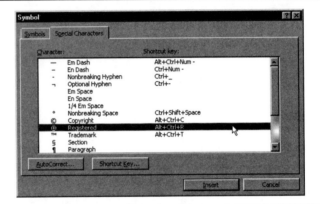

FIGURE 2.6: Choose a special character from the Special Characters tab of the Symbol dialog box and then click the Insert button.

4. To insert the symbol or special character, click the Insert button. Word will insert the character, and the Cancel button will change to a Close button.

   • You can also insert a symbol or special character by double-clicking it.

5. To insert more symbols or special characters, repeat steps 2 through 4.

6. Click the Close button to close the Symbol dialog box.

If you find yourself inserting a particular symbol or special character frequently, you can create a shortcut key combination for placing it more quickly. We'll look at how to do this in Skill 16. As you can see in the Symbol dialog box, many of the symbols and special characters already have shortcut keys assigned, but you can replace these with more convenient keyboard shortcuts of your own if you prefer.

Saving a Word Document

The first time you save a Word document, you assign it a name and choose the folder in which to save it. Thereafter, when you save the document, Word uses that name and folder and does not prompt you for changes to them—unless you decide to save the file under a different name or in a different folder, in which case you need to use the File ➤ Save As command rather than File ➤ Save. I'll discuss this in a moment.

TIP TIP TIP TIP TIP TIP TIP TIP TIP TIP TIP TIP TIP TIP TIP TIP TIP TIP TIP TIP TIP TIP TIP TIP TIP

You can also save different versions of the same document in the same file. We'll look at this in Skill 18.

Saving a Document for the First Time

To save a Word document for the first time:

1. Click the Save button or choose File ➤ Save. Word will display the Save As dialog box (see Figure 2.7).

NOTE NOTE NOTE NOTE NOTE NOTE NOTE NOTE NOTE NOTE NOTE NOTE NOTE NOTE NOTE

In dialog boxes that show filenames, you'll see file extensions (e.g., .doc at the end of a Word filename) only if you chose to see them in Windows Explorer. To display extensions in Explorer, choose View ➤ Options and clear the Hide MS-DOS File Extensions For File Types That Are Registered check box on the View tab of the Options dialog box or the Folder Options dialog box (these vary among Windows 95, Windows 98, and NT Workstation 4), then click the OK button.

2. In the Save In box at the top of the Save As dialog box, choose the folder in which to save the document.

    - Click the drop-down list button to the right of the Save In drop-down list to display the drop-down list of computers, folders, and locations accessible from your computer.

    - Click the Up One Level button (or press the Backspace key with the focus on the folder list) to move up one level of folders, or double-click a folder to open it and display its contents.

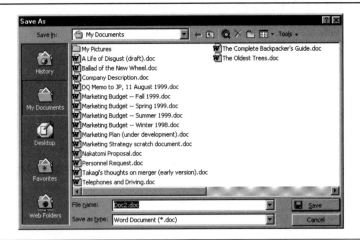

FIGURE 2.7: In the Save As dialog box, choose the folder in which to save your file, then enter a name for the file.

- Click the Back button (the button with the blue arrow pointing to the left) to move to the folder you were in previously. This button works like the Back button in Internet Explorer (or any other Web browser). When you display the ScreenTip for this button, it will show the name of the folder to which clicking the button will take you.

- Click the History button in the left panel of the dialog box to display the list of documents and folders you've worked with recently. (This list of documents is stored as links in the **\Office\Recent** folder.)

- Click the My Documents button in the left panel of the dialog box to display the **\My Documents** folder.

- Click the Desktop button in the left panel of the dialog box to display the computers and folders on your computer's desktop.

- Click the Favorites button in the left panel of the dialog box to display your list of Favorite folders and documents.

- Click the Web Folders button in the left panel of the dialog box to display your list of Web folders.

TIP TIP TIP TIP TIP TIP TIP TIP TIP TIP TIP TIP TIP TIP TIP TIP TIP TIP TIP TIP TIP TIP TIP

Like many Windows dialog boxes that provide access to files, Word's Save dialog box, Open dialog box, and others provide various ways in which to view and sort the files. The default view, shown in Figure 2.7, is List view, which shows an unadorned list of filenames. For more information, click the View drop-down list button and choose Details to show Details view, which shows the Name, Size, Type (for example, Microsoft Word Document), and Modified (i.e., last-modified) date for each file. You can also choose View ➢ Properties to show a panel of properties on the right-hand side of the dialog box or View ➢ Preview to display a preview panel on the right-hand side of the dialog box. To sort the files, choose View ➢ Arrange Icons and then By Name, By Type, By Size, or By Date, as appropriate, from the submenu. In Details view, you can click the column headings to sort the files by that column: Click once for ascending sort order, and click again to reverse the order.

3. In the File Name text box, enter a name for your file.

   - With Windows 95, Windows 98, and Windows NT's capacity for long filenames, you can enter a thorough and descriptive name—up to 255 characters, including the path to the file (i.e., the name of the folder or folders in which to save the file).

   - You can't use the following characters in filenames (if you do try to use one of these, Word will advise you of the problem):

Colon	:
Backslash	\
Forward slash	/
Greater-than sign	>
Less-than sign	<
Asterisk	*
Question mark	?
Double quotation mark	"
Pipe symbol	|

4. Click the Save button to save the file.

5. If Word displays a Properties dialog box for the document (see Figure 2.8), you can enter identifying information on the Summary tab.

   - In the Title box, Word displays the first paragraph of the document (or a section of it, if it's long). You'll often want to change this.

   - In the Author and Company boxes, Word displays the user name from the User Information tab of the Options dialog box.

- Use the Subject box to describe the subject of the document and enter any keywords that will help you remember the document in the Keywords box.

- Fill in other boxes as desired, then click OK to close the Properties dialog box and save the file.

NOTE NOTE NOTE NOTE NOTE NOTE NOTE NOTE NOTE NOTE NOTE NOTE NOTE NOTE

Whether the Properties dialog box appears depends on the Prompt For Document Properties setting on the Save tab of the Options dialog box. To have Word automatically prompt you for summary information, choose Tools ➢ Options, click the Save tab, select the Prompt For Document Properties check box, and click OK.

TIP TIP TIP TIP TIP TIP TIP TIP TIP TIP TIP TIP TIP TIP TIP TIP TIP TIP TIP TIP TIP TIP

To save all open documents at once, hold down one of the Shift keys on your keyboard, then, with your mouse, choose File ➢ Save All. Word will save each document that contains unsaved changes, prompting you for filenames for any document that has never been saved. If you have made changes to any of the templates on which the documents are based (for example, by creating a new keyboard shortcut, which I'll discuss in Skill 16), Word will prompt you to save the template as well.

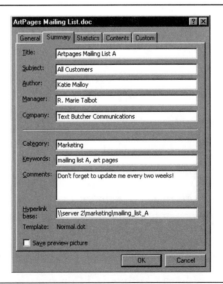

FIGURE 2.8: You can enter identifying information in the Properties dialog box.

Saving a Document Again

To save a document that you've saved before, click the Save button, choose File ➤ Save, or press Ctrl+S (the shortcut for Save). Word will save the document without consulting you about the location or filename.

Saving a Document under Another Name

One of the easiest ways to make a copy of a Word document is to open it and save it under a different name. This technique can be particularly useful if you've made changes to the document but don't want to replace the original document—for example, if you think you might need to revert to the original document and you've forgotten to make a backup before making your changes. The Save As command can also be useful for copying a document to a different folder or drive—for example, if you want to copy a document to a floppy drive or to a network drive.

To save a document under a different name or to a different folder:

1. Choose File ➤ Save As to display the Save As dialog box.

2. Enter a different name for the document in the File Name box or choose a different folder in the Save In area.

3. Click the Save button to save the document.

If the folder you chose already contains a document of the same name, Word will ask whether you want to overwrite it. Choose Yes or No. If you choose No, Word will return you to the Save As dialog box so that you can choose a different name or different folder.

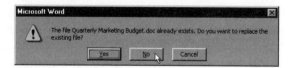

Saving a Word Document in a Different Format

Word lets you save documents in formats (file types) other than Word—for example, the file formats of other word processors. To save a file in a different format, you need to have Word's converter file for that format installed on your computer. If you don't, Word will prompt you to install the converter. Choose the Yes button, and the Windows installer will install the converter in question and notify you when it has finished doing so.

To save an existing file in a different format:

1.   Choose File ➢ Save As. Word will display the Save As dialog box.

2.   Scroll down the Save As Type drop-down list and choose the file type you want to save the current document as.

3.   If you want, enter a different filename for the file.

4.   Click the Save button or press Enter.

NOTE NOTE NOTE NOTE NOTE NOTE NOTE NOTE NOTE NOTE NOTE NOTE NOTE NOTE

If you haven't saved the file before, you can choose File ➢ Save instead of File ➢ Save As to open the Save As dialog box. You'll also need to specify a name for the document.

Closing a Document

To close the current document, choose File ➢ Close, press Ctrl+F4, or click the Close button on the document window. If the document contains unsaved changes, Word will prompt you to save them and will close the document when you're finished.

If the document has been saved before and if there are no new changes, Word will simply close the document. If you've created a new document but never changed it or saved it, Word will close it without prompting you to save it.

TIP TIP TIP TIP TIP TIP TIP TIP TIP TIP TIP TIP TIP TIP TIP TIP TIP TIP TIP TIP TIP TIP TIP

To close all open documents at once, hold down one of the Shift keys on your keyboard, then, with your mouse, choose File ➢ Close All. (Interestingly enough, the Close All choice appears on the File menu even when you have only one file open in Word.)

Opening a Word Document

To open a Word document:

1. Click the Open button on the Standard toolbar, choose File ➢ Open, or press Ctrl+O. Word will display the Open dialog box (see Figure 2.9). The Open dialog box provides several methods of navigating to the folder and file you want to open.

FIGURE 2.9: In the Open dialog box, use the Look In box to navigate to the folder that contains the document you want to open, then highlight the document and click the Open button.

2. If you're already in the right folder, proceed to step 3. If not, use the techniques described for the Save As dialog box in the section titled "Saving Documents for the First Time" to navigate to the folder holding the document you want to open. You'll notice that the Open dialog box has a Look In drop-down list rather than a Save In drop-down list, but otherwise everything works the same.

3. Choose the document to open, then click the Open button.

TIP TIP TIP TIP TIP TIP TIP TIP TIP TIP TIP TIP TIP TIP TIP TIP TIP TIP TIP TIP TIP TIP TIP TIP

To open several documents at once, click the first one in the Open dialog box to select it. Then, to select contiguous documents, hold down Shift and click the last document in the sequence to select it and all the ones between it and the first document. Then click the Open button. To select noncontiguous documents, hold down Ctrl and click each document you want to open and then click the Open button. (You can also combine the two methods of selection: First use Shift+click to select a sequence of documents, then use Ctrl+click to select others. To deselect documents within the range you have selected, use Ctrl+click.)

Opening Word Documents Using Windows Techniques

Windows 95, Windows 98, and Windows NT 4 offer several ways to open a Word document quickly. If you've used the document recently, pop up the Start menu, choose Documents, and choose the document from the list of the fifteen most recently used files (as shown here). If Word is already open, Windows will just open the document for you; if Word isn't open, Windows will open Word and the document at the same time.

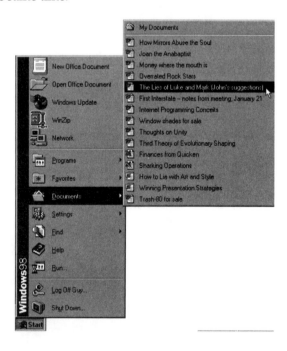

In Windows 98, the Documents menu also provides a shortcut to the **\My Documents** folder, the default location for storing your documents in Windows 98. In Windows NT 4 with Internet Explorer 4 or Internet Explorer 5 installed, the Documents menu provides a shortcut to the **\Personal** folder, the default location for storing your documents in NT. Click the My Documents shortcut or the Personal shortcut to display that folder in an Explorer window, which you can use to launch a document by double-clicking it.

If you need to open a Word document frequently but can't be sure that it will always be among your fifteen-most-wanted files on the Start menu's Documents menu, you can create an icon for it on the Desktop. To do so, either right-click the Desktop, choose New ➤ Shortcut, and then Browse for the document in the Create Shortcut dialog box; or, more simply, open an Explorer window, find the Word document you want to keep handy, and right-drag it to the Desktop. Windows will invite you to create a shortcut to the document; go right ahead.

TIP TIP TIP TIP TIP TIP TIP TIP TIP TIP TIP TIP TIP TIP TIP TIP TIP TIP TIP TIP TIP TIP TIP TIP

To quickly open one of the documents you worked on most recently from inside Word, pull down the File menu and choose one of the most recently used documents listed at the bottom of the menu. (By default, Word lists four files, but you can change this by using Tools ➤ Options, selecting the General tab, and changing the number in the Entries box for the Recently Used File List. Alternatively, you can turn off the display of recently used documents by clearing the Recently Used File List check box.

To keep a document in an even more handy place than the Desktop, you can create a shortcut for it on a Quick Launch toolbar if you're using the Active Desktop. To do so, open an Explorer window, find the document, right-drag it to the Quick Launch toolbar in question, and choose Create Shortcut Here from the resulting context menu. You'll then be able to launch the document (and Word, if it isn't already running) by clicking the icon on the Quick Launch toolbar.

NOTE NOTE NOTE NOTE NOTE NOTE NOTE NOTE NOTE NOTE NOTE NOTE NOTE NOTE NOTE

Word provides a feature for quickly finding documents by one or more pieces of information that you specify. For details, download the "Finding Word Documents" bonus item from the Sybex Web site.

Opening a Non-Word Document

Word can open files saved in a number of other formats, from plain-text ASCII files to spreadsheets (for example, Lotus 1-2-3) to calendar and address books. To open a file saved in a format other than Word, you need to have the appropriate converter file installed on your computer so that Word can read the file. Generally speaking, the easiest way to tell if you have the right converter installed for a particular file format is to try to open the file; if Word cannot open it, it will prompt you to install the converter. Choose the Yes button. The Windows Installer will install the converter and notify you when it has finished doing so.

To open a document saved in a format other than Word:

1. Select File ➤ Open to display the Open dialog box.

2. Choose the folder containing the document you want to open.

3. Click the drop-down list button on the Files Of Type list box at the bottom left-hand corner of the Open dialog box. From the list, select the type of file that you want to open. If Word doesn't list the file that you want to open, choose All Files (*.*) from the drop-down list to display all the files in the folder.

4. Choose the file in the main window of the Open dialog box, then click the Open button or press Enter to open the file.

Are You Experienced?

Now you can . . .

- ☑ create and save a new document

- ☑ enter text, dates, and special characters in a document

- ☑ use the Undo and Redo features

- ☑ open a document

- ☑ close a document

- ☑ open a non-Word document

Printing a Document

- → **Using Print Preview**
- → **Printing documents**
- → **Printing envelopes**
- → **Printing labels**

Once you've written, set up, and formatted your documents, you'll probably want to print them. As it does with its other features, Word offers a wealth of printing options. Printing can be as simple as clicking one button to print a whole document, or as complicated as choosing which parts of your document to print, what to print them on, how many copies to print, and even what order to print them in.

In this skill, we'll look first at how to use Word's Print Preview mode to nail down any glaring deficiencies in your text before you print it. Second, we'll tackle straightforward printing. And finally, we'll move on to the tricky stuff—envelopes and labels.

Using Print Preview

Before you print any document, you'll do well to use Word's Print Preview mode to establish that the document looks right before you print it.

To use Print Preview, click the Print Preview button or choose File ➤ Print Preview. Word will display the current document in Print Preview mode (see Figure 3.1).

In Print Preview mode, Word displays the Print Preview toolbar (see Figure 3.2), which has the following buttons:

Print	Prints the current document using the default print settings.
Magnifier	Switches between Magnifier mode and Editing mode. In Magnifier mode, the pointer appears as a magnifying glass containing a plus sign (when the view is zoomed out) or a minus sign (when the view is zoomed in). In Editing mode, the pointer appears as the insertion point, and you can use it to edit as usual.
One Page	Zooms the view to one full page.
Multiple Pages	Zooms the view to multiple pages. When you click the Multiple Pages button, Word displays a small grid showing the display combinations possible—one full page; two pages side by side; three pages side by side; two pages, one on top of the other; four pages, two on top, two below; and so on. Click the arrangement of pages you want. Click and drag to the right or bottom to extend out to more columns or rows of pages.
Zoom Control	Determines the size at which you view the document. Use the drop-down list to choose the zoom percentage that suits you.

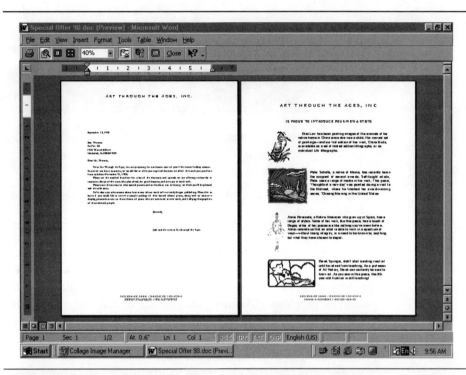

FIGURE 3.1: In Print Preview mode, Word displays your document as it will appear when you print it.

View Ruler	Toggles the display of the horizontal and vertical rulers on and off.
Shrink To Fit	Attempts to make your document fit on one fewer page (by changing the font size, line spacing, and margins). This is useful when your crucial fax strays a line or two on to an additional page and you'd like to shrink it down.
Toggle Full Screen Views	Maximizes Word and removes the menus, status bar, scroll bars, etc., from the display. This is useful for clearing more screen real estate to see exactly how your document looks before you print it.
Close Preview	Closes Print Preview, returning you to whichever view you were in before.
Help	Adds a question mark to the pointer so that you can click any screen element and receive pop-up help.

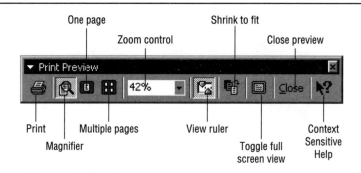

FIGURE 3.2: The Print Preview toolbar offers quick access to the Print Preview features.

You can explore Print Preview on your own, but here's one thing to try: Click and drag the gray margin borders in the rulers to quickly adjust the page setup of the document, or double-click in these borders to display the Page Setup dialog box. Print Preview will show you how the document will look on the printer you're currently using. If you're using Print Preview to check that your documents look OK before you print them, make sure that you've already selected the printer you're going to use for the document.

To exit Print Preview, click the Close button on the Print Preview toolbar to return to the view you were in before you entered Print Preview, or choose File ➤ Print Preview, or press the Escape key.

Printing a Document

Once you've checked a document in Print Preview and fixed any aberrations, you're ready to print it. Next, you need to choose whether to print the whole document at once or just part of it.

Printing a Whole Document Simply

The easiest way to print a document in Word is simply to click the Print button on the Standard toolbar. This prints the current document without offering you any options—to be more precise, it prints one copy of the entire document in page-number order (1, 2, 3) to the currently selected printer.

You can also print an entire document by using the procedure described in the next section and choosing All in step 2.

Printing a Document with Options

If you want to print only part of a document, don't click the Print button. Instead, choose File ➢ Print to display the Print dialog box (see Figure 3.3). Then:

TIP TIP TIP TIP TIP TIP TIP TIP TIP TIP TIP TIP TIP TIP TIP TIP TIP TIP TIP TIP TIP TIP
The keyboard shortcuts for the Print command are Ctrl+P and Ctrl+Shift+F12. I recommend using Ctrl+P for simplicity.

SKILL
3

1. Make sure the printer named in the Name drop-down list of the Printer group box is the one you want to use. If it's not, use the drop-down list to select the right printer.

2. Choose which pages to print in the Page Range group box by clicking one of the option buttons:

    - All prints the whole document.

    - Current Page prints the page on which the insertion point is currently located.

    - Selection prints only the selected text in your document. (If you haven't selected any text, this option button will be dimmed and unavailable.)

    - Pages lets you print individual pages by number or a range (or ranges) of pages. Use commas to separate the page numbers (e.g., 1, 11, 21) and a hyphen to indicate page ranges (e.g., 31-41). You can also combine the two: 1, 11, 21-31, 41-51, 61.

TIP TIP TIP TIP TIP TIP TIP TIP TIP TIP TIP TIP TIP TIP TIP TIP TIP TIP TIP TIP TIP TIP
To print from a particular page to the end of the document, you don't need to know the number for the last page of the document—simply enter the page number followed by a hyphen (e.g., 11-).

3. Make sure that Document is selected in the Print What drop-down list.

    - If you want to print a peripheral part of the document, select it in the Print What drop-down list. The choices are Document Properties (discussed in Skill 2), Comments (discussed in Skill 18), Styles (discussed in Skill 5), AutoText Entries (discussed in Skill 8) from the template, and Key Assignments (discussed in Skill 16) from the document or template.

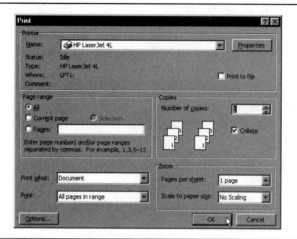

FIGURE 3.3: In the Print dialog box, choose the printer you want to use, which pages you want to print, the number of copies you want, and any zoom effects you want to apply. Then click the OK button to print.

4. If you want to print only odd pages or even pages, use the Print drop-down list at the bottom-left corner of the Print dialog box to specify Odd Pages or Even Pages instead of All Pages In Range. This can be useful for printing two-sided documents.

5. Choose how many copies of the document you want to print by using the Number Of Copies box in the Copies group box.

    • You can also choose whether to collate the pages—if you collate them, Word prints the first set of pages in order (1, 2, 3, 4, 5) and then prints the next set and subsequent sets; if you don't collate them, Word prints all the copies of page 1, then all the copies of page 2, and so on.

6. In the Zoom group box, you can choose whether to shrink the document down so that multiple pages fit on one sheet of paper. Choose the number of pages in the Pages Per Sheet drop-down list and select an option in the Scale To Paper Size drop-down list. For regular documents, you'll want to stick with 1 Page Per Sheet and No Scaling.

7. When you've made your choices in the Print dialog box, click the OK button to send the document to the printer.

Printing on Different Paper

So far we've looked only at printing on your default-sized paper (for example, $8\frac{1}{2}$x11" paper). Sooner or later you're going to need to print on a different size of paper, be it to produce a manual, an application to some bureaucracy, or a trifold birthday card. Not only can you use various sizes of paper with Word, but you can use different sizes of paper for different sections of the same document. (Skill 4 discusses sections.)

When you want to print on paper of a different size, you will need to set up your document suitably—paper size, margins, and orientation. (Look ahead to the "Page Setup" section of Skill 4 for more details on this if you need to.)

Next, choose the paper source for each section of your document.

SKILL 3

Choosing a Paper Source

If you're writing a letter or a report, you may want to put the first page on special paper. For example, the first page of a letter might be on company paper that contains the company's logo, name, address, and URL, while subsequent pages might be on paper that contains everything but the URL.

To choose the paper source for printing the current section of the current document:

1. Choose File ➤ Page Setup or double-click in the top half of the horizontal ruler or anywhere in the vertical ruler to display the Page Setup dialog box, then click the Paper Source tab (see Figure 3.4).

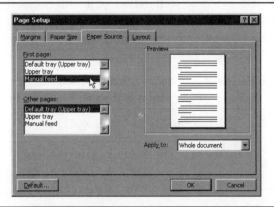

FIGURE 3.4: Choose the printer trays for the various sections of a document on the Paper Source tab of the Page Setup dialog box.

2. In the First Page list box, choose the printer tray that contains the paper for the first page. (If your printer has only one tray, choose Manual Feed so that you can feed the page of different paper separately from the main tray.)

3. In the Other Pages list box, choose the printer tray that contains the paper you want to use for the remaining pages of the document. Usually, you'll want to choose Default Tray here, but on occasion you may want to use either another tray or Manual Feed for special effects.

4. In the Apply To drop-down list box, choose the section of the document that you want to print on the paper you chose. (The default is Whole Document unless the document contains sections, in which case the default is This Section. You can also choose This Point Forward to print from the insertion point through the rest of the document on the paper you chose, the page containing the insertion point being the "first page" and the rest of the document being the "other pages.")

5. Click the OK button to close the Page Setup dialog box and save your changes.

NOTE NOTE NOTE NOTE NOTE NOTE NOTE NOTE NOTE NOTE NOTE NOTE NOTE NOTE

To set the paper source for another section of the document, click in that section and repeat the above steps.

Setting a Default Paper Source

If you always print from a different paper tray than your copy of Word is set up to use, you'd do well to change it. This might happen if you always need to use letterhead on a networked printer that has a number of paper trays, and your colleagues keep filling the default paper tray with flavorless white bond.

To set your default paper source:

1. Choose File ➤ Page Setup or double-click in the top half of the horizontal ruler (or anywhere in the vertical ruler) to display the Page Setup dialog box.

2. Click the Paper Source tab to display it.

3. Make your selections in the First Page list box and Other Pages list box.

4. Choose an option from the Apply To drop-down list if necessary.

5. Click the Default button. Word will display a message box asking for confirmation of your choice.

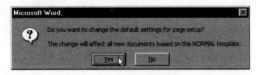

6. Click Yes. Word will close the Page Setup dialog box and make the change.

Printing Envelopes

Printing envelopes has long been the bane of the computerized office. Envelopes have been confusing to set up in word-processing applications and—worse— they tend to jam in laser printers and inkjet printers (and that's not even mentioning what dot-matrix printers think of them). There have been four traditional ways of avoiding these problems: hand-write the labels, use a typewriter, use window envelopes, or use sheets of labels. If none of these methods appeals to you, read on.

To print an envelope:

1. Choose Tools ➤ Envelopes And Labels. Word will display the Envelopes And Labels dialog box (see Figure 3.5).

    • If Word finds what it identifies as an address in the current document, it will display it in the Delivery Address box. If you don't think Word will find the address hidden in the document—for example, if the document contains more than one address or the address is not broken over several lines into a typical address format—highlight the address before choosing Tools ➤ Envelopes And Labels.

2. If Word hasn't found an address in the document, you'll need to choose it yourself.

    • To include a recently used address, click the Insert Address drop-down list button in the Envelopes And Labels dialog box and choose the name from the drop-down list.

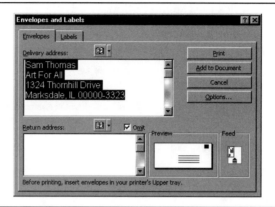

FIGURE 3.5: Word displays any address it finds in the document—or the address you selected—in the Delivery Address box on the Envelopes tab of the Envelopes And Labels dialog box.

- To include an address from an address book available to you (see the sidebar "Where Does the Address Book Live?" for more information on address books), click the Insert Address button and choose the address book from the Show Names From The drop-down list in the Select Name dialog box. If you aren't logged into Outlook (see the following sidebar), you will be prompted to choose a messaging profile (basically, an identity in Outlook) before the Select Name dialog box is displayed. Then choose the name, either by typing the first characters of the name into the Type Name Or Select From List text box or by selecting it from the list box. Click the OK button to insert the name in the Delivery Address box of the Envelopes And Labels dialog box.

- Alternatively, type the name and address into the Address box.

WHERE DOES THE ADDRESS BOOK LIVE?

If you've used other Office applications in addition to Word, you know that Microsoft has made the applications work with each other in its effort to deliver a comprehensive solution to your work needs. As you'll see in Skill 17, you can share data between applications (for example, you can insert part of an Excel spreadsheet or a PowerPoint slide in a Word document).

continued ▶

Along the same lines, the whole of Office shares an address book so that you can keep all your addresses in one convenient location.

Office keeps its address book in Outlook, the e-mail, calendaring, and scheduling application. The addresses available to you in the Envelopes And Labels dialog box will be those available in Outlook for the *messaging profile* (the Outlook identity) under which you logged into your computer or logged into Outlook. If you don't have Outlook installed on the computer you're using, the Envelopes And Labels dialog box will not contain an Insert Address button.

For information on creating and managing personal address books in Outlook, consult a book such as *Outlook 2000: No experience required* or *Mastering Outlook 2000* (both published by Sybex). If your computer is connected to a network and uses networked address books (such as those on an Exchange server), contact your network administrator for advice.

SKILL
3

3. Check the return address that Word has inserted in the Return Address box. Word automatically picks this information out of the User Information tab of the Options dialog box. If the information is incorrect, you can correct it in the Return Address box, but you'd do better to correct it in the Options dialog box if you regularly work with the computer you're now using. (Choose Tools ➢ Options, then click the User Information tab.) If no address is entered on the User Information tab of the Options dialog box, Word will leave the Return Address box blank.

   - You can also use the Insert Address button's drop-down list to insert a recently used address, or click the Insert Address button and choose a name in the Select Name dialog box.

   - Alternatively, you can omit a return address by checking the Omit check box.

4. Check the Preview box to see how the envelope will look and the Feed box to see how Word expects you to feed it into the printer. If either of these is not to your liking, click the Options button (or click the Preview icon or the Feed icon) to display the Envelope Options dialog box (see Figure 3.6).

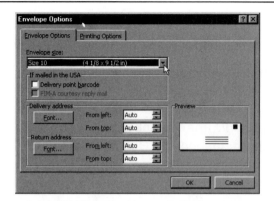

FIGURE 3.6: In the Envelope Options dialog box, use the Envelope Options tab to set the size of the envelope and the fonts for the delivery address and return address. Use the Printing Options tab to set the feed method you want to use with your printer.

5. On the Envelope Options tab of the Envelope Options dialog box (yes, this gets weird), use the Envelope Size drop-down list to choose the size of envelope you're using. (Check the envelope's packaging for the size before you get out your ruler to measure an envelope.)

6. If you want to customize the look of the addresses, use the options in the Delivery Address group box and Return Address group box. The Font button in these boxes opens the Envelope Address dialog box (which is a version of the Font dialog box that we'll examine in Skill 4). Choose the font and effects you want, then click the OK button to close the dialog box. Use the From Left and From Top boxes in the Delivery Address box and Return Address box to set the placement of the address on the envelope. Watch the Preview box to see how you're doing.

7. On the Printing Options tab of the Envelope Options dialog box, Word offers options for changing the feed method for the envelope—you have the choice of six different envelope orientations; the choice of placing the envelope Face Up or Face Down in the printer; and the choice of Clockwise Rotation. Again, choose the options you want. Click the OK button when you're satisfied.

If your printer is set up correctly, Word should be able to make a fair guess at how you'll need to feed the envelope for the printer to print it correctly. You probably won't need to change the settings on the Printing Options tab of the Envelope Options dialog box unless you find that Word won't print your envelope correctly.

SKILL
3

8. You can now print the envelope you've set up by clicking the Print button in the Envelopes And Labels dialog box, or by adding it to the current document by clicking the Add To Document button.

   - If you choose the Add To Document button, Word places the envelope on a new page at the start of the document and formats the page to require a manual envelope feed. When you print the document, you'll need to start the printer off with a manually fed envelope; once the envelope has printed, Word will resume its normal feeding pattern for the rest of the document (unless that too has abnormal paper requirements).

Printing Labels

If you don't want to mess with feeding envelopes into your printer and betting that it won't chew them up, sheets of labels provide a good alternative. What's more, Word makes it easy to set up labels.

In this section, we'll look at how to set up labels for one addressee—either a single label or a whole sheet of labels with the same address on each. For sheets of labels with a different address on each label, see Skill 13.

1. If the current document contains the address you want to use on the label, select the address.

2. Choose Tools ➤ Envelopes And Labels to display the Envelopes And Labels dialog box (see Figure 3.7) and select the Labels tab if it isn't currently displayed.

   - If you selected an address in step 1, or if Word found an address on its own, Word will display it in the Address box.

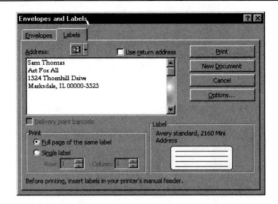

FIGURE 3.7: In the Envelopes And Labels dialog box, click the Labels tab if it isn't displayed.

3. Choose the type of labels you want. The current type of label is displayed in the Label box in the bottom-right corner of the Envelopes And Labels dialog box. To choose another type of label, click the Options button (or click anywhere in the Label group box). You'll see the Label Options dialog box (see Figure 3.8).

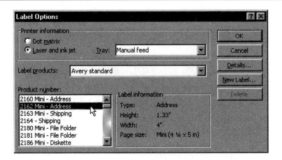

FIGURE 3.8: In the Label Options dialog box, pick the type of label you want to use.

- Choose the type of printer you'll be using: Dot Matrix, or Laser And Ink Jet.

- Choose the printer tray that you'll put the label sheets in by using the Tray drop-down list.

- Choose the category of label by using the Label Products drop-down list: Avery Standard, Avery A4 And A5 Sizes, MACO Standard, or Other. (Other includes labels by manufacturers other than Avery and MACO.)

- In the Product Number list box, choose the type of labels you're using—it should be on the box of labels. The Label Information group box will show the details for the type of labels you selected in the Product Number list box.

- For more details on the labels you chose, or to customize them, click the Details button to display the Information dialog box. Click OK when you're done.

- Click the OK button in the Label Options dialog box to return to the Envelopes And Labels dialog box. It will now display the labels you chose in the Label box.

4. Add the address (if you haven't already selected one):

   - To add a recently used address, choose it from the Insert Address button's drop-down list.

   - To include an address from an address book, click the Insert Address button and choose the address book from the Show Names From The drop-down list in the Select Name dialog box. If you aren't logged on to e-mail, you will be prompted to choose a messaging profile before the Select Name dialog box is displayed. Then choose the name, either by typing the first characters of the name into the Type Name or Select From List text box or by selecting it from the list box. Click the OK button to insert the name in the Address box of the Envelopes And Labels dialog box.

   - Alternatively, type the name and address into the Address box.

5. In the Print group box, choose whether to print a full page of the same label or a single label.

   - If you choose to print a single label, set the Row and Column numbers that describe its location on the sheet of labels.

6. If you chose to print a full page of the same label, you can click the New Document button to create a new document containing the labels, then print it and save it for future use. Alternatively, click the Print button to print the sheet of labels. (If you chose to print a single label, Word offers only the Print button.)

SKILL
3

If you want to customize your labels, choose the New Document button, then add any formatting that you like. You can also add graphics by using Word's Insert ➤ Picture command.

Are You Experienced?

Now you can . . .

- ☑ use Print Preview to see how your documents will look when you print them
- ☑ print documents
- ☑ print different parts of a document
- ☑ print envelopes
- ☑ print labels

SKILL 4

Formatting Documents

- → Formatting characters and words
- → Formatting paragraphs
- → Using tabs
- → Using language formatting
- → Setting up the page
- → Applying borders and shading

Word supplies you with enough formatting options to create anything from simple, typewriter-style documents up to a complex newsletter or book. The basic types of formatting options start with character formatting (how the individual letters look) and move through paragraph formatting (how paragraphs appear on the page) to style formatting (a combination of character and paragraph formatting, among other formatting) and, finally, page setup. In this skill, we'll look at character formatting, paragraph formatting, and page setup. In the next skill, I'll add styles to the mix.

Character Formatting

Character formatting is formatting that you can apply to one or more characters. A character is a letter, a number, a symbol, a space, or an object (such as a graphic). Character formatting consists of:

- character attributes (properties), such as bold, italic, underline, and strikethrough

- fonts (also known as typefaces) such as Courier New, Times New Roman, and Arial

- point size—the size of the font

- character spacing such as superscripts and subscripts (vertical spacing), and kerning (horizontal spacing)

You can apply character formatting in several ways: by using the Font dialog box, keyboard shortcuts, or the Formatting toolbar. Each of these methods has advantages and disadvantages depending on what you're doing when you decide to start applying formatting and how much of it you need to apply. We'll look at each of them in turn.

Character Formatting Using the Font Dialog Box

The Font dialog box offers you the most control over font formatting, providing all the character-formatting options together in one handy location.

To set character formatting using the Font dialog box:

1. Select the text whose formatting you want to change.

   - If you want to change the formatting of just one word, place the insertion point inside it.

2. Right-click in the text and choose Font from the context menu, or choose Format Font, to display the Font dialog box (see Figure 4.1). If the Font tab isn't displayed, click it to bring it to the front of the dialog box.

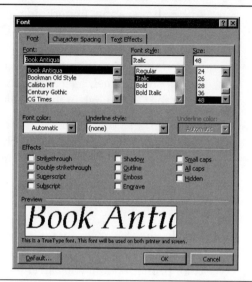

FIGURE 4.1: The Font dialog box gives you quick access to all the character formatting options Word offers.

3. Choose the formatting options you want from the Font tab:

   • In the Font list box, choose the font for the text.

   • In the Font Style list box, choose the font style: Regular, Italic, Bold, or Bold Italic.

TIP TIP TIP TIP TIP TIP TIP TIP TIP TIP TIP TIP TIP TIP TIP TIP TIP TIP TIP TIP TIP TIP TIP

Watch the Preview box at the bottom of the dialog box to see approximately how your text will look.

   • In the Size box, choose the font size you want. To choose a font size that Word doesn't list, type it into the top Size box—for example, enter **13** to produce 13-point text. (Word offers 12-point and 14-point options in the list box.)

- In the Underline box, choose the underlining style you want. The styles are mostly self-explanatory, with the possible exception of these two: (none) removes any existing underline, while Words Only adds a single underline underneath words, with no underline underneath spaces. If you apply underlining, you can select the color for the underline by using the Underline Color drop-down list. Automatic applies the default color (typically that of the current font). For colors beyond those shown on the drop-down panel, click the More Colors button on the panel, select the color you want on either the Standard tab or the Custom tab of the Colors dialog box, and click the OK button to apply the color.

- For any special effects, select the check boxes in the Effects area for Strikethrough, Double Strikethrough, Superscript, Subscript, Shadow, Outline, Emboss, Engrave, Small Caps, All Caps, or Hidden. (Hidden text is invisible under normal viewing conditions and does not print unless you choose to include it.)

- Finally, choose a color for your text from the Font Color drop-down list. This will affect the text on screen—and on printouts if you have a color printer. Again, you can choose colors other than those on the drop-down palette by clicking the More Colors button to display the Colors dialog box.

4. For special effects, adjust the settings on the Character Spacing tab of the Font dialog box.

- The Scale drop-down list controls the horizontal scaling of the text. By default, this is set to 100%—full size. You can change this value to anything from 1% to 600% to squeeze or stretch the text horizontally.

- The Spacing option controls the horizontal placement of letters relative to each other—closer to each other or farther apart—by adjusting the space between the letters. From the Spacing drop-down list, you can choose Expanded or Condensed, then use the up and down spinner arrows in the By box to adjust the degree of expansion or condensation. (Alternatively, simply click the spinner arrows and let Word worry about making the Spacing drop-list match your choice.) Again, watch the Preview box for a simulation of the effect your current choices will have.

- The Position option controls the vertical placement of letters relative to the baseline they're theoretically resting on. From the Position list, you can choose Normal, Raised, or Lowered, then use the spinner arrows in the By box to raise or lower the letters—or simply click the spinner arrows and let Word determine whether the text is Normal, Raised, or Lowered.

- To turn on automatic kerning for fonts above a certain size, select the Kerning For Fonts check box and adjust the point size in the Points And Above box if necessary.

NOTE NOTE NOTE NOTE NOTE NOTE NOTE NOTE NOTE NOTE NOTE NOTE NOTE NOTE NOTE

Kerning **is adjusting the space between letters so that no letter appears too far from its neighbor. For example, if you type WAVE in a large font size without kerning, Word will leave enough space between the W and the A, and the A and the V, for you to slalom a small truck through. With kerning, you'll only be able to get a motorcycle through the gap.**

SKILL 4

5. To really enliven a document, try one of the six options on the Text Effects tab of the Font dialog box: Blinking Background, Las Vegas Lights, Marching Black Ants, Marching Red Ants, Shimmer, and Sparkle Text. Use these options in moderation for best effect on Web pages, and be aware that they can look bad in printed documents. To remove an animation, select (none) in the Animations list box.

6. When you've finished making your choices in the Font dialog box, click the OK button to close the dialog box and to apply your changes to the selected text or current word.

Setting a New Default Font

To set a new default font for all documents based on the current template, make all your choices on the Font and Character Spacing tabs (you probably won't want to set any Text Effects options as defaults) of the Font dialog box, then click the Default button (on any tab). Word will display a message box to confirm that you want to change the default font. Click the Yes button to make the change.

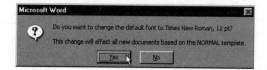

Character Formatting Using the Formatting Toolbar

The Formatting toolbar offers a quick way to apply some of the most-used character formatting options: font, font size, bold, italic, underline, highlighting, and font color (see Figure 4.2).

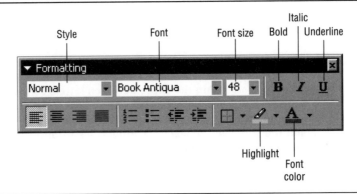

FIGURE 4.2: The Formatting toolbar provides a quick way to apply formatting to your documents.

To change fonts with the Formatting toolbar, select the text you want to affect, then click the drop-down list button on the Font box and select the new font from the list that appears.

- The fonts you've used most recently will be listed at the top of the list, with an alphabetical listing of all the fonts underneath.

- To move quickly down the list of fonts, type the first letter of the font's name.

To change font size, select the text to change, then click the drop-down list button on the Font Size box and select the font size from the list that appears. To choose a font size that Word doesn't list, type it into the Font Size box and press Enter.

TIP TIP TIP TIP TIP TIP TIP TIP TIP TIP TIP TIP TIP TIP TIP TIP TIP TIP TIP TIP TIP TIP TIP TIP

To change the font or font size of just one word, you don't need to select it—just placing the insertion point within the word does the trick.

To apply bold, italic, or underline, select the text you want to emphasize, then click the Bold, Italic, or Underline button on the Formatting toolbar. When you've applied one of these attributes, the relevant button will appear to be pushed in.

To remove bold, italic, or underline, select the emphasized text, then click the Bold, Italic, or Underline button again to remove the formatting.

To apply highlighting to one instance of text, select the text, then click the Highlight button.

To apply highlighting to several instances of text easily, click the Highlight button before selecting any text. Your mouse pointer will take on a little highlighter pen when moved into the document window. Click and drag this over text to highlight it.

To turn the highlighting off, click the Highlight button again or press the Esc key.

To change the color of the highlighting, click the drop-down list arrow next to the Highlight button and choose another color from the list. (The default color for highlighting is the classic fluorescent yellow—Enhanced French Headlamp, as it's known in the trade—beloved of anyone who's ever had a highlighter pen break in their shirt pocket.)

To remove highlighting, click and drag the highlighter pen over the highlighted text.

To change the font color of the current selection or current word, click the Font Color drop-down palette button and choose the color you want from the palette. You can then apply that color quickly to selected text by clicking the Font Color button.

Character Formatting Using Keyboard Shortcuts

Word offers the following keyboard shortcuts for formatting text with the keyboard. For all of them, select the text you want to affect first, unless you want to affect only the word in which the insertion point is currently resting.

Action	Keyboard Shortcut
Increase font size (in steps)	Ctrl+Shift+.
Decrease font size (in steps)	Ctrl+Shift+,
Increase font size by 1 point	Ctrl+]
Decrease font size by 1 point	Ctrl+[
Change case (cycle)	Shift+F3
All capitals	Ctrl+Shift+A
Small capitals	Ctrl+Shift+K
Bold	Ctrl+B
Underline	Ctrl+U

Action	Keyboard Shortcut
Underline (single words)	Ctrl+Shift+W
Double-underline	Ctrl+Shift+D
Hidden text	Ctrl+Shift+H
Italic	Ctrl+I
Subscript	Ctrl+=
Superscript	Ctrl+Shift+= (i.e., Ctrl++)
Remove formatting	Ctrl+Shift+Z
Change to Symbol font	Ctrl+Shift+Q

Paragraph Formatting

With paragraph formatting, you can set a number of parameters that influence how your paragraphs look:

- Alignment
- Indentation
- Line spacing
- Text flow
- Tabs

The following sections of this skill discuss each of these paragraph formatting options in turn.

Setting Alignment

Word provides the standard four kinds of paragraph alignment: left-aligned (the default and normal alignment), centered, right-aligned (aligned with the right margin), and justified (aligned with both the left margin and the right margin). Alignment is also called *justification*.

There are several ways to set paragraph alignment: You can align new text (more exactly, a new paragraph) quickly in Print Layout view, you can use the alignment buttons on the Formatting toolbar, you can use the keyboard shortcuts, or you can use the options in the Paragraph dialog box. Using the buttons on the Formatting toolbar is the easiest way of aligning existing text.

Aligning New Text by Using Click and Type

If you need to quickly align a new paragraph you're adding to a page, your best bet is to use the Click and Type feature, which we examined in Skill 2. Double-click to place the insertion point where you want it in blank space on the page, and Word handles the intervening paragraphs, any necessary tabs, and the alignment automatically.

Setting Alignment Using the Formatting Toolbar

To set alignment using the Formatting toolbar:

1. Place the insertion point in the paragraph that you want to align. To align more than one paragraph, select all the paragraphs you want to align.

2. Click the Align Left, Center, Align Right, or Justify button on the Formatting toolbar (see Figure 4.3).

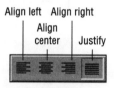

FIGURE 4.3: To align the current paragraph or selected text quickly, click the appropriate button on the Formatting toolbar.

Setting Alignment Using Keyboard Shortcuts

When you're typing, the quickest way to set the alignment of paragraphs is by using these keyboard shortcuts:

Shortcut	Effect
Ctrl+L	Align left
Ctrl+E	Center
Ctrl+R	Align right
Ctrl+J	Justify

Setting Alignment Using the Paragraph Dialog Box

The third way to set alignment—and usually the slowest—is to use the Paragraph dialog box. Why discuss this? Because you're very likely to be making other formatting changes in the Paragraph dialog box, so sometimes you may find it useful to set alignment there too.

To set alignment using the Paragraph dialog box:

1. Place the insertion point in the paragraph you want to align. To align several paragraphs, select all the paragraphs you want to align.

2. Right-click and choose Paragraph from the context menu, or choose Format ➢ Paragraph, to display the Paragraph dialog box (see Figure 4.4).

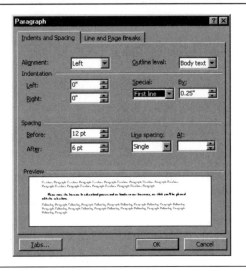

FIGURE 4.4: In the Paragraph dialog box, you can set many paragraph-formatting options, including alignment.

3. Choose the alignment you want from the Alignment drop-down list.

4. Click the OK button to close the Paragraph dialog box.

Setting Indents

As with setting alignment, you can set indents in more than one way. Again, the quickest way is with the ruler, but you can also use the Paragraph dialog box and keyboard shortcuts.

Before we get into setting indents, you need to know a little about how Word handles them. Briefly, the size of the page you're working with is set via the Page Setup dialog box, which we'll examine in the section titled "Page Setup" later in this skill. For most documents, Word starts you off with an $8\frac{1}{2}$" × 11" page—standard letter-sized paper. You can then set top, bottom, left, and right margins for the page. Again, Word starts you off with default margins, but you can set your own margins whenever you want (we'll examine this in "Page Setup" too). Any indents you set are relative to the margins, not to the edges of the page. You can set both positive indents (in from the margin) and negative indents (out from the margin).

Setting Indents with the Ruler

To set indents using the ruler, click and drag the indent markers on it (see Figure 4.5).

FIGURE 4.5: Click and drag the indent markers on the ruler to change the indentation of the current paragraph or selected paragraphs.

- The first-line indent marker (the downward-pointing arrow) specifies the indentation of the first line of the paragraph (this could be a hanging indent).

- The left indent marker (the upward-pointing arrow) specifies the position of the left indent.

NOTE NOTE NOTE NOTE NOTE NOTE NOTE NOTE NOTE NOTE NOTE NOTE NOTE NOTE

To move the left indent marker and first-line indent marker together, drag the left indent marker by the square box at its base rather than by the upward-pointing mark. Dragging by the upward-pointing mark will move the left indent marker but leave the first-line indent marker where it was.

- The right indent marker specifies the position of the right indent.

Setting Indents with the Paragraph Dialog Box

Depending on whether you have a graphical or literal mindset, you may find setting indents in the Paragraph dialog box easier than setting them with the ruler. To set paragraph indents with the Paragraph dialog box:

1. Place the insertion point in the paragraph for which you want to set indents. To set indents for several paragraphs, select all the paragraphs you want to set indents for.

2. Right-click and choose Paragraph from the context menu, or choose Format ➤ Paragraph, to display the Paragraph dialog box.

3. Make sure the Indents And Spacing tab is selected (if it's not visible, click it to bring it in front of the Line And Page Breaks tab).

4. In the Left box, enter the distance to indent the paragraph from the left margin.

5. In the Right box, enter the distance to indent the paragraph from the right margin.

6. In the Special box, choose from (none), First Line, and Hanging:

   - (none) formats the paragraph as a regular paragraph, with indents controlled solely by the Left and Right settings.

   - First Line adds an indent to the first line of the paragraph. This indent is in addition to the Left setting. For example, if you choose a Left setting of 0.5" and a First Line setting of 0.5", the first line of the paragraph will be indented one inch. By using a first-line indent, you can avoid having to type a tab at the beginning of a paragraph.

   - Hanging makes the first line of the paragraph hang out to the left of the rest of the paragraph. (This is sometimes referred to as an *outdent*.) Hanging indents are great for bulleted or numbered paragraphs—the bullet or number hangs out to the left of the paragraph, and the wrapped lines of the paragraph align neatly with the first line.

   Figure 4.6 illustrates the different types of indentation Word provides for paragraphs.

7. If you chose a Special setting of First Line or Hanging, enter a measurement in the By box.

8. Click the OK button to close the Paragraph dialog box.

TIP TIP TIP TIP TIP TIP TIP TIP TIP TIP TIP TIP TIP TIP TIP TIP TIP TIP TIP TIP TIP TIP TIP

When setting indents, you can use negative values for Left and Right indents to make the text protrude beyond the margin. Negative indents can be useful for special effects, but if you find yourself using them all the time, you probably need to adjust your margins. One other thing—for obvious reasons, you can't set a negative hanging indent, no matter how hard you try.

SKILL
4

> This paragraph is **not indented at all** and looks suitably dense as a result. If you are going to use no indentation, set extra space between paragraphs so that the reader can tell where a paragraph begins and ends.
>
> **First-line indents** save you from having to create an indent at the start of each new paragraph by pressing the tab button. The lines that follow a first-line indent are flush left.
>
> - Hanging indents are most useful for bulleted lists and the like; the bullet stands clear of the text.
>
> To set off a quotation, you can **indent** it **from both margins**. This way, the reader's can easily identify it as quoted material. Common practice is to run short sections of quoted material into paragraphs (using quotation marks), and to place longer quotes self-standing, with a smaller font size.

FIGURE 4.6: Word provides these different types of indentation for formatting paragraphs.

Setting Indents by Using Keyboard Shortcuts

Here are the keyboard shortcuts for setting indents:

Indent from the left	Ctrl+M
Remove indent from the left	Ctrl+Shift+M
Create (or increase) a hanging indent	Ctrl+T
Reduce (or remove) a hanging indent	Ctrl+Shift+T
Remove paragraph formatting	Ctrl+Q

Choosing Measurement Units

You may have noticed that the measurement units (inches, centimeters, etc.) in the Paragraph dialog box on your computer are different from those in the screens shown here—for example, you might be seeing measurements in centimeters or picas rather than in inches. If you're using Word's Web features, you may even be seeing measurements in pixels (abbreviated *px*). A pixel is one of the tiny glowing phosphors that goes to make up a monitor screen.

If so, don't worry. Word lets you work in any of four measurements: inches, centimeters, points, and picas. Points and picas—$\frac{1}{72}$ of an inch and $\frac{1}{6}$ of an inch, respectively—are most useful for page layout and typesetting, but if you're not doing those, you might want to switch between inches and centimeters.

To change your measurement units:

1. Choose Tools ➤ Options to display the Options dialog box.

2. Click the General tab to bring it to the front.

3. Choose Inches, Centimeters, Millimeters, Points, or Picas as your measurement unit from the Measurement Units drop-down list.

4. Click the OK button to close the Options dialog box.

Setting Line Spacing

In most documents, Word starts you off with single-spaced lines, with only enough spacing between the lines to prevent the descenders on characters in one line from touching the ascenders on characters in the next line. You can change the line spacing of all or part of a document by using either the Paragraph dialog box or keyboard shortcuts:

1. Place the insertion point in the paragraph you want to adjust, or select several paragraphs whose line spacing you want to change.

    - To select the whole document quickly, choose Edit ➤ Select All, or hold down the Ctrl key and click once in the selection bar at the left edge of the Word window. Alternatively, press Ctrl+5 (that's the 5 on the numeric keypad, not the 5 above the letters R and T).

2. Right-click in the selection and choose Paragraph from the context menu, or choose Format ➤ Paragraph, to display the Paragraph dialog box (shown in Figure 4.4).

3. If the Indents And Spacing tab isn't at the front of the Paragraph dialog box, click it to bring it to the front.

4. Use the Line Spacing drop-down list to choose the line spacing you want:

Line Spacing	Effect
Single	Single spacing, based on the point size of the font.
1.5 lines	Line-and-a-half spacing, based on the point size of the font.

Line Spacing	Effect
Double	Double spacing based on the point size of the font.
At least	Sets a minimum spacing for the lines, measured in points. This can be useful for including fonts of different sizes in a paragraph or for including in-line graphics.
Exactly	Sets the exact spacing for the lines, measured in points.
Multiple	Multiple line spacing, set by the number in the At box to the right of the Line Spacing drop-down list. For example, to use triple line spacing, enter 3 in the At box; to use quadruple line spacing, enter 4.

5. If you chose At Least, Exactly, or Multiple in the Line Spacing drop-down list, adjust the setting in the At box if necessary.

6. Click the OK button to apply the line spacing setting to the chosen text.

TIP TIP TIP TIP TIP TIP TIP TIP TIP TIP TIP TIP TIP TIP TIP TIP TIP TIP TIP TIP TIP TIP TIP

To set line spacing with the keyboard, press Ctrl+1 to single-space the selected paragraphs, Ctrl+5 to set 1.5-line spacing, and Ctrl+2 to double-space paragraphs.

Setting Spacing Before and After Paragraphs

As well as setting the line spacing within any paragraph, you can adjust the amount of space before and after any paragraph to position it more effectively on the page. So instead of using two blank lines (i.e., two extra paragraphs with no text) before a heading and one blank line afterward, you can adjust the paragraph spacing to give the heading plenty of space without using any blank lines.

TIP TIP TIP TIP TIP TIP TIP TIP TIP TIP TIP TIP TIP TIP TIP TIP TIP TIP TIP TIP TIP TIP TIP

The easiest way to set consistent spacing before and after paragraphs of a particular type is to use Word's *styles*, which I'll discuss in the next skill.

To set the spacing before and after a paragraph:

1. Place the insertion point in the paragraph whose spacing you want to adjust, or select several paragraphs to adjust their spacing all at once.

2. Right-click and choose Paragraph from the context menu, or choose Format ➤ Paragraph, to display the Paragraph dialog box (shown in Figure 4.4).

SKILL 4

3. Make sure the Indents And Spacing tab is foremost. If it isn't, click it to bring it to the front.

4. In the Spacing box, choose a Before setting to specify the number of points of space before the selected paragraph. Watch the Preview box for the approximate effect this change will have.

5. Choose an After setting to specify the number of points of space after the current paragraph. Again, watch the Preview box.

NOTE NOTE NOTE NOTE NOTE NOTE NOTE NOTE NOTE NOTE NOTE NOTE NOTE NOTE NOTE

The Before setting for a paragraph adds to the After setting for the paragraph before it; it does not change it. For example, if the previous paragraph has an After setting of 12 points, and you specify a Before setting of 12 points for the current paragraph, you'll end up with 24 points of space between the two paragraphs (in addition to the line spacing you've set).

6. Click the OK button to close the Paragraph dialog box and apply the changes.

TIP TIP TIP TIP TIP TIP TIP TIP TIP TIP TIP TIP TIP TIP TIP TIP TIP TIP TIP TIP TIP TIP

To quickly add or remove one line worth of space before a paragraph, select the paragraph or place the cursor within it and press Ctrl+0 (Ctrl+zero).

Using the Text Flow Options

Word offers six options for controlling how your text flows from page to page in the document. To select these options, click in the paragraph you want to apply them to or select a number of paragraphs. Then choose Format ➤ Paragraph to display the Paragraph dialog box, click the Line And Page Breaks tab to bring it to the front of the dialog box (unless it's already at the front), and select the options you want to use:

Widow/Orphan Control

A *widow* (in typesetting parlance) is when the last line of a paragraph appears by itself at the top of a page; an *orphan* is when the first line of a paragraph appears by itself at the foot of a page. Leave the Widow/Orphan Control box selected to have Word rearrange your documents to avoid widows and orphans.

Keep Lines Together	Tells Word to prevent the paragraph from breaking over a page. If the whole paragraph will not fit on the current page, Word moves it to the next page. If you write long paragraphs, choosing the Keep Lines Together option can produce painfully short pages.
Keep With Next	Tells Word to prevent a page break from occurring between the selected paragraph and the next paragraph. This option can be useful for making sure that a heading appears on the same page as the paragraph of text following it or that an illustration appears together with its caption—but be careful not to set Keep With Next for body text paragraphs or other paragraphs that will need to flow normally from page to page.
Page Break Before	Tells Word to force a page break before the current paragraph. This is useful for making sure that, for example, each section of a report starts on a new page.
Suppress Line Numbers	Tells Word to turn off line numbers for the current paragraph. This applies only if you are using line numbering in your document.
Don't Hyphenate	Tells Word to skip the current paragraph when applying automatic hyphenation.

SKILL 4

When you've chosen the options you want, click the OK button to apply them to the paragraph or paragraphs.

Setting Tabs

To align the text in your documents, Word provides five kinds of tabs:

- Left-aligned
- Centered
- Right-aligned
- Decimal-aligned
- Bar (a vertical line at the tab's position)

Setting Tabs Using the Ruler

The quickest way to set tabs for the current paragraph, or for a few paragraphs, is to use the ruler. If the ruler isn't visible, choose View ➤ Ruler to display it, or simply pop it up by sliding the mouse pointer onto the gray bar at the top of the screen once you've selected the paragraphs you want to work on.

Adding a Tab

To add a tab:

1. Display the ruler if necessary.

2. Place the insertion point in a single paragraph or select the paragraphs to which you want to add the tab.

3. Choose the type of tab you want by clicking the tab selector button at the left end of the ruler to cycle through left tab, center tab, right tab, and decimal tab.

4. Click the ruler in the location where you want to add the tab. The tab mark will appear in the ruler:

TIP TIP TIP TIP TIP TIP TIP TIP TIP TIP TIP TIP TIP TIP TIP TIP TIP TIP TIP TIP TIP TIP TIP

When adding a tab, you can click with either the left or the right mouse button. For moving or removing a tab, only the left button works.

Moving a Tab

To move a tab, display the ruler if necessary, then click the tab marker and drag it to where you want it.

Removing a Tab

To remove a tab, display the ruler if it's not visible, then click the marker for the tab you want to remove and drag it into the document. The tab marker will disappear from the ruler.

Setting Tabs Using the Tabs Dialog Box

When you need to check exactly where the tabs are in a paragraph, or if you set too many tabs in the ruler and get confused, turn to the Tabs dialog box to clear everything up.

First, place the insertion point in a single paragraph or select the paragraphs whose tabs you want to change, then choose Format ➣ Tabs to display the Tabs dialog box (see Figure 4.7) and follow the procedures described in the next sections.

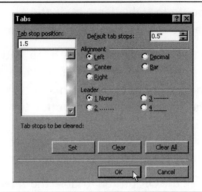

FIGURE 4.7: The Tabs dialog box gives you fine control over the placement and types of tabs in your document.

TIP TIP TIP TIP TIP TIP TIP TIP TIP TIP TIP TIP TIP TIP TIP TIP TIP TIP TIP TIP TIP TIP TIP TIP

To quickly display the Tabs dialog box, double-click an existing tab in the bottom half of the ruler. (If you double-click in any open space in the bottom half of the ruler, the first click will place a new tab for you; if you double-click in the top half of the ruler, Word will display the Page Setup dialog box.) You can also get to the Tabs dialog box quickly by clicking the Tabs button on either panel of the Paragraph dialog box.

Setting Default Tabs

To set different spacing for default tabs, adjust the setting in the Default Tab Stops box at the top of the Tabs dialog box. For example, a setting of 1" will produce tabs at 1", 2", 3", and so on.

Setting Tabs

To set tabs:

1. Enter a position in the Tab Stop Position box.

    *   If you're using the default unit of measurement set in the copy of Word you're using, you don't need to specify the units.

    *   If you want to use another unit of measurement, specify it: for example, 2.3", 11 cm, 22 pi, 128 pt, 66px.

2. Specify the tab alignment in the Alignment box: Left, Center, Right, Decimal, or Bar. (Bar inserts a vertical bar— | —at the tab stop.)

3. In the Leader area, specify a tab leader if you want one: periods, hyphens, or underlines leading up to the tabbed text. (Periods are often used as tab leaders for tables of contents, between the heading and the page number.) Choose the None option button to remove leaders from a tab.

4. Click the Set button.

5. Repeat steps 1 through 4 to specify more tabs if necessary.

6. Click the OK button to close the Tabs dialog box and apply the tabs you set.

Clearing Tabs

To clear a tab, select it in the Tab Stop Position list and click the Clear button. Word will list the tab you chose in the Tab Stops To Be Cleared area of the Tabs dialog box. Choose other tabs to clear if necessary, then click the OK button.

 To clear all tabs, simply click the Clear All button, then click the OK button.

Moving Tabs

To move tabs using the Tabs dialog box, you need to clear them from their current position and then set them elsewhere—you can't move them as such. (To move tabs easily, use the ruler method described earlier in this skill.)

Language Formatting

You can format text as being written in a language other than English. Not only can you spell-check text written in other languages, but you can use the Find feature to search for text formatted in those languages for quick reference. (Skill 7 discusses spell-checking, while Skill 6 discusses the Find feature.)

To format selected text as another language:

1. Choose Tools ➤ Language ➤ Set Language to display the Language dialog box (see Figure 4.8).

FIGURE 4.8: In the Language dialog box, choose the language in which to format the selected text, then click OK.

2. In the Mark Selected Text As list box, choose the language in which to format the text.

    • Selecting the Do Not Check Spelling Or Grammar check box tells Word not to use the spell checker and other proofing tools on the selected text. This can be useful for one-off technical terms that you don't want to add to your custom dictionaries (which we'll look at in Skill 7). But if you find the spell checker suddenly failing to catch blatant spelling errors, check to see if the Do Not Check Spelling Or Grammar check box is selected for the text in question.

3. Click the OK button to apply the language formatting to the selected text.

WARNING WARNING WARNING WARNING WARNING WARNING WARNING WARNING

If Word does not have the dictionary files installed for a language that you have formatted text as, it will display a warning message box when you run a spell-check on the text. After checking other text formatted as languages whose dictionaries it does have, Word will then tell you that the spell-check is complete. This can be deceptive, because it will not have checked the text for whose language it does not have the dictionary.

SKILL
4

You can also apply language formatting from the Spelling context menu, which we'll look at in Skill 7: Right-click a word with the wavy red underline and choose Language from the context menu. Then either select a language from the list of languages you've been using or choose Set Language to display the Language dialog box.

Page Setup

If you're ever going to print a document, you need to tell Word how it should appear on the page. You can change the margins, paper size, layout of the paper, and even which printer tray the paper comes from (as we saw in Skill 3).

The best time to set paper size is at the beginning of a project. While you can change it at any time during a project without trouble, having the right size (and orientation) of paper from the start will help you lay out your material.

To alter the page setup, double-click in the top half of the horizontal ruler (or anywhere in the vertical ruler), or choose File ➤ Page Setup, to display the Page Setup dialog box, then follow the instructions for setting margins, paper size, and paper orientation in the next sections. If you want to change the page setup for only one section of a document, place the insertion point in the section you want to change before displaying the Page Setup dialog box. Alternatively, you can choose This Point Forward from the Apply To drop-down list on any tab of the Page Setup dialog box to change the page setup for the rest of the document.

To quickly display the Page Setup dialog box, double-click in the top half of the ruler. (Double-clicking in the bottom half of the ruler displays the Tabs dialog box, so be precise.)

Setting Margins

To set the margins for your document, click the Margins tab in the Page Setup dialog box (see Figure 4.9). In the boxes for Top, Bottom, Left, and Right margins, use the spinner arrows to enter the measurement you want for each margin; alternatively, type in a measurement.

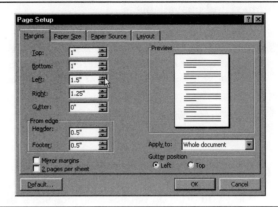

FIGURE 4.9: The Margins tab of the Page Setup dialog box

If you're typesetting documents (rather than simply using the word processor to put them together), you may want to select the Mirror Margins check box. This makes the two inner-margin measurements the same as each other, and the two outer-margin measurements the same as each other. It also changes the Left and Right settings in the column under Margins in the Page Setup dialog box to Inside and Outside, respectively. (If you're having trouble visualizing the effect that mirror margins produce, try opening a few books on your bookshelf and looking to see if the margins will mirror each other when the book is closed. This book doesn't use mirror margins, but many others do.)

To print two pages per sheet of paper, select the 2 Pages Per Sheet check box. This is especially useful with the Landscape paper orientation (discussed in the section later in this skill titled "Setting Paper Orientation") for creating folded booklets on standard letter-sized paper. When you select 2 Pages Per Sheet, the Mirror Margins check box becomes dimmed and unavailable.

The *gutter measurement* is the space that your document will have on the inside of each facing page. For example, if you're working with mirror-margin facing pages, you could choose to have a gutter measurement of 1" and inside and outside margins of 1.25 inches. That way, your documents would appear with a 1.25" left margin on left-hand pages, a 1.25" right margin on right-hand pages, and a 2.25" margin on the inside of each page (the gutter plus the margin setting). The two Gutter Position option buttons (Left and Top) control where Word positions the gutter margin on your pages. The default position of the gutter margin is left, but you can change the gutter margin to the top by selecting the Top option button. When Top is selected, the Mirror Margins and 2 Pages Per Sheet check boxes are dimmed and unavailable.

TIP TIP TIP TIP TIP TIP TIP TIP TIP TIP TIP TIP TIP TIP TIP TIP TIP TIP TIP TIP TIP TIP TIP

Use gutters for documents you're planning to bind. That way, you can be sure that you won't end up with text bound unreadably into the spine of the book.

Use the Preview box in the Page Setup dialog box to get an idea of how your document will look when you print it.

Setting Paper Size

Word lets you print on paper of various sizes, offering a Custom option to allow you to set a paper size of your own, in addition to various standard paper and envelope sizes.

To change the size of the paper you're printing on, click the Paper Size tab of the Page Setup dialog box (see Figure 4.10).

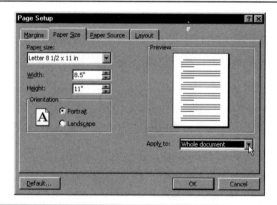

FIGURE 4.10: The Paper Size tab of the Page Setup dialog box

In the Paper Size drop-down list box, choose the size of paper you'll be working with (for example, Letter $8\frac{1}{2} \times 11$ in). If you can't find the width and height of paper you want, use the Width and Height boxes to set the width and height of the paper you're using; Word will automatically set the Paper Size box to Custom Size.

Setting Paper Orientation

To change the orientation of the page you're working on, click the Paper Size tab of the Page Setup dialog and choose Portrait or Landscape in the Orientation group box. (Portrait is taller than it is wide; Landscape is wider than it is tall.)

Borders and Shading

If a part of your document—whether it be text, a graphic, or an entire page— needs a little more emphasis, you can select it and add borders and shading by using either the Tables And Borders toolbar or the Borders And Shading dialog box. In general, the Tables And Borders toolbar is easier to use, as you can immediately see the effects it's producing.

Adding Borders and Shading Using the Tables And Borders Toolbar

To display the Tables And Borders toolbar, right-click the menu bar or any displayed toolbar and choose Tables And Borders from the context menu. Figure 4.11 shows the Tables And Borders toolbar with the buttons related to borders and shading identified. We'll look at the buttons related to tables in Skill 9.

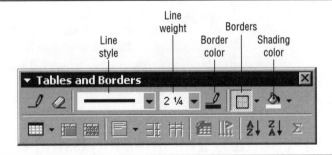

FIGURE 4.11: Use the border-related buttons on the Tables And Borders toolbar to apply borders.

First, choose the style of border you want to apply:

- Click the Line Style button and choose a suitable style of line from the drop-down list: single, dotted, dashed, dotted-and-dashed, multiple lines, and so on.

- Click the Line Weight button and choose a suitable weight from the drop-down list.

- Click the Border Color button and choose a color from the palette of available colors. The Automatic choice applies the default color of border for the font color of the text or object selected. To see more colors, click the More Line Colors button to display the Colors dialog box, select a color on either the Standard tab or the Custom tab, and click the OK button to apply it.

Next, apply the border:

- To apply the current style of border to the current selection, just click the Border button.

- To apply a different style of border, click the drop-down list button and choose a type of border from the border palette. If you're not clear which style of border one of the buttons on the palette represents, hover the mouse pointer over it to display the ScreenTip for the button.

- To remove the border from the current selection, click the No Border button on the border palette.

Then apply shading if you want to:

- To apply the current shading color to the selection, click the Shading Color button.

- To change the current shading color, click the drop-down list button and choose a color from the palette. To see more fill colors, click the More Fill Colors button to display the Colors dialog box, select a color on either the Standard tab or the Custom tab, and click the OK button to apply it.

- To remove shading from the current selection, click the No Fill button on the Shading Color palette.

Adding Borders and Shading Using the Borders And Shading Dialog Box

For more control over the borders and shading you apply, use the Borders And Shading dialog box:

1. Select the text or objects to which you want to apply borders or shading and choose Format ➤ Borders And Shading to display the Borders And Shading dialog box (see Figure 4.12).

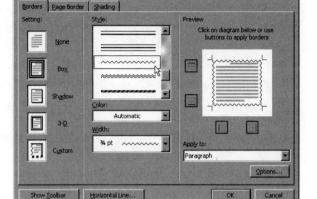

FIGURE 4.12: Apply borders and shading to items from the Borders And Shading dialog box.

2. On the Borders tab, choose the type of border you want to add from the options displayed:

   • In the Settings area, choose one of the settings: None, Box, Shadow, Grid (for tables and cells), 3-D (not available for tables and cells), or Custom. Watch the effect in the Preview box.

   • Next, choose the type of line you want from the Style list, choose a color from the Color drop-down list, and choose a weight from the Width drop-down list. To change one of the lines, click the appropriate icon in the Preview area to apply it or remove it.

   • For text, you can choose Text or Paragraph in the Apply To drop-down list below the Preview area. If you apply the border to a paragraph, you can specify the distance of the border from the text by clicking the Options button and specifying Top, Bottom, Left, and Right settings in the Border And Shading Options dialog box. Then click the OK button.

3. On the Page Border tab, choose the type of border you want to add to the page. The controls on this tab work in the same way as those described in step 2. The important difference is that the Apply To drop-down list allows you to choose between the Whole Document, This Section, This Section—First Page Only, and This Section—All Except First Page. Again, clicking the

Options button displays the Border And Shading Options dialog box, which allows you to place the border precisely on the page. The Art drop-down list provides decorative page borders suitable for cards, notices, and the like. Depending on your installation of Office, you may need to install the Art files separately; if so, choose Yes when Word prompts you to do so, and the Windows Installer will handle the process.

4.   On the Shading tab, choose the type of shading to add:

- Choose the color for the shading from the Fill palette.

- Choose a style and color for the pattern in the Style And Color drop-down list boxes in the Patterns area.

- Finally, use the Apply To list to specify whether to apply the shading to the paragraph or just to selected text.

WARNING WARNING WARNING WARNING WARNING WARNING WARNING WARNING

Go easy with shading on printed documents, especially if you're using a monochrome printer. Any shading over 20 percent will completely mask text on most black-and-white printouts (even if it looks wonderfully artistic on screen). For Web documents, you can be a little more liberal with shading, but be careful not to make the pages difficult to read.

5.   Click OK to close the Borders And Shading dialog box and apply your changes to the selection.

Removing Borders and Shading

To remove borders and shading, select the item, then choose Format ➤ Borders And Shading to display the Borders And Shading dialog box. Then:

- To remove a border, choose None in the Settings area on the Borders tab.

- To remove a page border, choose None in the Settings area on the Page Border tab.

- To remove shading, choose No Fill in the Fill palette and Clear in the Style drop-down list on the Shading tab.

Click OK to close the Borders And Shading dialog box.

Inserting Decorative Horizontal Lines

To insert a decorative horizontal line in a document:

1. Choose Format ➤ Borders And Shading to display the Borders And Shading dialog box.

2. Click the Horizontal Lines button on any one of the three tabs. Word will close the Borders And Shading dialog box and display the Horizontal Line dialog box.

3. On the Pictures tab, select the style of line you want.

4. Click the OK button to insert the line and close the Horizontal Line dialog box.

Are You Experienced?

SKILL
4

Now you can...

☑ **format characters and words**

☑ **format paragraphs**

☑ **set up pages**

☑ **use language formatting**

☑ **apply borders and shading**

☑ **insert horizontal lines**

SKILL 5

Using Styles and Complex Formatting

- Understanding what styles are
- Applying styles
- Creating and modifying styles
- Creating and using sections
- Using automatic bullets and numbering
- Using AutoCorrect
- Using AutoFormat
- Creating footnotes and endnotes

In this skill, we'll examine the more complex formatting options that Word provides for making your documents look as you want them to. We'll start by discussing styles, which draw together the different types of formatting that we looked at in the previous skill. Styles are a powerful tool for applying complex, frequently used formatting. From there, you'll see how you can use sections to apply substantially different formatting to different parts of the same document. After that, we'll examine three key automation features: Word's automatic bullets and numbering for creating quick lists; the AutoCorrect feature, which enables you to correct misspellings automatically and expand designated abbreviations; and the AutoFormat feature, which automatically applies formatting as you work. Finally, we'll look at creating footnotes and endnotes in your documents.

Style Formatting

Word's *paragraph styles* bring together all the formatting elements discussed in Skill 4–character formatting, paragraph formatting (including alignment), tabs, language formatting, and borders and shading. Each style contains complete formatting information that you can apply with a click of the mouse or a single keystroke.

NOTE NOTE NOTE NOTE NOTE NOTE NOTE NOTE NOTE NOTE NOTE NOTE NOTE NOTE

Word also offers character styles, which are similar to paragraph styles but contain only character formatting. Character styles are suitable for picking out elements in a paragraph formatted with paragraph styles.

Using styles not only gives your documents a consistent look—every Heading 1 paragraph will appear in the same font and font size, with the same amount of space before and after it, and so on—but also saves you a great deal of time in formatting your documents.

You can either use Word's built-in styles (which are different in Word's various predefined templates) or create your own styles. Every paragraph in Word uses a style; Word starts you off in the Normal style unless the template you're using dictates otherwise.

Applying Styles

To apply a style, place the insertion point in the paragraph or choose a number of paragraphs, then click the Style drop-down list button on the Formatting toolbar and choose the style you want from the list:

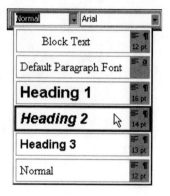

Some of the most popular styles have keyboard shortcuts: Ctrl+Shift+N for Normal style; Ctrl+Alt+1 for Heading 1, Ctrl+Alt+2 for Heading 2, Ctrl+Alt+3 for Heading 3; and Ctrl+Shift+L for List Bullet style.

You can also apply a style by choosing Format ➢ Style to display the Style dialog box (see Figure 5.1), choosing the style in the Styles list box, and clicking the Apply button.

If you have many styles defined or a slow computer (or both), the style list may be slow to appear the first time you summon it for any given document. To speed this up, you can make Word display styles in a standard font. Choose Tools ➢ Customize to display the Customize dialog box, click the Options tab, clear the List Font Names In Their Font check box, and click the OK button. This also speeds up the display of the Font drop-down menu.

SKILL 5

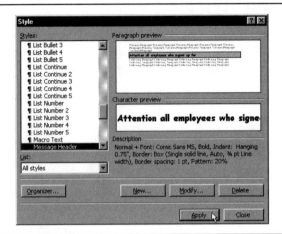

FIGURE 5.1: To apply a style, choose it in the Styles list box and click the Apply button.

To tell which style paragraphs are in, you can display the *style area*, a vertical bar at the left side of the Word window that displays the style name for each paragraph, as shown here. You can display the style area in Normal view and Outline view, but not in Web Layout view, Print Layout view, or Print Preview.

Inside Address	1324 Thornhill Drive
Inside Address	Marksdale, IL 00000-3323
Salutation	
	Dear Mr. Thomas,
Body Text	We at Art Through the Ages, Inc. are preparing for our busi
Body Text	As one of our best customers, we would like to offer you a sp

To display the style area, choose Tools ➤ Options to display the Options dialog box and click the View tab to bring it to the front. Enter a measurement in the Style Area Width box in the Window area and then click OK.

To alter the width of the style area once you've displayed it, click and drag the dividing line. To remove it, drag the dividing line all the way to the left of the Word window.

Creating a New Style

As you can see in the Styles list box shown in Figure 5.1, Word's templates come with a number of built-in styles. If they're not enough for you, you can create your own styles in three ways: by example, by definition, or by having Word do all the work for you.

Creating a New Style by Example

The easiest way to create a style is to set up a paragraph of text with the exact formatting you want for the style–character formatting, paragraph formatting, borders and shading, bullets or numbers, and so on. Then click the Style drop-down list, type the name for the new style into the box, and press Enter. Word will create the style, which you can immediately select from the Style drop-down list and apply to other paragraphs as necessary.

Creating a New Style by Definition

The more complex way of creating a style is by definition:

1. Choose Format ➢ Style to display the Style dialog box.

2. Click the New button. Word will display the New Style dialog box (see Figure 5.2).

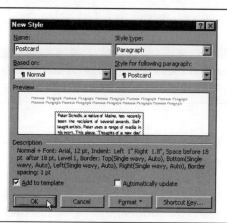

FIGURE 5.2:   Creating a new style in the New Style dialog box

3. Set the information for your new style:

    - In the Name box, enter a name for the style. Word will accept style names over 100 characters, but you'll do better to keep them short enough to fit in the Style box on the Formatting toolbar. If your style name is over 20 characters long, you should probably rethink your naming conventions.

    - In the Based On drop-down list box, choose the style on which you want to base the new style. Bear in mind that if you change the base style later, the new style will change too. The Preview box will show what the Based On style looks like.

    - In the Style Type box, choose whether you want a paragraph style or a character style.

    - In the Style For Following Paragraph box (which is not available for character styles), choose the style that you want Word to apply to the paragraph immediately after this style. For example, after the Heading 1 style, you might want Body Text, or after Figure, you might want Caption. But for many styles, you'll want to continue with the style itself.

4. To adjust the formatting of the style, click the Format button and choose Font, Paragraph, Tabs, Border, Language, Frame, or Numbering from the drop-down list. This will display the dialog box for that type of formatting. When you've finished, click the OK button to return to the New Style dialog box.

NOTE NOTE NOTE NOTE NOTE NOTE NOTE NOTE NOTE NOTE NOTE NOTE NOTE NOTE NOTE

Some of these dialog boxes, such as Character, Paragraph, and Tabs, we've already looked at in the previous skill; others we'll examine in subsequent skills.

5. Repeat step 4 as necessary, selecting other formatting characteristics for the style.

6. Select the Add To Template check box to add the new style to the template.

7. Select the Automatically Update check box if you want Word to automatically update the style when you change it. (We'll look at this option more in a minute.)

8. To set up a shortcut key for the style, click the Shortcut Key button. Word will display the Customize Keyboard dialog box. With the insertion point in the Press New Shortcut Key box, press the shortcut key combination you'd like to set, click the Assign button, then click the Close button.

WARNING WARNING WARNING WARNING WARNING WARNING WARNING WARNING

Watch the Currently Assigned To area of the Customize Keyboard dialog box (which you'll see after typing in the combination) when selecting your shortcut key combination. If Word already has assigned that key combination to a command, macro, or style, it will display its name there. If you choose to assign the key combination to the new style, the old assignment for that combination will be deactivated.

9. In the New Style dialog box, click the OK button to return to the Style dialog box.

10. To create another new style, repeat steps 2 through 9.

11. To close the Style dialog box, click the Apply button to apply the new style to the current paragraph or current selection, or click the Close button to save the new style without applying it.

Having Word Create Styles Automatically

Creating styles yourself can get tedious—why not have Word create them for you? And when you change the formatting of a paragraph that has a certain style, you can have Word update the style for you, so that every other paragraph that has the same style takes on that formatting too.

To have Word automatically create styles for you:

1. Choose Tools ➤ AutoCorrect to display the AutoCorrect dialog box.

2. Click the AutoFormat As You Type tab to display it.

3. In the Automatically As You Type area at the bottom of the tab, select the Define Styles Based On Your Formatting check box. (This is selected by default.)

4. Click the OK button to close the AutoCorrect dialog box.

Once you've set this option (or if it was set already), Word will attempt to identify styles you're creating and will supply names for them. For example, if you

SKILL
5

start a new document (with paragraphs in the Normal style, as usual) and bold and center the first paragraph, Word may define that bolding and centering as a Title style; if you simply increase the font size, Word may define that paragraph Heading 1 instead. This sounds creepy but works surprisingly well; and if it doesn't suit you, you can easily turn it off by clearing the Define Styles Based On Your Formatting check box.

Modifying a Style

You can modify a style by example and by definition. You can also choose to have Word automatically identify and apply changes you make to the style.

Modifying a Style by Example

To modify a style by example, change the formatting of a paragraph that currently has the style assigned to it, then choose the same style again from the Style drop-down list. Word will display the Modify Style dialog box (see Figure 5.3). Make sure the Update The Style To Reflect Recent Changes option button is selected, then click the OK button to update the style to include the changes you just made to it. If you want Word to automatically update the style without displaying this dialog box when you make changes in the future, select the Automatically Update The Style From Now On check box first.

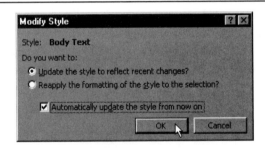

FIGURE 5.3:   Modifying a style in the Modify Style dialog box

Modifying a Style by Definition

Modifying a Word style by definition is similar to creating a new style, except that you work in the Modify Style dialog box, which offers one fewer option than the New Style dialog box offers (you don't get to choose whether the style is a paragraph style or a character style because Word already knows which it is).

Open the Style dialog box by choosing Format ➢ Style, then choose the style you want to work on from the Styles list. (If you can't see the style you're looking for, make sure the List box at the bottom-left corner of the Style dialog box is showing All Styles rather than Styles In Use or User-Defined Styles.)

Click the Modify button. Word will display the Modify Style dialog box. From there, follow steps 3 through 9 in the section titled "Creating a New Style by Definition" (except for selecting the style type) to modify the style and step 11 to exit the Style dialog box.

Removing a Style

Removing a style is much faster than creating one. Simply open the Style dialog box by choosing Format ➢ Style, select the style to delete in the Styles list, and click the Delete button. Word will display a message box confirming that you want to delete the style; click the Yes button.

You can then delete another style the same way, or click the Close button to leave the Style dialog box.

SKILL
5

TIP TIP TIP TIP TIP TIP TIP TIP TIP TIP TIP TIP TIP TIP TIP TIP TIP TIP TIP TIP TIP TIP

Keep in mind that you can't delete a Heading style once you've started using it. Also, when you delete a style that's in use (other than a Heading style), Word applies the Normal style to those paragraphs. (If you do this by mistake, choose Edit ➢ Undo Style to make Word both restore the style to the list of available styles and reapply it to the paragraphs it was previous applied to.)

Styles and Templates

As you learned in Skill 2, a template is a special type of document on which you can base other documents. In fact, every document you create in Word is based on a template. If you do not specify a particular template when you create a new document, Word bases the document on a default template called the Normal template, which in essence creates a blank document. If you need to, you can subsequently attach a different template to the document; I'll describe how to do this in the next section.

When you create a document, it inherits the styles in the template. You can subsequently create new styles in the document itself or in the template.

Each template has a built-in set of styles. You can modify these styles or create new styles, as described in the preceding sections. You can also copy styles from one template to another, as described in the section after next.

Changing the Template a Document Is Based On

To change the template attached to a document:

1. Choose Tools ➤ Templates And Add-Ins to display the Templates And Add-Ins dialog box (see Figure 5.4). The template currently attached to the document appears in the Document Template text box.

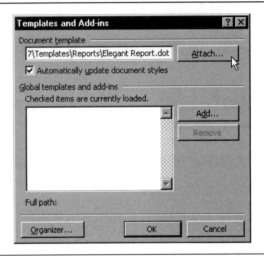

FIGURE 5.4: The Templates And Add-Ins dialog box displays the name of the template currently attached to the document. To attach the document to a different template, click the Attach button. Word will display the Attach Template dialog box.

2. Click the Attach button to display the Attach Template dialog box.

3. Select the template you want to attach to the document. (You may need to navigate to a different location to find the template.)

4. Click the Open button. Word will close the Attach Template dialog box, returning you to the Templates And Add-Ins dialog box.

5.   If you want the document to take on the styles contained in the new template, select the Automatically Update Document Styles check box. (This is usually a good idea.)

6.   Click the OK button to close the Templates And Add-Ins dialog box.

Copying Styles from One Document or Template to Another

To copy styles from one document or template to another:

1.   Choose Tools ➤ Templates And Add-Ins to display the Templates And Add-Ins dialog box.

2.   Click the Organizer button to display the Organizer dialog box (see Figure 5.5).

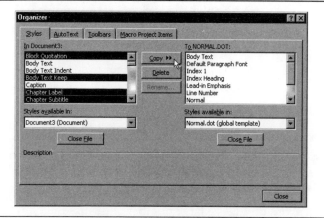

FIGURE 5.5:   Use the Organizer dialog box to copy styles from one template to another.

SKILL
5

3.   If the Styles tab of the Organizer dialog box isn't displayed, click it to display it.

4.   Open the document or template from which you want to copy the styles in one of the two list boxes and the document or template to which you want to copy the styles in the other list box. (It doesn't matter which is in the left-hand list box and which is in the right-hand list box.)

   •   The left-hand list box at first displays the active document, and the right-hand list box the Normal template. If the active document is attached to a template other than the Normal template, you can select it in the Styles Available In drop-down list.

- To close the document or template currently open in a list box, click the corresponding Close File button. The Close File button will become an Open File button.

- To open a document or template, click the Open button. Word will display the Open dialog box. Navigate to the document or template and open it.

5. In one list box, select the styles you want to copy. Use Shift+click to select multiple contiguous styles, or Ctrl+click to select multiple noncontiguous styles.

6. Click the Copy button to copy the styles to the other template.

7. When you've finished copying styles, click the Close button to close the Organizer dialog box:

- If you've made changes to a template that currently does not have a document open, or a document that was not open, Word will prompt you to save the changes to the template or document.

- If you've made changes to a template that is attached to an open document, Word will prompt you to save the changes the next time you save the document.

- If you've made changes to a document that is open, Word will save those changes the next time you save the document.

Using Themes

 Word provides a large number of themes that you can apply to your documents to give them a particular look. A *theme* is essentially a design scheme and color scheme for a document. A theme typically consists of a background color or background graphic; horizontal lines or other design elements; and fonts, colors, and sizes for regular items such as heading styles, body text styles, and bullets. Some themes have different colors for hyperlinks and table borders as well. When you apply a theme to a document, Word applies these colors, fonts, and graphics to the document, changing (and perhaps unifying) its look.

As you may have noticed from the previous description, themes have a certain amount of overlap with templates in that they affect the look of the document you apply them to. Themes are different from templates in that templates can contain customized toolbars, menus, and keyboard shortcuts. Further, templates can contain default text and AutoText entries, while themes cannot.

Usually, the best way to work with themes is to start a document based upon a particular template and then apply a suitable theme to the document to achieve a certain look with it. By using a consistent theme, you can provide a degree of unity among documents that are based on different templates.

As you might imagine, themes are especially useful for Web pages. You can also use themes for e-mail messages you create in WordMail for Outlook.

To apply a theme to a document:

1. Choose Format ➤ Theme to display the Theme dialog box (see Figure 5.6).

SKILL
5

FIGURE 5.6: Use the Theme dialog box to apply a theme (a unified look) to a document.

2. Select a theme in the Choose A Theme list box. The Sample Of Theme box will display a preview of how the theme will look.

   - Many themes are not installed in the default installation of Word. When you choose a theme in the Choose A Theme list box that is not installed, Word will display a message in the preview area telling you this and providing an Install button that you can click to install the theme.

3. Below the Choose A Theme list box, select options for the theme. Watch the preview as you try these options:

   - The Vivid Colors check box applies higher-contrast colors to the theme. This check box is cleared by default.

- The Active Graphics check box controls whether the theme displays any animated graphics it contains when viewed with a Web browser.

- The Background Image check box controls whether the theme uses its background image for this document.

4. Click the OK button to apply the theme to the document.

To change the theme of a document, repeat the above procedure and choose a different theme.

To remove a theme from a document, choose Format ➤ Theme, select the (No Theme) option at the top of the Choose A Theme list box, and click the OK button.

Using the Style Gallery

Word provides the Style Gallery to give you a quick overview of its many templates and the myriad styles they contain. To open the Style Gallery, choose Format ➤ Theme to display the Theme dialog box, then click the Style Gallery button. Word will display the Style Gallery dialog box (see Figure 5.7).

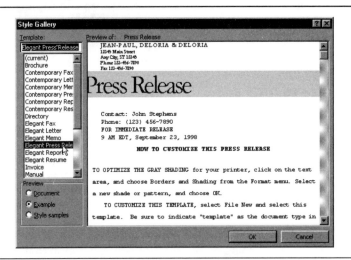

FIGURE 5.7: The Style Gallery dialog box gives you a quick view of the styles in Word's templates.

To preview a template in the Preview Of box, select it in the Template list box. Then choose the preview you want in the Preview box:

- Document shows you how your current document looks with the template's styles applied.

- Example shows you a sample document that uses the template's styles.

- Style Samples shows each of the styles in the document.

NOTE NOTE NOTE NOTE NOTE NOTE NOTE NOTE NOTE NOTE NOTE NOTE NOTE NOTE NOTE

If the template you select in the Template list box is not yet installed on your computer, Word will prompt you to install it by clicking the OK button in the Style Gallery dialog box.

To apply the template you've chosen to your document, click the OK button.

Section Formatting

Often you'll want to create documents that use different page layouts, or even different sizes of paper, for different pages. Word handles this by letting you divide documents into *sections*, each of which can have different formatting characteristics. For example, you could use sections to set up a document to contain both a letter and an envelope, or to have one-column text and then multi-column text, and so on.

SKILL 5

Creating a Section

To create a section:

1. Place the insertion point where you want the new section to start.

2. Choose Insert ➤ Break. Word will display the Break dialog box (see Figure 5.8).

3. Choose the type of section break to insert by clicking an option button in the Section Breaks area:

   - Next Page starts the section on a new page. Use this when you have a drastic change in formatting between sections—for example, an envelope on one page and a letter on the next.

   - Continuous starts the section on the same page as the preceding paragraph. This is useful for creating layouts with differing numbers of columns on the same page.

   - Even Page starts the section on a new even page.

   - Odd Page starts the section on a new odd page. This is useful for chapters or sections that should start on a right-hand page for consistency.

FIGURE 5.8: In the Break dialog box, choose the type of section break to insert and then click the OK button.

4. Click the OK button to insert the section break. It will appear in Normal view and Outline view as a double dotted line across the page containing the words *Section Break* and the type of section break.

Section Break (Continuous)

The Sec indicator on the status bar will indicate which section you're in.

Page 3   Sec 2   3/7

TIP TIP TIP TIP TIP TIP TIP TIP TIP TIP TIP TIP TIP TIP TIP TIP TIP TIP TIP TIP TIP TIP

If you need to try a different type of section break (for example, Next Page instead of Continuous), you can change the type of section break on the Layout tab of the Page Setup dialog box: Place the insertion point in the relevant section, then choose File ➤ Page Setup, select the type of section you want from the Section Start drop-down list on the Layout tab, and click the OK button. The advantage of changing the break rather than deleting it and then creating a new break of a different type is that changing the break does not affect the formatting of the section, while deleting the break does (as explained next).

Deleting a Section

To delete a section break, place the insertion point at its beginning (or select it) and press the Delete key.

 WARNING WARNING WARNING WARNING WARNING WARNING WARNING WARNING
When you delete a section break, the section before the break will take on the formatting characteristics of the section after the break.

Automatic Bullets and Numbering

In this section, we'll look at the options Word offers for adding automatic bullets and numbering to your documents. First, we'll look at straightforward bullets and numbering; then we'll look at how to modify the bullets and numbers to produce special effects; and finally we'll look at heading numbering, which can almost magically speed up the creation of long documents that consist of numbered sub-items.

The bullets and numbering that Word applies automatically are paragraph formatting rather than individual characters on the page. In other words, once you've added a bullet to a list, you can't just select the bullet and delete it as you might delete a character—you have to remove it from the paragraph's formatting. We'll look at this process later in the section titled "Removing Bullets and Numbering."

Adding Bullets and Numbering

You can add straightforward bullets and numbering to existing text by using the buttons on the Formatting toolbar.

 To add bullets, first select the paragraphs you want to add bullets to and then click the Bullets button on the Formatting toolbar. Word will add the bullets and apply a hanging indent to each of the paragraphs but leave the paragraphs in their current style.

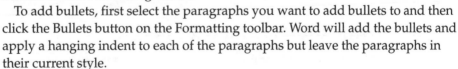 TIP TIP TIP TIP TIP TIP TIP TIP TIP TIP TIP TIP TIP TIP TIP TIP TIP TIP TIP TIP TIP TIP TIP TIP TIP
To continue a numbered or bulleted list, press Enter at the end of the list. To discontinue the list, press Enter twice at the end of the list.

 To add numbers, select the paragraphs you want to number and then click the Numbering button on the Formatting toolbar.

For a variety of styles of bullets and numbering, select the paragraphs you want to apply them to, then either right-click in the selection and choose Bullets And Numbering from the context menu or choose Format ➢ Bullets And Numbering to open the Bullets And Numbering dialog box (see Figure 5.9).

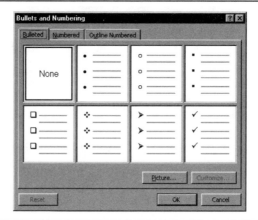

FIGURE 5.9:   The Bullets And Numbering dialog box gives you plenty of choices for bulleting and numbering your lists.

Choose the tab that corresponds to the type of list you want to create: Bulleted, Numbered, or Outline Numbered, then click the style that suits you best. Click the OK button to apply the bullets or numbering and close the Bullets And Numbering dialog box.

NOTE NOTE NOTE NOTE NOTE NOTE NOTE NOTE NOTE NOTE NOTE NOTE NOTE NOTE NOTE
We'll look at outline numbering in detail in Skill 14.

Removing Bullets and Numbering

To remove bullets or numbering from selected paragraphs, either click the Bullets button or the Numbering button, or choose Format ➢ Bullets And Numbering to display the Bullets And Numbering dialog box. Select the None option and click the OK button.

Modifying the Bullets and Numbering Styles

If you find the choices offered in the Bullets And Numbering dialog box inadequate for your needs, you can create your own bullets or numbers to adorn your text.

To create your own styles of bullets and numbering:

1. Select the paragraphs you want to add bullets or numbers (or both) to.

2. Right-click and select Bullets And Numbering from the context menu, or choose Format ➤ Bullets And Numbering, to display the Bullets And Numbering dialog box.

3. Select the appropriate tab and the format that suits you best, then click the Customize button. Word will display the Customize Bulleted List dialog box, the Customize Numbered List dialog box, or the Customize Outline Numbered List dialog box as appropriate. Figure 5.10 shows the Customize Bulleted List dialog box, and the steps that follow discuss the options available in this dialog box. The Customize Numbered List dialog box and Customize Outline Numbered List dialog box look a little different, but the options work in similar ways.

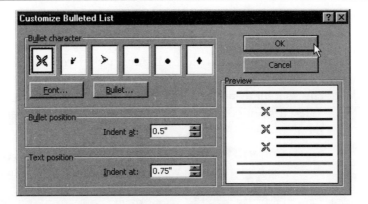

FIGURE 5.10: In the Customize Bulleted List dialog box, you can choose almost any bullet character that your computer can produce.

4. In the Bullet Character group box, choose from one of the six bullets displayed; or click the Bullet button to open the Symbol dialog box, choose a character, and click OK to return to the Customize Bulleted List dialog box. Then click the Font button to display the Font dialog box and choose a suitable font, font size, and other formatting for the bullet. Click the OK button to close the Font dialog box and return to the Customize Bulleted List dialog box.

5. In the Bullet Position group box, use the Indent At measurement to specify any indent the bullet should receive.

6. In the Text Position group box, use the Indent At measurement to specify the indent of the text. Usually, you'll want this to be more than the indent for the bullet.

7. Click the OK button to apply the formatting to your list.

NOTE NOTE NOTE NOTE NOTE NOTE NOTE NOTE NOTE NOTE NOTE NOTE NOTE NOTE NOTE

You can also customize a bulleted list by using pictures for bullets. To do so, click the Picture button in the Bullets And Numbering dialog box to display the Picture Bullet dialog box. On the Pictures tab, select the type of bullet you want to use, then click the OK button to apply the bullet to the current selection.

AutoCorrect

AutoCorrect offers five features that help you quickly enter your text in the right format. Every time you finish typing a word and press the spacebar, press Enter, press Tab, or type any form of punctuation (comma, period, semicolon, colon, quotation marks, exclamation point, question mark, or even a % sign), Word checks it for a multitude of sins and, if it finds it guilty, takes action immediately.

The first four of AutoCorrect's features are straightforward; the fifth is a little more complex:

Correct TWo INitial CApitals   Stops you from typing an extra capital at the beginning of a word. If you need to type technical terms that need two initial capitals, clear the check box to turn this option off or create AutoCorrect exceptions for them. We'll look at exceptions later in this skill.

TIP TIP TIP TIP TIP TIP TIP TIP TIP TIP TIP TIP TIP TIP TIP TIP TIP TIP TIP TIP TIP TIP

If you type three initial capitals in a word, Word will not try to correct the second and third, figuring you're typing an acronym of some sort. (It will still query the spelling of the word if it doesn't recognize it.)

Capitalize First Letter Of Sentences   Does just that. If you and Word disagree about what constitutes a sentence, turn this option off by clearing the check box. For example, if you start a new paragraph without ending the one before it with a period, Word will not capitalize the first word. On the other hand, if you want to create a sentence fragment that shouldn't start with a capital but that comes after a period, you're out of luck—Word will capitalize the first word.

Capitalize Names Of Days   Does just that.

Correct Accidental Usage Of cAPS lOCK key   A neat feature that works most of the time. If Word thinks you've got the Caps Lock key down and you don't know it, it will turn Caps Lock off and change the offending text from upper- to lowercase and vice versa. Word usually decides that Caps Lock is stuck when you start a new sentence with a lowercase letter and continue with uppercase letters; however, the end of the previous sentence may remain miscased.

Replace Text As You Type   The best of the AutoCorrect features. We'll look at it in detail in the next section.

Replace Text As You Type

The AutoCorrect Replace Text As You Type feature keeps a list of AutoCorrect entries. Each time you finish typing a word, AutoCorrect scans this list for that word. If the word is on the list, Word substitutes the replacement text for the word. AutoCorrect keeps a separate list of entries for each language that you use in your document via language formatting (Tools ➢ Language ➢ Set Language). When you display the AutoCorrect dialog box, it identifies itself by the current language: **AutoCorrect: English (US)**, **AutoCorrect: French**, and so on.

Replace Text As You Type is a great way of fixing typos you make regularly, and Word comes with a decent list of AutoCorrect entries already configured—if you type *awya* instead of *away* or *disatisfied* instead of *dissatisfied*, Word will automatically fix the typo for you. But AutoCorrect is even more useful for setting up abbreviations for words or phrases that you use frequently, saving you not only time and keystrokes but also the effort of memorizing complex spellings or details. For example, suppose you write frequently to your bank manager demanding an explanation of charges to your account: You could set up one AutoCorrect entry containing the address and salutation, another containing your account details, a third containing your ritual complaint, and a fourth containing your name and signature. You would have the bulk of the letter written in a four-fold flurry of keystrokes. (You could also use a template to achieve a similar savings of time.)

You can add AutoCorrect entries to Word's list in two ways—either automatically while running a spelling check, or manually at any time.

Adding AutoCorrect Entries While Spell-Checking

Adding AutoCorrect entries while spell-checking a document is a great way to teach Word the typos you make regularly. When the spell checker finds a word it doesn't like, make sure the appropriate replacement word is highlighted in the

Suggestions box; if the word selected in the Suggestions box isn't the appropriate one, type in the right word. Then click the AutoCorrect button in the Spelling dialog box. Word will add the word from the Not In Dictionary box to the Replace list in AutoCorrect and the word selected in the Suggestions box to the With list in AutoCorrect. This way, you can build an AutoCorrect list tailored precisely to your typing idiosyncrasies.

You can also add AutoCorrect entries during on-the-fly spell-checks by choosing AutoCorrect from the context menu and selecting the word to map the current typo to in the submenu that appears.

NOTE NOTE NOTE NOTE NOTE NOTE NOTE NOTE NOTE NOTE NOTE NOTE NOTE NOTE NOTE
You'll learn more about spell-checking (both on-the-fly and automatic) in Skill 7.

Adding AutoCorrect Entries Manually

Adding AutoCorrect entries while spell-checking is great for building a list of your personal typos in Word, but it's of little use for setting up AutoCorrect with abbreviations that will increase your typing speed dramatically. For that, you need to add AutoCorrect entries manually.

To add AutoCorrect entries manually:

1. If the replacement text for the AutoCorrect entry is in the current document, select it.

TIP TIP TIP TIP TIP TIP TIP TIP TIP TIP TIP TIP TIP TIP TIP TIP TIP TIP TIP TIP TIP TIP
To create an AutoCorrect entry that contains formatting—bold, italic, paragraph marks, tabs, and so on—or a graphic, you need to select the formatted text (or the graphic) in a document before opening the AutoCorrect dialog box.

2. Choose Tools ➤ AutoCorrect to display the AutoCorrect dialog box (see Figure 5.11).

3. Make sure that the Replace Text As You Type check box is selected.

4. Enter the typo or abbreviation to replace in the Replace box.

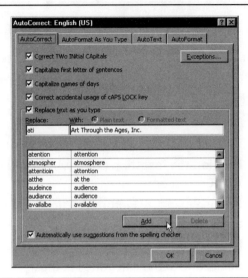

FIGURE 5.11: The AutoCorrect dialog box

TIP TIP TIP TIP TIP TIP TIP TIP TIP TIP TIP TIP TIP TIP TIP TIP TIP TIP TIP TIP TIP TIP TIP TIP TIP

When choosing the Replace text for an abbreviated AutoCorrect entry, avoid using a regular word that you might type in a document and not want to have replaced. Try reducing the word or phrase to an abbreviation that you'll remember—for example, omit all the vowels and include only the salient consonants.

5. Enter the replacement text in the With box.

- If you selected text before opening the AutoCorrect dialog box, that text will appear in the With box. If the text needs to retain its formatting, make sure the Formatted Text option button has been selected. (The Formatted Text option button also needs to be selected if your selection contains a paragraph mark or tab—that counts as formatting.)

6. Click the Add button or press Enter to add the AutoCorrect entry to the list.

- If Word already has an AutoCorrect entry stored for that Replace text, you'll see a Replace button instead of the Add button. When you press Enter or click this button, Word will display a confirmation dialog box to make sure that you want to replace the current AutoCorrect entry.

7. To add another AutoCorrect entry, repeat steps 3 through 6.

8. To close the AutoCorrect dialog box, click the Close button.

GETTING CREATIVE WITH AUTOCORRECT ENTRIES: INCLUDING GRAPHICS

You can include inline graphics, text boxes, borders, and so on in Auto-Correct entries. (In Skill 10 you'll learn how to incorporate graphics into Word documents.) For example, you can easily include your company's logo in an AutoCorrect entry for the company address for letterhead:

1. Enter the text of your company's address and format it as appropriate.

2. Position the insertion point where you want the graphic to appear in the AutoCorrect entry text.

3. Choose Insert ➤ Picture ➤ Clip Art to display the Microsoft Clip Gallery application.

4. Make sure the Pictures tab is displayed. (If it isn't, click it to display it.)

5. Select one of the categories in the list box to display its contents.

6. Click the picture you want, then choose the Insert Clip item (the top item) from the context menu to insert the picture in the document at the insertion point.

7. Resize the picture if necessary, crop it, or add a border to it. (Again, we'll look at the details of these procedures in Skill 10.)

8. Select the text and the picture of the address.

9. Choose Tools ➤ AutoCorrect. Word will display the AutoCorrect dialog box with the selected text and picture in the With text box. It will select the Formatted Text option button, because the picture counts as formatting.

10. Enter the abbreviation for the address and picture in the Replace text box.

11. Click the Add button to add the AutoCorrect entry.

12. Click the OK button to close the AutoCorrect dialog box.

Now you can enter the address and its picture in a document by typing the text of the abbreviation and then pressing a punctuation key. Be imaginative like this, and AutoCorrect can save you plenty of time in your work, a few seconds at a time.

The Automatically Use Suggestions From The Spelling Checker check box controls whether AutoCorrect includes suggestions from the spell checker in the list of words it provides when you right-click a misspelled word and choose Auto-Correct from the context menu.

Deleting AutoCorrect Entries

To delete an AutoCorrect entry, open the AutoCorrect dialog box (by choosing Tools ➤ AutoCorrect) and select the entry from the scroll list at the bottom of the dialog box. (You can type the first few letters of an entry's Replace designation in the Replace box to scroll to it quickly.) Then click the Delete button.

You can then either delete further AutoCorrect entries or click the OK button to close the AutoCorrect dialog box.

Using AutoCorrect Exceptions

If you've already managed to think up a couple of things that could cause problems with AutoCorrect, hold up a moment: AutoCorrect has an Exceptions feature that you can use to prevent specific items from triggering AutoCorrect corrections.

From the AutoCorrect tab of the AutoCorrect dialog box, click the Exceptions button to display the AutoCorrect Exceptions dialog box (see Figure 5.12).

SKILL 5

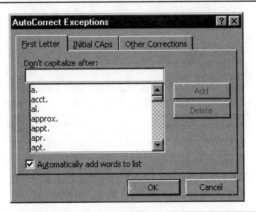

FIGURE 5.12: In the AutoCorrect Exceptions box, set exceptions to prevent specific terms you use from being corrected automatically.

When Word doesn't recognize an abbreviation, it'll think the period that denotes the abbreviation is the end of a sentence instead. On the First Letter tab, you can prevent this from happening by adding to the list of abbreviations any abbreviation that Word does not recognize. Simply type the word into the Don't Capitalize After text box and click the Add button.

When the Automatically Add Words To List check box at the bottom of the First Letter tab is selected, Word will automatically add first-letter exceptions to the list when you use Backspace to undo AutoCorrect's correction of them. For example, say you're writing about syntax and you need to use the abbreviation *prep.* for *preposition*. If you type *prep. used*, AutoCorrect will change *used* to *Used* because it thinks the period ends a sentence. But if you now use Backspace to delete *Used* and then type in *used* to replace it, Word will create a first-letter exception for *prep.*

To delete a first-letter exception, select it in the Don't Capitalize After list box and click the Delete button.

On the INitial CAps tab, you can create exceptions for those rare terms that need two initial capitals (for example, IPng, the next-generation Internet Protocol). Enter the text in the Don't Correct text box, then click the Add button.

To delete an initial-cap exception, select it in the Don't Correct list box and click the Delete button.

When the Automatically Add Words To List check box at the bottom of the INitial CAps tab is selected, Word will automatically add two-initial-cap words to the list when you use Backspace to undo AutoCorrect's correction of them and then retype them. For example, if you're writing about the next-generation Internet protocol and you type *IPng* and a space, AutoCorrect will change *IPng* to *Ipng*. But if you press Backspace four times (once for the space, once for the *g*, once for the *n*, and once for the *p*, leaving the *I* there) and then type *Png* and a space, Word will create a two-initial-cap exception for *IPng* and will cease and desist from lowercasing the second letter.

On the Other Corrections tab, you can create exceptions for other words. Type the word into the Don't Correct text box, then click the Add button. To delete an entry, select it in the list box and click the Delete button.

When the Automatically Add Words To List check box on the Other Corrections tab is selected, Word will automatically add other words to the list when you correct AutoCorrect's correction of them by backspacing over the correction and retyping the word.

Using AutoFormat

To automate the creation of documents, Word offers automatic formatting with its AutoFormat features: AutoFormat regular, which applies styles when you choose the Format ➤ AutoFormat command, and AutoFormat As You Type, which applies automatic formatting to paragraphs as you finish them.

To set AutoFormat options:

1. Choose Tools ➤ AutoCorrect to display the AutoCorrect dialog box.

2. Click the AutoFormat tab or AutoFormat As You Type tab of the AutoCorrect dialog box. Figure 5.13 shows the AutoFormat As You Type tab.

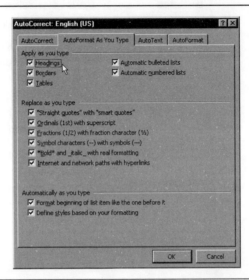

FIGURE 5.13: On the AutoFormat As You Type tab (and the AutoFormat tab, which is not shown here) of the AutoCorrect Options dialog box, set the autoformatting options you want.

3. In the Apply or Apply As You Type box, select the check boxes next to the autoformatting options you want to use. For AutoFormat, the options are: Headings, Lists, Automatic Bulleted Lists, and Other Paragraphs; and for AutoFormat As You Type the options are: Headings, Borders, Tables, Automatic Bulleted Lists, and Automatic Numbered Lists.

Headings	Word applies Heading 1 style when you press Enter, type a short paragraph starting with a capital letter and not ending with a period, and press Enter twice. Word applies Heading 2 when that paragraph starts with a tab.

Automatic Numbered Lists	Word creates a numbered list when you type a number followed by a punctuation mark (such as a period, hyphen, or closing parenthesis) and then a space or tab and some text.
Automatic Bulleted Lists	Word creates a bulleted list when you type a bullet-type character (e.g., a bullet, an asterisk, a hyphen) and then a space or tab followed by text.
Borders	Word adds a border to a paragraph that follows a paragraph containing three or more dashes, underscores, or equal signs: Dashes produce a thin line for dashes, underscores produce a thicker line, and equal signs produce a double line.
Tables	Word creates a table when you type an arrangement of hyphens and plus signs (e.g., +--+--+--+). This is one of the more bizarre and inconvenient ways of creating a table; we'll look at better ways in Skill 9.
Other Paragraph	Word applies styles based on what it judges your text to be.

TIP TIP TIP TIP TIP TIP TIP TIP TIP TIP TIP TIP TIP TIP TIP TIP TIP TIP TIP TIP TIP TIP TIP TIP TIP

You can stop the automatic numbered or bulleted list by pressing Enter twice.

4. Choose Replace or Replace As You Type options as necessary.

5. In the Automatically As You Type area of the AutoFormat As You Type tab, select the Format Beginning Of List Item Like The One Before It check box if you want Word to try to mimic your formatting of lists automatically. Select the Define Styles Based On Your Formatting check box if you want Word to automatically create styles whenever it feels that it's appropriate.

6. In the Always AutoFormat area of the AutoFormat tab, select the Plain Text WordMail documents check box if you want Word to automatically format plain-text e-mail in WordMail. (We'll look at WordMail in Skill 12.)

7. Click the OK button to close the AutoCorrect dialog box.

AutoFormat As You Type options will now spring into effect as you create your documents.

If you decide to use the regular AutoFormat feature instead of AutoFormat As You Type, create your document and then choose Format ➤ AutoFormat. Word will display an AutoFormat dialog box (see Figure 5.14), which lets you access the AutoFormat dialog box to refine your predefined AutoFormat settings if necessary. Choose a type of document from the drop-down list, then click the OK button to start the autoformatting.

FIGURE 5.14: In the AutoFormat dialog box, choose a type of document and whether you want to review the changes Word proposes, then click the OK button.

Footnotes and Endnotes

Footnotes are notes placed at the foot of the page that refers to them. *Endnotes* are notes placed at the end of a document, as with magazine articles that cite references. Footnotes and endnotes were incredibly tedious to handle in the days of typewriters and hot metal, but Word handles them like a pro.

Word automates the numbering of footnotes and endnotes (maintaining separate numbering for each), adjusts pages so that footnotes fit, and can even manage *Continued. . .* notices for footnotes that need to run to the next page. If your document has sections, you can choose to place the endnotes for any given section either at the end of the section or at the end of the document.

Inserting a Footnote or Endnote

To insert a footnote or endnote:

1. Choose Insert ➤ Footnote. Word will display the Footnote And Endnote dialog box (see Figure 5.15).

SKILL
5

FIGURE 5.15: To insert a footnote, choose Insert ➤ Footnote and select Footnote in the Footnote And Endnote dialog box.

2. To insert a footnote, choose Footnote in the Insert area; to insert an endnote, choose Endnote.

3. To choose footnote or endnote options, click the Options button. Word will display the Note Options dialog box (see Figure 5.16) with either the All Footnotes tab or the All Endnotes tab displayed, as appropriate. Choose options as follows:

   - In the Place At drop-down list, choose whether to place footnotes at the bottom of the page or beneath the text on the page (i.e., higher than the bottom of the page if the text is short), and endnotes at the end of the document or the end of the section.

   - In the Number Format drop-down list, choose an appropriate number format for your footnotes.

   - In the Start At box, choose the number with which to start numbering the footnotes or endnotes.

TIP TIP TIP TIP TIP TIP TIP TIP TIP TIP TIP TIP TIP TIP TIP TIP TIP TIP TIP TIP TIP TIP TIP TIP

When you're building a long document out of subdocuments, you may want to number footnotes or endnotes consecutively throughout the whole work. To do so, enter the appropriate number in the Start At box for the notes in each successive document.

   - In the Numbering area, choose whether the note numbering should be continuous, if it should restart at each section, or if (for footnotes only) it should restart on each page.

- Click the OK button when you've chosen the note options.

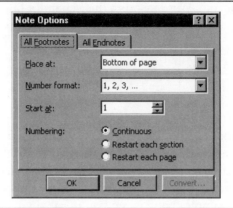

FIGURE 5.16: Choose options for footnotes and endnotes in the Note Options dialog box.

4. If you want your footnote or endnote to be numbered with special symbols of your choosing, select Custom Mark in the Numbering box and click the Symbol button. In the Symbol dialog box, choose the symbol you want to use (use the Font drop-down list to see symbols from other character sets) and click OK. If you're using AutoNumber and it's showing an inappropriate format, go back to step 3 and change the numbering scheme in the Options dialog box.

5. Click OK to insert the footnote or endnote in your document.

    - If you're in Normal view, Word will display a Footnote pane or Endnote pane at the bottom of your screen.

    - If you're in Print Layout view, Word will move the insertion point to the bottom of the page (for footnotes) or the end of the section or document (for endnotes).

6. Type the text of the footnote or endnote after the reference mark that Word inserts.

7. Return to your document by choosing Close (from the Footnotes or Endnotes pane), by clicking in the main document text, or by pressing Shift+F5.

When you insert further footnotes or endnotes, Word will synchronize their numbering with the existing footnotes or endnotes.

Changing Footnote and Endnote Separators

By default, Word inserts a fine separator line across part of the page between the body text and footnotes and between the body text and endnotes:

> deployment of high-speed technologies was hindered by the lack of DSLAMs[1] at many
>
> _____
> [1] Digital Subscriber Line Access Multiplexers

To change this line, choose View ➤ Footnotes in Normal view to display the Footnotes pane, then choose Footnote Separator from the drop-down list. The line then appears as a paragraph that you can select and delete (or edit). You can also add pictures using Insert ➤ Picture, or you can change to Print Layout view and add drawings by using the Drawing toolbar. Click the Close button to close the Footnotes pane when you're satisfied with the result.

Adding Continued Notices to Footnotes

To add *Continued. . .* notices to footnotes, choose View ➤ Footnotes in Normal view and choose Footnote Continuation Notice from the drop-down list on the Footnotes pane. Enter the text for the footnote continuation notice and format it using normal formatting techniques. Click the Close button to close the Footnotes pane and return to your document; Word will then display your *Continued. . .* message whenever a footnote runs over to the next page.

> However, when we understand that: Frugality is not poverty; it is a mid-point between scarcity and opulence[2], we can come to understand one of the underpinnings of living in
>
> _____
> [1] Derek Springer quoted by R. Robert Moss in Art and All, August 20, 1994, pg. 67.
> [2] Adrian Aguirre in *Circles of strength: Community Alternatives to Alienation*, Krutsio: A Desert
> *Continued on the next page*

TIP TIP TIP TIP TIP TIP TIP TIP TIP TIP TIP TIP TIP TIP TIP TIP TIP TIP TIP TIP TIP TIP

You can also edit the separator between footnotes and *Continued...* notices by choosing Footnote Continuation Separator from the drop-down list on the Footnotes pane—for example, you might want to use a line as a separator.

Moving and Copying Footnotes and Endnotes

You can quickly move a footnote or endnote by selecting its reference mark within the text and using Cut and Paste or drag-and-drop to move the reference mark to a different location. If need be, Word will renumber that footnote or end-note and all affected footnotes or endnotes.

To copy a footnote or endnote, select its reference mark within the text and use Copy and Paste (or Ctrl+drag-and-drop) to copy it to another location. Again, Word will renumber the copied footnote or endnote and all affected footnotes or endnotes accordingly.

Deleting a Footnote or Endnote

To delete a footnote or endnote, simply select its reference mark within the text and press Delete (or right-click and choose Cut from the context menu). Word will renumber all subsequent footnotes or endnotes accordingly.

Viewing Footnotes or Endnotes

To view a footnote or endnote in a document, move the mouse pointer over the reference mark for that footnote or endnote. Word will display the text of the footnote or endnote in a pop-up box, as shown here; it will not display any graphical elements in the footnote.

> Theodoraki (ibid.) disputes that vampires would be content with the flesh of goats.

The Diet of Vampires[2]

To work with footnotes or endnotes in Normal view, choose View ➤ Footnotes. If you have both footnotes and endnotes in the same document, Word will display the View Footnotes dialog box. Choose the View Footnotes Area option button or the View Endnote Area option button and click the OK button.

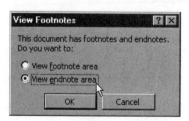

SKILL
5

Converting Footnotes to Endnotes (and Vice Versa)

You can convert footnotes to endnotes (or vice versa) by choosing Insert ➢ Footnote to display the Footnote And Endnote dialog box, clicking the Options button to display the Note Options dialog box, and clicking the Convert button. In the Convert Notes dialog box (shown below), choose Convert All Footnotes To Endnotes, Convert All Endnotes To Footnotes, or Swap Footnotes And Endnotes; then click the OK button.

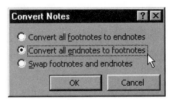

Word will perform the conversion you specified. If you convert footnotes to endnotes or endnotes to footnotes, Word will renumber the resulting notes so they're in sync with the existing notes.

Click the OK button in the Note Options dialog box, then click the Close button in the Footnote And Endnote dialog box.

Are You Experienced?

Now you can...

- ☑ use styles to apply complex formatting quickly to paragraphs
- ☑ create a new style
- ☑ modify an existing style
- ☑ use themes to give your documents a distinctive look
- ☑ use sections to divide your documents into differently formatted parts
- ☑ use automatic bullets and numbering
- ☑ use, create, and delete AutoCorrect entries
- ☑ use AutoFormat to format your documents automatically
- ☑ work with footnotes and endnotes

Skill 6: Using Find and Replace

- ⊙ Finding and replacing text
- ⊙ Using Find and Replace to format text
- ⊙ Using special characters and wildcards for powerful searches
- ⊙ Using advanced Find and Replace features

Word's Find and Replace features are powerful tools for changing your documents rapidly. At their simplest, the Find and Replace features let you search for any *string* of text (a letter, several letters, a word, or a phrase) and replace either chosen instances or all instances of that string. For example, you could replace all instances of *dangerous* with *unwise*, or you could replace selected instances of *this fearful lunatic* with *the Vice President of Communications*. You can also use Find independently of Replace to locate strategic parts of your document or to get to specific words in order to change the text around them.

Beyond the simple uses of Find and Replace, you can search for special characters (such as tabs or paragraph marks), for special operators (such as a digit, a character, or a range of characters), for particular formatting (such as double underline, bold, or italic in Engravers Gothic font), or for a particular Word style (such as Heading 9 or Body Text). You can search for text in a particular language, for paragraphs with particular tab formatting, or for text that sounds like other text. You can even combine many of these elements to conduct searches of truly fiendish complexity that will confound your colleagues and impress your friends—while speeding up your work.

In this skill, I'll start with the basics of Find and Replace. I'll then move to more complicated Find and Replace operations. Even if at the moment you think you need only use the simplest aspects of Find and Replace, I'd encourage you to read about the others as well, so that you know they're available when you need them.

Finding Text

Word offers a large number of features for finding text. You can search for text without worrying about its formatting; you can search for text with particular formatting (such as bold, double underline, or 44-point Allegro font), or you can search for a particular style.

NOTE NOTE NOTE NOTE NOTE NOTE NOTE NOTE NOTE NOTE NOTE NOTE NOTE NOTE
You can also combine these Find operations with Replace operations. I'll get to this a little later in the skill in the sections titled "Finding and Replacing Text," "Finding and Replacing Formatting," and "Finding and Replacing Styles."

To find text:

1. Choose Edit ➤ Find to display the Find And Replace dialog box (see Figure 6.1). If you see only the top half of the dialog box shown here, click the More button to display the rest of it.

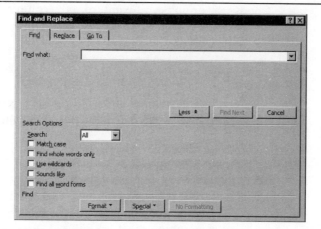

FIGURE 6.1: The Find And Replace dialog box gives you a quick way to access any combination of characters or formatting in your document. If you're seeing a smaller version of the Find And Replace dialog box, click the More button to expand it.

2. In the Find What box, enter the text you're looking for.

    - You can use *wildcard* characters to find a variety of characters. I'll get into this in a moment in the section "Finding Special Characters and Using Wildcards."

    - Word stores the Find operations from the current session in a drop-down list that you can access by clicking the arrow at the right-hand end of the Find What box.

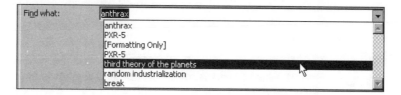

3. Choose the direction to search from the Search drop-down list: Down, Up, or All.

    - If you choose Down or Up, Word will prompt you to continue when it reaches the end or beginning of the document (unless you started Find at the beginning or end of the document).

4. Choose the options you want from the column of check boxes in the Search Options area of the dialog box. Each option you choose will be listed under the Find What box.

- Match Case makes Word use the capitalization of the word in the Find What box as a search constraint. For example, with Match Case selected and *laziness* entered in the Find What box, Word will ignore instances of *Laziness* or *LAZINESS* in the document and find only *laziness.*

- Find Whole Words Only makes Word look only for the exact word entered in the Find What box and not for the word when it is part of another word. For example, by selecting the Find Whole Words Only check box, you could find *and* without finding *land, random, mandible,* and so on. Find Whole Words Only is not available if you type a space in the Find What box.

- Use Wildcards provides special search options that we'll look at in the section "Finding Special Characters and Using Wildcards" later in this skill.

- Sounds Like finds words that Word thinks sound like those in the Find What box. Your mileage may vary depending on your own pronunciation. For example, if you select the Sounds Like check box and enter *meddle* in the Find What box, Word will find both *middle* and *muddle,* but it won't find rhyming words such as *peddle* and *pedal.*

- Find All Word Forms attempts to find all forms of the verb or noun in the Find What box. This is particularly useful with Replace operations: Word can change *break, broken, breaking,* and *breaks* to *fix, fixed, fixing,* and *fixes.* Enter the basic form of the words in the Find What and the Replace With boxes on the Replace tab of the Find And Replace dialog box–in this example, use *break* and *fix.*

WARNING WARNING WARNING WARNING WARNING WARNING WARNING WARNING

Find All Word Forms is an ambitious feature prone to random behavior if you use it unwisely. To give Microsoft credit, Word will warn you that choosing Replace All with Find All Word Forms selected may not be advisable—it's likely to find (and change) more than you bargained for. If you use it, use it carefully, and be especially careful with words such as *lead* because the metal "lead" will likely be misinterpreted as the verb "to lead."

5. Make sure no formatting information appears in the box under the Find What text box. If the No Formatting button at the bottom of the dialog box is

active (not dimmed), that means Word will look for words only with the selected formatting; click the button to remove the formatting. If the No Formatting button is dimmed, you're OK.

6. Click the Find Next button to find the next instance of your chosen text. If Word finds the text, it will stop; otherwise, it will tell you that it was unable to find the text.

7. Click the Find Next button again to keep searching, or click the Cancel button to close the Find dialog box.

Once you perform a Find operation (or a Find and Replace operation), Word sets the Object Browser to browse by the item you last found. You'll see that the Next Page and Previous Page buttons at the foot of the vertical scroll bar turn from black to blue, and if you move the mouse pointer over them, the ScreenTips identify them as Next Find/Go To and Previous Find/Go To, respectively. You can then click these buttons to move to the next or previous instance of the item you last found; you can also press Ctrl+PageDown or Ctrl+PageUp for the same effect.

To reset the Object Browser to browse by page, click the Select Browse Object button and choose the Browse By Page icon from the pop-up panel, as shown here. (To switch back to Browse By Find after that, you can click the Select Browse Object button again and choose the Browse By Find icon—the binoculars—from the pop-up panel.)

SKILL
6

Finding Special Characters and Using Wildcards

Often, you'll want to search for something more complex than plain text. Perhaps you'll need to search for an em dash (—), a paragraph mark, or any number—or you may want to search for words beginning with a specific character or for words that begin with a certain range of letters. For the first three of these, you'll need to use Word's special characters; for the last two, you'll need Word's special search operators.

Special Characters

To find a special character such as a paragraph mark, a tab character, or a graphic, click the Special button on the Find dialog box and choose the character from the drop-down list that appears (see Figure 6.2).

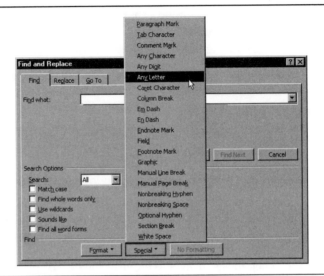

FIGURE 6.2: You can find special characters, such as page breaks or endnote marks, by using the Special drop-down list in the Find dialog box.

You can combine special characters with regular text to make your Find operations more effective. For example, the special character for a paragraph mark is **^p**; so to find every instance where *Joanne* appears at the beginning of a paragraph, you could search for **^pJoanne**.

It's usually easiest to enter special characters from the Special drop-down list, but you can enter them faster with keystrokes. Here's the full list of characters and what they find:

Character	Finds
^?	Any one character
*	A string of characters. Select the Use Wildcards check box when you use this (it's actually a wildcard rather than a special character, but it's simpler to use than the other wildcards).
^p	A paragraph mark
^t	A tab
^a	A comment mark
^#	Any digit
^$	Any letter

Character	Finds
^^	A caret (^)
^n	A column break
^+	An em dash (—)
^=	An en dash (–)
^e	An endnote mark
^d	A field
^f	A footnote mark
^g	A graphic
^l	A manual line break
^m	A manual page break
^~	A nonbreaking hyphen
^s	A nonbreaking space
^-	An optional hyphen
^b	A section break
^w	A white space

Of these, you'll probably find yourself using ^? and * the most. For example, you could use sh^?p to find *ship* or *shop* and f*d to find *fad*, *fatherhood*, and *flustered*—not to mention the phrase "*after the tragic d*eath of Don Quixote."

WARNING WARNING WARNING WARNING WARNING WARNING WARNING WARNING

As you can see from the Don Quixote example, you need to be a little careful when using the * special character, particularly with only one identifying letter on either side of it. For a more realistic example of how you might actually use * in a search, see the section "Advanced Find and Replace" on the Sybex Web site.

Using Wildcards

Word's wildcards go one stage beyond the special characters. You can search for one out of several specified characters, any character in a range, any character except the given one, and even a string of characters at the beginning or end of a word only. To enter these operators, select the Use Wildcards check box and then click the Special button to display the drop-down list (see Figure 6.3).

SKILL 6

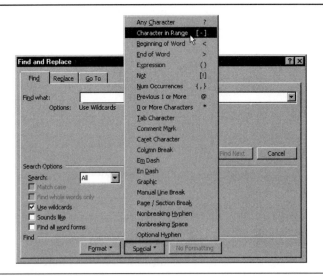

FIGURE 6.3: To search for wildcards, select the Use Wildcards check box and then choose the wildcards from the Special drop-down list.

Here is the list of wildcards and what they find:

Wildcard	Finds	Examples
[ ]	Any one of the given characters	**s[iou]n** finds *sin*, *son*, and *sun*
[-]	Any one character in the range	**[g-x]ote** finds *note, mote, rote,* and *tote*; enter the ranges in alphabetical order
[!]	Any one character except the characters inside the brackets	**[!f][!a]therhood** finds *mother-hood* but not *fatherhood*
[!x-z]	Any one character except characters in the range inside the brackets	**a[!b-l]e** finds *ape, are,* and *ate,* but not *ace, age,* or *ale*
{x}	Exactly *x* number of occurrences of the previous character or expression	**we{2}d** finds *weed* but not *wed,* because weed has two *es*

Wildcard	Finds	Examples
{x,}	At least *x* occurrences of the previous character or expression	**we{1,}d** finds *weed* and *wed*, because both words have at least one *e*
{x,y}	From *x* to *y* occurrences of the previous character or expression	**40{2,4}** finds *400*, *4000*, and *40000*, because each has between two and four zeroes; it won't find *40*, because it has only one zero
@	One or more occurrences of the previous character or expression	**o@h!** finds *oh!* and *ooh!*, which both contain one or more *o*s followed by an *h*
<	The following search string (in parentheses) at the beginning of a word	**<(work)** finds *working* and *workaholic*, but not *groundwork*
>	The preceding search string (in parentheses) at the end of a word	**(sin)>** finds *basin* and *moccasin*, but not *sinful*

SKILL 6

Finding and Replacing Text

To find and replace text:

1. Choose Edit ➤ Replace to display the Replace tab of the Find And Replace dialog box (see Figure 6.4).

   - If you're already working on the Find tab of the Find And Replace dialog box, click the Replace tab.

2. In the Find What box, enter the text to find.

   - To find text you've searched for before in the current session, click the arrow at the right-hand end of the Find What box and choose the text from the drop-down list.

3. In the Replace With box, enter the text you want to replace the found text with.

   - To reuse replacement text from the current session, click the arrow at the right-hand end of the Replace With box and choose the text from the drop-down list.

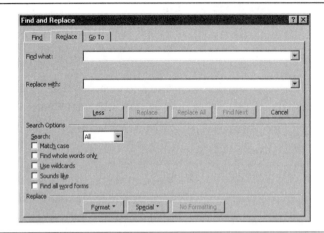

FIGURE 6.4: The Replace tab of the Find And Replace dialog box.

4. Choose a search direction from the Search drop-down list: All, Down, or Up.

5. Choose Replace options such as Match Case and Find Whole Words Only, as appropriate (see the section "Finding Text" earlier in this skill for an explanation of these options).

6. Start the Replace operation by clicking the Find Next button, the Replace button, or the Replace All button:

   • The Find Next button and the Replace button will find the next instance of the text in the Find What box. Once you've found it, click the Find Next button to skip to the next occurrence of the text without replacing anything, or click the Replace button to replace the text with the contents of the Replace With box and have Word find the next instance of the Find What text.

   • The Replace All button will replace all instances of the text in the Find What box with the text in the Replace With box. If you've chosen Up or Down in the Search drop-down list and started the search anywhere other than the end or the beginning of the document (respectively), Word will prompt you to continue when it reaches the beginning or end of the document.

7. When you've finished your Replace operation, click the Close button to close the Replace dialog box (this button will be Cancel if you haven't made any replacements).

When replacing simple text, make sure that Word is displaying no formatting information below the Find What and Replace With boxes—otherwise Word will find only instances of the text that have the appropriate formatting information (bold, italic, Book Antiqua font, Heading 4 style, and so on), or it will replace the text in the Find What box with inappropriately formatted text from the Replace With box. To remove formatting information from the Find What and Replace With boxes, click in the appropriate box and then click the No Formatting button.

Finding and Replacing Formatting

There's no need to use text for Replace operations in Word—you can simply find one kind of formatting and replace it with another. For example, say you received an article for your newsletter in which the author had used boldface rather than italic for emphasizing words she intended to explain. To convert these words from bold to italic, you could replace all Bold text with text with No Bold, Italic formatting.

This replacing function sounds suspiciously utopian, but it works well. Alternatively, you can replace particular strings of text that have one kind of formatting with the same strings of text that have different kinds of formatting; or you can replace formatted strings of text with other formatted strings of text.

SKILL 6

To replace one kind of formatting with another kind of formatting:

1. Choose Edit ➤ Replace to display the Replace tab of the Find And Replace dialog box.

2. With the insertion point in the Find What box, click the Format button and choose Font, Paragraph, Tabs, or Language from the drop-down list. Word will display the Find Font, Find Paragraph, Find Tabs, or Find Language dialog box. These are versions of the Font, Paragraph, Tabs, and Language dialog boxes discussed in Skill 4.

3. Choose the formatting you want Word to find, then click the OK button to return to the Find And Replace dialog box. Word will display the formatting you chose in the Format box underneath the Find What box.

4.   Add further formatting to the mix by repeating steps 2 and 3 with font, paragraph, tab, or language formatting.

5.   With the insertion point in the Replace With box, click the Format button and choose Font, Paragraph, Tabs, or Language from the drop-down list. Word will display the Replace Font, Replace Paragraph, Replace Tabs, or Replace Language dialog box. Again, these are versions of the regular Font, Paragraph, Tabs, and Language dialog boxes discussed in Skill 4.

6.   Choose the replacement formatting, then click the OK button to return to the Find And Replace dialog box. Word will display this formatting in the Format box under the Replace With box.

7.   Again, add further font, paragraph, tab, or language formatting, this time by repeating steps 5 and 6.

8.   Start the search by clicking the Find Next, Replace, or Replace All buttons.

TIP TIP TIP TIP TIP TIP TIP TIP TIP TIP TIP TIP TIP TIP TIP TIP TIP TIP TIP TIP TIP TIP TIP TIP

Without any text entered in the Find What and Replace With boxes, Word will replace all instances of the formatting you chose. For example, you could replace all boldface with italic, no boldface. You can also enter text in the Find What box and nothing in the Replace With box to have Word remove that text and put different formatting where it was—or vice versa. (This seems a bizarre concept until you find out how useful it is. We'll look at an example of this in the "Advanced Find and Replace" item in the Web component for this book.) Or you can enter replacement text in both the Find What box and in the Replace With box and replace both the text and the formatting at once. For example, you could replace all boldfaced instances of the word *break* with italicized (without boldface) instances of the word *fix*.

Finding and Replacing Styles

To replace one style with another:

1.   Choose Edit ➤ Replace to display the Find And Replace dialog box.

2.   Make sure that the Format boxes under the Find What box and the Replace With box don't contain any formatting information. To clear formatting information from the boxes, click in the appropriate box and then click the No Formatting button.

3. With the insertion point in the Find What box, click the Format button and choose Style from the drop-down list. Word will display the Find Style dialog box (see Figure 6.5).

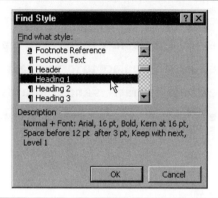

FIGURE 6.5: In the Find Style dialog box, choose the style you want Word to find.

4. Choose the style you want to find from the Find What Style list, then click the OK button to return to the Find And Replace dialog box. The area underneath the Find What box will display the style you chose.

5. Click in the Replace With box (or press Tab to move the insertion point there), then click the Format button and choose Style once more. Word will display the Replace Style dialog box, which is almost identical to the Find Style dialog box.

6. Choose the replacement style from the Replace With Style list and then click the OK button to return to the Find And Replace dialog box. The area underneath the Replace With box will display the style you chose.

7. Choose a search direction from the Search drop-down list if necessary.

8. Start the search by clicking the Find Next, Replace, or Replace All buttons.

TIP TIP TIP TIP TIP TIP TIP TIP TIP TIP TIP TIP TIP TIP TIP TIP TIP TIP TIP TIP TIP TIP TIP TIP

To replace words or characters in one style with words or characters in another style, choose the styles as described above and then enter the appropriate text in the Find What box and the Replace With box.

Are You Experienced?

Now you can...

- ☑ use Find and Replace to find and replace text
- ☑ use Find and Replace to find and replace formatting
- ☑ use Find and Replace to format text
- ☑ use special characters and wildcards with Find and Replace
- ☑ use Find and Replace to make major formatting changes to documents

SKILL 7

Spelling, Grammar, and Word Count

- ➔ **Checking spelling and grammar**
- ➔ **Using the Thesaurus**
- ➔ **Getting a word count**
- ➔ **Creating, loading, and editing custom dictionaries**
- ➔ **Customizing the grammar checker**

In this chapter, you'll use four Word tools to check and improve your documents. I'll start with the spell checker and grammar checker, which can check your spelling, your grammar, or the two together. I'll then move on to using Word's built-in thesaurus, which you can use to quickly look up words or phrases that have similar or opposite meanings. Finally, I'll show you how to get a word count for a document or a selected part of a document.

Checking Spelling and Grammar

Word provides a spell checker and a grammar checker to help improve the spelling and grammar in your documents. Before you start using these tools, you need to be aware of their differing goals and success rates. The two tools are integrated to a large extent, so it's a good idea to understand what each does and a little about how each works.

The spell checker is a great tool for making sure your document contains no embarrassing typos. But bear in mind that the spell checker is limited in its goal—it simply tries to match words that you type against the lists in its dictionary files, flagging any words it does not recognize and suggesting replacements that seem to be close in spelling. It does not consider words in context, beyond making sure that you meant to repeat any word that appears twice in a row. Anything more than that is the job of the grammar checker.

The grammar checker works by applying grammatical rules to your sentences; you can customize the assortment of rules it uses to make it match your writing style a little more closely. The grammar checker can be helpful for pointing out some problems with your writing—it can nail passive constructions and subject-verb disagreement every time and will try to tell you if you're being politically incorrect—but its suggestions are often unsuitable, and there are many grammatical problems that it cannot identify. If you want to use the grammar checker, remember that *it does not understand the meaning of your writing*, even though it can identify many of the parts of speech. For example, it finds no complaint with this sentence:

> Indigenously life beckons diligently sea pre-diet in queasy sand fun for fat delirium.

As far as the grammar checker is concerned, this is a fine sentence—it has nouns, a verb, prepositions, adverbs, adjectives, nothing is obviously out of place, and so on. We know that this sentence is gibberish (with perhaps a nod at William Carlos Williams), but the grammar checker hasn't a clue.

These severe limitations aside, the grammar checker will occasionally save you from yourself. And you can either have it critique your prose surreptitiously in the background as you write, or switch it off altogether. Read on.

NOTE NOTE NOTE NOTE NOTE NOTE NOTE NOTE NOTE NOTE NOTE NOTE NOTE NOTE NOTE

> **As described in detail in Skill 5, Word's AutoCorrect feature offers other forms of spell-checking.**

On-the-Fly Spell-Checking and Grammar-Checking

On-the-fly spell-checking and grammar-checking offers you the chance either to correct each spelling error and grammatical error the moment you make it or to highlight all the spelling errors and grammatical errors in a document and deal with them one by one. This is one of those partially great features that isn't right for everybody. The spell checker in particular can be intrusive when you're typing like a maniac trying to finish a project on time and it keeps popping up typos, interrupting your flow. Nonetheless, try these features and see how you do with them. (If you've just installed Word, you'll find the spell checker and grammar checker are enabled by default.)

To enable Word's on-the-fly spell-checking and grammar-checking:

1. Choose Tools ➤ Options to display the Options dialog box.

2. Click the Spelling & Grammar tab to bring it to the front.

3. In the Spelling area, select the Check Spelling As You Type check box.

4. In the Grammar area, select the Check Grammar As You Type check box.

5. Click the OK button to close the Options dialog box.

The spell checker will now put a squiggly red line under any word that doesn't match an entry in its dictionary. To spell-check one of these words quickly, right-click it. Word will display a spelling menu with suggestions for other spellings of the word (or what it thinks the word is) along with four other options:

- Ignore All tells Word to ignore all instances of this word.

SKILL
7

- Add adds the word to the Word spelling dictionary currently selected (I'll get to dictionaries in a minute).

- AutoCorrect offers a submenu replicating the suggestions Word displayed at the top of the spelling menu. By choosing one of these, you can quickly create an AutoCorrect entry for this particular typo. (If Word has no suggestions for the word it doesn't recognize, it will show no AutoCorrect submenu.)

- Language displays a submenu that lets you assign one of the languages you've been using. To assign a different language, choose Set Language from the submenu to display the Language dialog box.

- Spelling fires up a full-fledged spell-check (see the next section for details on this, too).

Once you have chosen either Add or Ignore All for one instance of a word that the spell checker has flagged, Word removes the squiggly red underline from all other instances of that word. (If you have chosen another spelling for a flagged word, either from the main portion of the context menu or the AutoCorrect submenu of the context menu, Word doesn't change all instances of that word.)

If you type the same word twice, Word will flag the second instance of the word and offer you a different menu—Delete Repeated Word, Ignore, and Spelling, as shown here. (In this case, if you choose Spelling, the Spelling dialog box will appear to tell you that you've repeated the word.)

NOTE NOTE NOTE NOTE NOTE NOTE NOTE NOTE NOTE NOTE NOTE NOTE NOTE NOTE NOTE
As described in Skill 4, the Do Not Check Spelling Or Grammar language attribute (set via the Language dialog box; Tools ➢ Language ➢ Set Language, then select the Do Not Check Spelling Or Grammar check box) tells Word not to spell-check the text, no matter which language it is formatted as. If on-the-fly spell-checking seems to stop working, check the language formatting of the text in question—it may have this attribute set.

The grammar checker will put a squiggly green line under any word or construction that runs afoul of the rules that the grammar checker is currently using. To see what the grammar checker thinks is wrong with one of these words, right-click it and see what suggestions Word offers from the context menu.

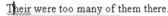

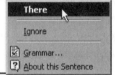

The grammatical suggestion may consist of a single word, as it does here. In other instances, Word may suggest a way of rewriting the whole sentence.

The Spelling And Grammar Status indicator on the status bar shows the status of spell- and grammar-checking. While you're typing (or otherwise inserting text), the icon will show a pen moving across the book; when Word has time to check the text, you'll see a check mark on the right page of the book if everything's fine, and a cross on the page if there's one or more mistakes.

Static Spell-Checking and Grammar-Checking

If you don't like Word's on-the-fly spell- and grammar-checking, or if you simply want to be sure that you have corrected all the spelling errors in that vital report you've written before you submit it to your boss, run Word's regular spell and grammar checker instead.

1. Click the Spelling And Grammar button, choose Tools ➢ Spelling And Grammar, or press F7 to start the spell and grammar checker.

NOTE NOTE NOTE NOTE NOTE NOTE NOTE NOTE NOTE NOTE NOTE NOTE NOTE NOTE NOTE

If you have selected any text (or a picture), Word assumes that you want to check it. After Word has finished checking the selected text (or picture—which it usually finds to be correctly spelled), it then displays a message box asking if you want to check the rest of the document. If you have not selected anything, Word will automatically start checking from the beginning of the document.

- If Word does not find any words that it does not recognize, it will display either a message saying that the spell- and grammar-check is complete or the Readability Statistics dialog box, which we'll examine in a minute.

2. As soon as Word encounters either a word that does not match an entry in its dictionary or what it considers a grammatical error, it displays the Spelling And Grammar dialog box. Figure 7.1 shows how Word responds to a spelling error: The Not In Dictionary box shows the offending word in its sentence, and the Suggestions box shows Word's best guess at the word highlighted, with lesser suggestions below it.

NOTE NOTE NOTE NOTE NOTE NOTE NOTE NOTE NOTE NOTE NOTE NOTE NOTE NOTE NOTE

Again, text with the Do Not Check Spelling Or Grammar language attribute turned on will not be checked by the spell and grammar checker.

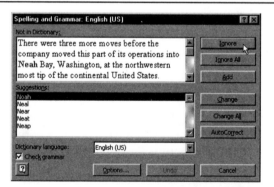

FIGURE 7.1: The Spelling And Grammar dialog box tackles a spelling problem.

3. You now have several choices:
- If you think this is the only instance of a particular spelling in a document and you don't want to change it, click the Ignore button to ignore this instance of the apparent misspelling.

- Click the Ignore All button to have Word skip all instances of this word. This is useful for names or technical terms (or foreign words) that will appear in only one document and that you don't want to add to your custom dictionaries.

- Click the Change button to change this instance of the word marked in the Not In Dictionary box to the word selected in the Suggestions list. (If Word has not suggested a different spelling for the word, the Change button will be dimmed.)

- Accept the word selected in the Suggestions list (or choose another of the suggested words) and click the Change All button to change all instances of the marked word in the Not In Dictionary box to the word you chose. (Again, the Change All button will be dimmed if Word has not suggested any alternative spellings or words.) Use Change All when you're sure about the correct spelling of a word.

- Click the Add button to add the word marked in the Not In Dictionary box to the custom dictionary currently selected. Once you've added the word to the dictionary, Word will not flag it again. (We'll look at selecting dictionaries in a minute.)

- If Word has found a typo that you feel you're likely to repeat, click the AutoCorrect button to add the marked word to the Not In Dictionary box and the chosen suggestion to the list of AutoCorrect entries.

- Click the Undo button to undo the last spell-checking change you made.

- Click the Cancel button or Close button to stop the spell-check.

4. When the spell and grammar checker encounters a grammatical problem, you'll see a Spelling And Grammar dialog box like the one shown in Figure 7.2: The upper box displays the type of grammatical rule the guilty sentence has supposedly violated, and the Suggestions box contains purported remedies. The Office Assistant (if you are using it) will display any additional information that Word can supply about the rule. Your choices here are correspondingly fewer:

   - Click the Ignore button to ignore the ostensible problem Word has pointed out.

   - Click the Ignore Rule button to ignore all instances of this ostensible problem. This is the quickest way to establish your authority when you and Word disagree on issues such as subject-verb agreement. (The alternative, as we'll see in a minute, is to turn off grammatical rules that irritate you.)

SKILL 7

- Click the Next Sentence button to ignore not only this problem, but also any others that Word may say that this sentence has.

- Choose a suggestion from the Suggestions list box or change the text on your own, then click the Change button to implement the change.

- Clear the Check Grammar check box at the bottom of the Spelling And Grammar dialog box to proceed with the spell-check without checking any more grammar.

- Click the Cancel button or Close button to stop the spell- and grammar-check.

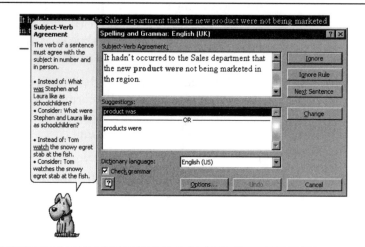

FIGURE 7.2: The Spelling And Grammar dialog box tackles a grammatical problem, with the aid of the Office Assistant.

To see readability statistics for the document you are spell-checking, select the Show Readability Statistics check box on the Spelling & Grammar tab of the Options dialog box (Tools ➤ Options) before running a spell- and grammar-check.

To stop the grammar checker from running, clear the Check Grammar With Spelling check box on the Spelling & Grammar tab of the Options dialog box.

Working with Dictionaries

Word comes with a built-in dictionary that it uses for spell-checking. You can't change this dictionary, but you can create and use custom dictionaries to supplement it. You can open and close these as needed for the particular documents you're working on; however, the more dictionaries you have open, the slower Word's spell-checking will be, so it pays to think ahead and coordinate your efforts a little.

The Default Custom Dictionary

Word starts off with a default custom dictionary named `Custom.dic`, which you'll usually find in the `\Application Data\Microsoft\Proof\` folder under the `Windows` folder (for Windows 95 and Windows 98) or the appropriate `Profiles` folder (for Windows NT). Whenever you run the spell and grammar checker, Word adds any words that you add to your custom dictionary by using the Add command during a spell-check to the `Custom.dic` dictionary—unless you tell it otherwise by selecting another dictionary, which we'll look at in a moment.

TIP TIP TIP TIP TIP TIP TIP TIP TIP TIP TIP TIP TIP TIP TIP TIP TIP TIP TIP TIP TIP TIP TIP TIP TIP

When adding words to your custom dictionary, use lowercase letters unless the words require special capitalization. If you add a word in lowercase, Word will recognize it when you type it in uppercase or with an initial capital letter; but if you add a word with an initial capital letter, Word will not recognize it if you type it using all lowercase letters.

Creating a Custom Dictionary

To create a new custom dictionary—for example, for foreign words you use in your English documents (as opposed to foreign words you use in your foreign-language documents) or for technical terms that you don't want to keep in `Custom.dic`—here's what to do:

1. Choose Tools ➢ Options to display the Options dialog box, then click the Spelling & Grammar tab. (If you're in the middle of spell-checking, click the Options button in the Spelling dialog box instead.)

2. Click the Dictionaries button to display the Custom Dictionaries dialog box (see Figure 7.3).

3. Click the New button to open the Create Custom Dictionary dialog box.

4. Enter a name for the dictionary in the File Name text box, then click the Save button to create the dictionary and close the Create Custom Dictionary dialog box. Word will return you to the Custom Dictionaries dialog box, where you will see the new dictionary in the Custom Dictionaries list box.

FIGURE 7.3: In the Custom Dictionaries dialog box, click the New button to create a new dictionary.

5. If you want to specify a different language for the new custom dictionary, select it in the Custom Dictionaries list box and choose a language from the Language drop-down list.

6. Make sure that the check box for the new dictionary is selected, then click the OK button to close the Custom Dictionaries dialog box and return to the Options dialog box.

7. If you want to add new terms to the new dictionary rather than to the currently selected one, select the new dictionary in the Custom Dictionary drop-down list.

8. Click the OK button to close the Options dialog box.

Adding Custom Dictionaries from Other Folders

If you have custom dictionaries stored in folders other than the \Proof\ folder, you may need to tell Word where they are.

To add a custom dictionary:

1. Choose Tools ➢ Options to display the Options dialog box, then click the Spelling & Grammar tab. (If you're in the middle of spell-checking, click the Options button in the Spelling And Grammar dialog box instead.)

2. Click the Dictionaries button to display the Custom Dictionaries dialog box.

3. Click the Add button to display the Add Custom Dictionary dialog box.

4. Navigate to the folder containing the custom dictionary you want to add using standard Windows navigation techniques.

5. Select the dictionary to add, then click the OK button. Word will add the dictionary to the list of custom dictionaries and then return you to the Custom Dictionaries dialog box.

6. Make sure the check box for the new dictionary in the Custom Dictionaries list box is selected, then click the OK button to close the Custom Dictionaries dialog box.

7. If you want to add new terms to the new dictionary rather than to the currently selected one, select the new dictionary in the Custom Dictionary drop-down list.

8. Click the OK button to close the Options dialog box.

> NOTE NOTE NOTE NOTE NOTE NOTE NOTE NOTE NOTE NOTE NOTE NOTE NOTE NOTE NOTE
>
> **To remove a custom dictionary from the Custom Dictionaries list in the Custom Dictionaries dialog box, select the dictionary you want to remove and then click the Remove button. (This option just removes the dictionary from the list—it does not delete the dictionary file.)**

Editing a Custom Dictionary

One way of adding words to your custom dictionaries is by clicking the Add button whenever you run into one of them during a spell-check. However, Word also lets you open and edit your custom dictionaries. This is particularly useful when you have added a misspelled word to a dictionary, and the spell checker is now merrily accepting a mistake in every document you write.

SKILL
7

To edit a custom dictionary:

1. Choose Tools ➤ Options to display the Options dialog box, then click the Spelling & Grammar tab.

2. Click the Dictionaries button to display the Custom Dictionaries dialog box.

3. In the Custom Dictionaries list box, choose the dictionary you want to edit and click the Edit button. Word will display a warning telling you that it is about to turn automatic spell-checking off; click the OK button, and Word will open the dictionary as a Word file.

4. Edit the dictionary as you would any other document, making sure you have only one word per line.

5. Choose File ➤ Save to save the dictionary.

6. Choose File ➤ Close to close the dictionary and return to your document.

7.   Choose Tools ➤ Options to display the Options dialog box, then turn automatic spell-checking back on by selecting the Check Spelling As You Type check box on the Spelling & Grammar tab. Click OK to close the Options dialog box.

Customizing the Grammar Check

If you find the grammar checker helpful but think it offers some suggestions that you could do without, try customizing it to use only those rules that you need. You can either select one of the grammar checker's existing sets of rules or edit a set of rules and turn off those you don't want to use.

To choose a set of rules for the grammar checker:

1.   Choose Tools ➤ Options to display the Options dialog box, then click the Spelling & Grammar tab.

2.   In the Grammar area, choose the style of writing you're aiming for from the Writing Style drop-down list: Casual, Standard, Formal, Technical, or Custom.

3.   To customize the rules, click the Settings button to display the Grammar Settings dialog box (see Figure 7.4).

    • In the Require area, choose whether Word should check for Comma Before Last List Item (also known as *serial comma*), Punctuation With Quotes, and Spaces Between Sentences.

    • In the Grammar And Style Options list box, select the check boxes for the items you want to have the grammar checker apply to your text.

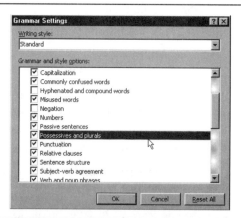

FIGURE 7.4: In the Grammar Settings dialog box, customize the set of rules that you want the grammar checker to apply when checking your document.

4. Click the OK button to apply your choices and close the Grammar Settings dialog box.

5. Click the OK button in the Options dialog box to close it.

Using the Thesaurus

If you've ever had a word right on the tip of your tongue but just out of your grasp, Word's thesaurus will prove a welcome tool. The thesaurus gives you a hand in unlocking the power and richness of the English language by offering synonyms (words with the same meaning) and antonyms (words with the opposite meaning) of the word or phrase you select.

Word provides a quick list of synonyms on the context menu for regular text paragraphs. Right-click a word or a selected phrase, choose Synonyms from the context menu, and choose a word or phrase from the submenu to insert it in place of your original word or phrase. If there are no suggestions, or none you like, choose Thesaurus to display the Thesaurus dialog box.

You can also invoke the thesaurus directly as follows:

1. Select the word or phrase you want to look up, or just place the insertion point within the word.

2. Choose Tools ➤ Language ➤ Thesaurus or press Shift+F7 to start the Thesaurus. You'll see the Thesaurus dialog box (see Figure 7.5) with the word you chose displayed in the Looked Up box.

SKILL 7

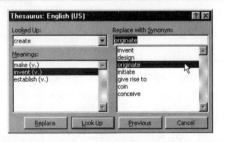

FIGURE 7.5: The Thesaurus dialog box provides you with a way of digging the depths of the English language for the precise word you need. These are the possibilities the thesaurus offers for "create."

3. In the Meanings box, highlight the word that is closest in meaning to the one you're searching for.

   - If Word finds any antonyms for the word in the Looked Up box, you'll see the word *Antonyms* at the bottom of the list. Highlight it to see the list of antonyms.

   - If Word finds any related words that aren't actually synonyms, it will offer the choice Related Words in the Meanings list box (sometimes Word finds synonyms *and* related words). Click Related Words to see a list of related words in the Replace With Related Word list box (which is the Related Words version of the Replace With Synonym list box) and choose one of those words.

   - If Word doesn't find any words it can identify with the word you looked up, the Looked Up box will become the Not Found box, and the Meanings list box will become the Alphabetical List list box. In this list box, you will find a listing of words closest in spelling to the original word. Double-click the word you want in the Alphabetical List list box to display its synonyms in the Replace With Synonym box, or click the Cancel button and select a different word to look up.

TIP TIP TIP TIP TIP TIP TIP TIP TIP TIP TIP TIP TIP TIP TIP TIP TIP TIP TIP TIP TIP TIP TIP

The thesaurus isn't much good at the declension of nouns or the conjugation of verbs—in most cases, you'll do better to look up a singular noun rather than a plural one (for example, *case* rather than *cases*) and the basic form of a verb rather than the past tense or the present or past participle. Going for the root word will also get you results more quickly—for example, if you look up *charm*, you'll see far more possibilities than if you look up *charming*.

4. Once you've found the meaning you want in the Meanings list box, choose the most appropriate synonym (or antonym or related word) from the Replace With Synonym (or Replace With Antonym or Replace With Related Word) list box. You can then:

   - Click the Replace button to replace the word you looked up in text with the synonym, antonym, or related word.

   - Click the Look Up button to look up the meanings and synonyms for the synonym (or antonym or related word).

- Click the Previous button to go back a step in your pursuit of the right word; this restores the previous word to the Looked Up box.

- Click the Cancel button to cancel the search and return to your document.

Getting a Word Count

To get a quick count of the words in your document—not to mention the number of pages, characters, paragraphs, and lines—choose Tools ➢ Word Count. Word will calculate the numbers and display them in the Word Count dialog box (see Figure 7.6).

- To include footnotes and endnotes in the count, select the Include Footnotes And Endnotes check box in the Word Count dialog box. If you're getting the word count for a selection, this check box will be dimmed and unavailable.

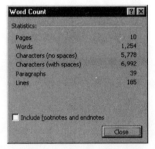

SKILL 7

FIGURE 7.6: Use Tools ➢ Word Count to find out how many words your document contains.

For a word count of just a part of your document, select that part first. Use Outline view (discussed in Skill 14) to quickly select one or more heading sections of a document.

TIP TIP TIP TIP TIP TIP TIP TIP TIP TIP TIP TIP TIP TIP TIP TIP TIP TIP TIP TIP TIP TIP TIP

Another text-improvement feature that Word offers is hyphenation. For coverage of hyphenation, see the Web component for this book on the Sybex Web site, www.sybex.com.

Are You Experienced?

Now you can...

- ☑ check the spelling and grammar of your documents
- ☑ create a new dictionary
- ☑ load an existing dictionary
- ☑ add words to a dictionary of your choice
- ☑ customize the grammar checker
- ☑ count the characters, words, sentences, or paragraphs in a document

AutoText, Captions, Bookmarks, and Fields

- → **Creating and using AutoText entries**
- → **Using automatic captioning**
- → **Using bookmarks**
- → **Using fields**

In this skill, we'll examine four features that Word provides for automating different parts of the creation of a document: AutoText, automatic captions, bookmarks, and fields. AutoText lets you create abbreviations for text you enter frequently in documents. Word also gives you the advantage of automatic bullets and numbering, including heading numbering, along with automatic captioning for figures and tables, and more. Word's bookmarks give you quick access to parts of your documents; and fields provide a way of entering information.

AutoText

Similar to AutoCorrect (which you met in Skill 5), AutoText provides a way to insert frequently used text and graphics in your documents. AutoText has several components that we'll look at in the following sections. Essentially, you create AutoText entries, then insert them in the way you find easiest. Word has a number of built-in AutoText entries that range from your username and company to sundry closing lines for letters ("Cordially," "Best Regards," and so on), but you'll benefit most from AutoText by creating your own entries.

Creating an AutoText Entry

To create an AutoText entry:

1. Select the text (and/or graphics, etc.) from your document for the AutoText entry. Make sure that it contains all the formatting it needs.

2. Click the Create AutoText button on the AutoText toolbar or press Alt+F3 to display the Create AutoText dialog box (see Figure 8.1).

FIGURE 8.1: In the Create AutoText dialog box, select a name for your Auto-Text entry and then click the OK button.

3. In the Please Name Your AutoText Entry text box, enter the name you'll use to identify the AutoText entry.

   • If you chose text for the AutoText entry, Word will automatically display the first couple of words from your selection in the Please Name Your AutoText Entry box. Often, you'll want to change this and use something catchy that you won't forget.

   • Unlike AutoCorrect entries, AutoText entries can have plain English names that you'll type all the time because AutoText does not automatically replace your typing.

4. Click the OK button to add the AutoText entry to Word's list and close the Create AutoText dialog box.

   • If an AutoText entry with the same name already exists, Word will ask if you want to redefine it. Choose Yes or No; if you choose No, Word will let you choose another name for the AutoText entry; if you choose Yes, Word will replace the existing AutoText entry with the new one.

Inserting an AutoText Entry

You can insert an AutoText entry in several ways:

   • by using the AutoText toolbar

   • by typing and using the AutoComplete feature

   • by typing and choosing the entry manually

   • by using the Insert ➤ AutoText menu item

Inserting an AutoText Entry from the AutoText Toolbar

To insert an AutoText entry from the AutoText toolbar, use the Insert AutoText button. This button will bear the name of the style of the current paragraph, such as **Heading 1** or **Body Text**. If there are no AutoText entries defined for the style of the current paragraph, the button will be identified as All Entries. Click the button to display a list of the AutoText entries associated with the current style.

To insert an entry associated with another style or with one of Word's pre-defined entries, hold down the Shift key as you click the Insert AutoText button. Word will display a menu of all the AutoText categories that it contains, including its predefined categories (Attention Line, Closing, Header/Footer, and so on) and all the styles that have AutoText entries defined. Select the category you want, then choose the item from the submenu that appears.

Inserting an AutoText Entry by Using the AutoComplete Feature

To insert an AutoText entry using the AutoComplete feature, start typing the name of the entry. As soon as you've typed four letters of it, or enough of it to distinguish it from any other AutoText entry that starts with the same four letters, AutoComplete will pop up a suggestion box, as shown here. Press Enter or F3 to replace the name of the entry with the full text of the entry; keep typing to ignore the suggestion.

You can turn off the AutoComplete feature as follows:

1. Click the AutoText button or choose Insert ➤ AutoText ➤ AutoText to display the AutoText tab of the AutoCorrect dialog box.

2. Clear the Show AutoComplete Tip For AutoText And Dates check box.

3. Click the OK button to close the AutoCorrect dialog box.

Inserting an AutoText Entry Manually

When you've turned off AutoComplete, you can insert an AutoText entry by typing the first few letters of its name and then pressing F3 to insert the entry. You have to type enough letters of the name to distinguish it from any other AutoText entry; if you have few AutoText entries, one letter might be enough, but usually you'll need three or four letters.

Inserting an AutoText Entry from the Insert Menu

You can also insert an AutoText entry from the Insert menu:

1. Display the appropriate AutoText submenu:

   - To display the AutoText submenu of AutoText entries associated with the current style, choose Insert ➤ AutoText.

   - To display the AutoText submenu of all AutoText categories, pull down the Insert menu and hold down the Shift key as you select AutoText.

2. Choose the entry you want either from the AutoText submenu or from a category from the AutoText submenu, as shown in Figure 8.2.

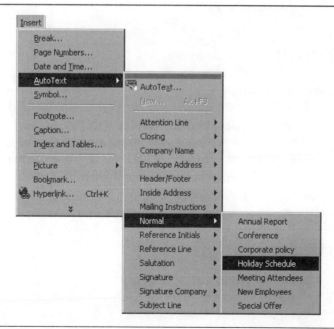

SKILL 8

FIGURE 8.2: You can also insert AutoText entries from the Insert ➤ AutoText submenu.

Changing an AutoText Entry

You can't edit an AutoText entry on the AutoText tab of the AutoCorrect dialog box. Instead, to change an AutoText entry, simply insert it in text (as described in the previous section), then make edits to it by using regular Word editing techniques. Once you have the material for the entry to your satisfaction, select it, choose Insert ➤ AutoText ➤ New to display the Create AutoText dialog box, enter the name of the existing AutoText entry in the Please Name Your AutoText Entry text box, click the OK button, and confirm that you want to replace the entry.

Deleting an AutoText Entry

To delete an AutoText entry:

1. Click the AutoText button or choose Insert ➤ AutoText ➤ AutoText to display the AutoText tab of the AutoCorrect dialog box.

2. Select the entry in the list box.

3. Click the Delete button to delete the entry.

4. Either delete more AutoText entries or click the Close button to close the AutoCorrect dialog box.

Captioning

Word's captioning features offer relief for those needing to ensure that the figures, graphics, tables, slides, video clips, equations, and so on throughout their long documents are numbered consistently and sequentially. You can forget about laboriously renumbering all subsequent figures when you delete one at the beginning of a chapter—Word will handle it for you in seconds.

You can add either automatic numbering to captions of your own devising or you can designate standard captions that Word will add automatically to every table, equation, video clip, or whatever you insert in your document.

Inserting a Caption

To insert a caption:

1. Select the item that you want to caption. For example, select a picture or a table.

2. Choose Insert ➤ Caption. Word will display the Caption dialog box (see Figure 8.3).

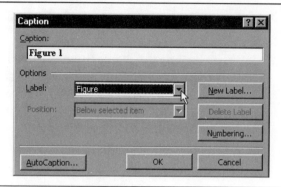

FIGURE 8.3: The Caption dialog box

3. From the Label drop-down list, choose Figure, Equation, or Table. Word will display your choice in the Caption text box.

    - To add a new label to the list (and to the Caption text box), click the New Label button. In the New Label dialog box that Word displays, enter the text for the new label in the Label box and click the OK button. Word will insert the new label in the Caption box with its regular numbering.

SKILL
8

TIP TIP TIP TIP TIP TIP TIP TIP TIP TIP TIP TIP TIP TIP TIP TIP TIP TIP TIP TIP TIP TIP TIP

To delete a caption you've created, select the caption in the Label drop-down list and click the Delete Label button. You can tell which captions are Word's and which are yours because Word won't let you delete any of its captions (the Delete Label button will be dimmed when one of Word's captions is selected).

4. Adjust the numbering of the caption if necessary: Click the Numbering button to display the Caption Numbering dialog box (see Figure 8.4). Click the OK button when you've finished.

    -   From the Format drop-down list, choose the numbering format you want: 1, 2, 3; a, b, c; A, B, C; i, ii, iii; or I, II, III.

    -   To include the chapter number with the illustration (for example, to produce "Figure 8.4" and so on), select the Include Chapter Number check box. Specify the style at the beginning of each chapter from the Chapter Starts With Style drop-down list and then choose a separator character from the Use Separator drop-down list. Word offers periods, hyphens, colons, and em and en dashes as separator characters.

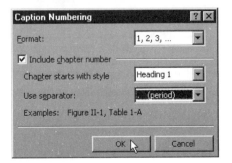

FIGURE 8.4: Specify different numbering for your caption in the Caption Numbering dialog box.

5. In the Position drop-down list, choose whether you want the caption to appear above or below the selected item.

6. Click the OK button in the Caption dialog box to apply the caption numbering and return to your document. Add your specific caption to the generic caption that Word has inserted.

Using AutoCaption for Truly Automatic Captions

You can also choose to add automatic captions to recurring elements in a Word document. For example, if you're adding a number of tables to a document, you can have Word automatically add captions to each table as you insert it to prevent you from missing a table or using a wrong or inconsistent caption.

To add automatic captions to an element:

1. Choose Insert ➤ Caption to display the Caption dialog box.

2. Click the AutoCaption button to display the AutoCaption dialog box (see Figure 8.5).

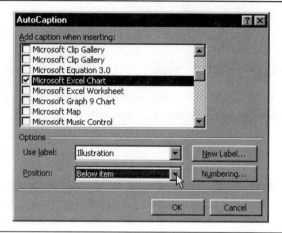

FIGURE 8.5: In the AutoCaption dialog box, choose the element or elements to which you want to add automatic captions and then customize the captions and numbering.

3. In the Add Caption When Inserting list box, select the check box for the element you want to have captioned automatically.

    -   If you want several elements to have the same caption, select each one.

4. In the Options area, specify what the label should be and whether Word should position it above or below the element.

    -   The Use Label drop-down list offers standard choices: Equation, Figure, or Table. If you chose Microsoft Equation or Microsoft Word Table in the Add Caption When Inserting box, Word will offer you Equation and Table, respectively. Otherwise, it will offer you Figure as a generic title.

    -   To change the label, click the New Label button and insert the text of the new label in the New Label dialog box.

    -   To specify the numbering for the element, click the Numbering button and make your choices in the Caption Numbering dialog box. (For

**SKILL
8**

details, see the previous section, "Inserting a Caption.") Click the OK button when you've finished.

- Use the Position drop-down list to specify the position of the caption: Above Item or Below Item.

5. To add a different AutoCaption to another item, repeat steps 3 and 4 ad lib.

6. Click the OK button to close the AutoCaption dialog box and return to your document.

Updating Captions

Word renumbers captions whenever you insert a new caption. If you move a caption to a different position in the document or delete one altogether, you'll need to tell Word to update the captions. To do so, select the whole document (choose Edit ➢ Select All or Ctrl+click in the selection bar) and press the F9 key.

TIP TIP TIP TIP TIP TIP TIP TIP TIP TIP TIP TIP TIP TIP TIP TIP TIP TIP TIP TIP TIP TIP

If you want to update only one caption (or a number of captions one-by-one) without updating other fields in the document, select that caption and press F9.

Using Bookmarks

Word's electronic bookmarks provide a way of assigning names to parts of your documents so that you can access them swiftly. A bookmark can mark a single point in the text, one or more characters, a table, a graphic—pretty much any item in a document.

Adding a Bookmark

To add a bookmark:

1. Position the insertion point where you want to insert the bookmark.

- If you want the bookmark to mark a particular section of text, a graphic, a text box, a table, or another element, select that item.

2. Choose Insert ➢ Bookmark to display the Bookmark dialog box (see Figure 8.6).

FIGURE 8.6: In the Bookmark dialog box, enter the name for the bookmark and click the Add button.

3. Enter the name for the bookmark in the Bookmark Name text box.

- Bookmark names can be up to 40 characters long, must start with a letter, and can contain letters, numbers, and underscores, but no spaces or symbols.

- To reuse an existing bookmark name, select it in the Bookmark Name list box.

4. Click the Add button to add the bookmark and close the Bookmark dialog box.

Going to a Bookmark

Once you've added bookmarks to a document, you can quickly move to them by using either the Bookmark dialog box or the Go To dialog box.

To move to a bookmark using the Bookmark dialog box:

1. Choose Insert ➤ Bookmark to display the Bookmark dialog box.

2. In the Bookmark Name list box, select the bookmark you want to move to.

- To sort the bookmarks alphabetically by Name, select the Name option button in the Sort By area; to sort them by their location in the document (i.e., from first to last), select the Location option button.

- To display hidden bookmarks such as those that Word uses to mark cross references, select the Hidden Bookmarks check box.

3. Click the Go To button to move to the bookmark and then click the Close button (into which the Cancel button will have changed) to close the Bookmark dialog box.

To move to a bookmark by using the Go To dialog box:

1. Double-click in open space in the page/section or current-position areas of the status bar, press F5, or choose Edit ➢ Go To to display the Go To tab of the Find And Replace dialog box (see Figure 8.7).

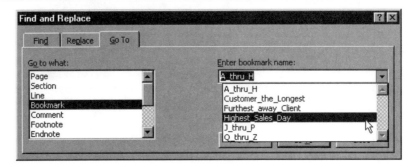

FIGURE 8.7: Choose the bookmark to move to on the Go To tab of the Find And Replace dialog box and then click the Go To button.

2. Choose Bookmark in the Go To What list box.

3. Select the bookmark from the Enter Bookmark Name drop-down list and then click the Go To button.

4. Click the Close button to close the Go To dialog box.

Viewing Bookmarks

Word doesn't normally display bookmarks, which makes it easier to read your documents. But when you do need to see where your bookmarks are, choose Tools ➢ Options to display the Options dialog box, and select the Bookmarks check box in the Show area on the View tab. Then click the OK button to close the Options dialog box.

An empty bookmark appears as a heavy I-beam—like a mouse pointer on steroids—while a bookmark that contains text or another item encloses it within square brackets. The following illustration shows both types of bookmarks.

Please let us know if you]will be available to atten the creative

Deleting a Bookmark

To delete a bookmark:

1. Choose Insert ➢ Bookmark to display the Bookmark dialog box.

2. In the Bookmark Name list box, select the bookmark you want to delete.

3. Click the Delete button to delete the bookmark. The bookmark's contents will not be affected.

4. Repeat steps 2 and 3 as necessary and then click the Close button to close the Bookmark dialog box.

TIP TIP TIP TIP TIP TIP TIP TIP TIP TIP TIP TIP TIP TIP TIP TIP TIP TIP TIP TIP TIP TIP TIP TIP TIP
You can also delete a bookmark by selecting it and pressing the Delete key. Using this method will delete the bookmark's contents as well.

Fields

In this section, we'll look at how to use Word's fields in your documents. Fields have the reputation of being difficult to understand and difficult to use. Fortunately, neither part of this is really true: Like many features of Word, fields *can* be extremely complex—but the basic idea behind fields is simple, and they can be straightforward and extremely useful to use. In fact, many people use fields in their day-to-day work without realizing it: Word uses fields for items such as page numbering and dates, which show up in pretty much every other document.

What Is a Field?

A field is a special code that tells Word to insert particular information in a document. For example, you can use fields to insert information such as page numbers and dates in your documents and have them updated automatically.

Word lets you view either the field *codes* (the instructions that tell Word what information to put in your document) or the *results* of the field codes (the information the codes produce). Usually, you'll want to see the results, but when you're creating a document that contains many fields, you may find it easier to display the codes.

Fields get their information from a variety of sources, such as the following:

- Date and time information comes from your computer's clock. (If it's wrong, the fields will be wrong too.)

- User information comes from the information stored on the User Info tab of the Options dialog box.

- File information comes from the Properties dialog box—some of it you can fill in when you save the document (Keywords, Comments, and so on), and some of it is generated automatically (details on who last saved the file and when, and so on).

Inserting Fields

For the most-often used fields, such as dates and page numbers, Word provides special ways of inserting them. To insert a date (or time), you can use the Date And Time dialog box (Insert ➢ Date And Time), as discussed in Skill 2. You can also choose whether to insert the information as a field (by selecting the Update Automatically check box in the Date And Time dialog box) or as text (by leaving the check box cleared). To insert a page number in a header or footer, use the Page Number button on the Header And Footer toolbar, which we'll examine in Skill 11. But you can also insert most any field code from the Field dialog box.

To insert a field code manually at the insertion point:

1. Choose Insert ➢ Field to display the Field dialog box (see Figure 8.8).

2. Choose the category of field in the Categories list. (The first choice, All, shows the fields in alphabetical order and is helpful if you know the name of the field but not which category Word lumps it into. Otherwise, choose a category, and Word will display all the fields for that category in the Field Names list box.)

3. Choose the field name you want from the Field Names list box.

4. To set options for the field, click the Options button to display the Field Options dialog box (see Figure 8.9). Choose formatting, formats, or switches for the field—the contents of the Field Options dialog box will vary depending on the field you've chosen—and click the Add To Field button to add them to the field. Use the Undo Add button to correct any mistakes. When the field in the Field Codes box looks right, click the OK button to return to the Field dialog box.

5. Click OK to close the Field dialog box and insert the field (and any formatting or switches) in the document.

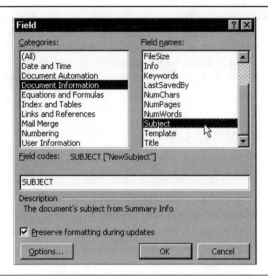

FIGURE 8.8: Choose the field you want to insert in the Field dialog box.

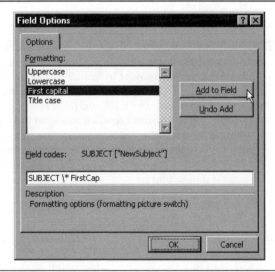

SKILL 8

FIGURE 8.9: Choose formatting or formats for the field in the Field Options dialog box.

WARNING WARNING WARNING WARNING WARNING WARNING WARNING WARNING

You *can* type field codes straight into your document, provided you press Ctrl+F9 to insert the {~TS} field-delimiter characters rather than try to type them in from the keyboard—but it's a great waste of time and effort. Using the Insert ➤ Field command is almost always faster and simpler.

Viewing Field Codes

By default, Word displays the *results* of field codes rather than the codes themselves, so if you insert a data code in your document, you'll see something like **July 16, 1999** rather than { **TIME \@"M/d/yy"** } or a similar code.

To display a field code rather than the field result, right-click in any field and choose Toggle Field Codes from the context menu. (To display the field result again, repeat the maneuver.) Alternatively, click in the field and press Shift+F9.

To toggle between field codes and field results for all fields in a document, either press Alt+F9 or choose Tools ➤ Options to display the Options dialog box, then bring the View tab to the front. Select the Field Codes check box in the Show area to display field codes; clear it to display field results. Click the OK button to close the Options dialog box.

NOTE NOTE NOTE NOTE NOTE NOTE NOTE NOTE NOTE NOTE NOTE NOTE NOTE NOTE NOTE

You may find it helpful to display field codes when arranging documents (e.g., forms, which we'll look at in Bonus Skill 2 on the Sybex Web site) that contain many of them. You may find it even more helpful to split the window and view field codes in one half and field results in the other. To do this, choose Window ➤ Split or double-click the split bar located at the top of the vertical scroll bar. Display the field codes in one pane by choosing Tools ➤ Options, which will display the Options dialog box. Then select the Field Codes check box in the Show area of the View tab box and click OK. Do not use the Alt+F9 or Shift+F9 shortcuts.

WARNING WARNING WARNING WARNING WARNING WARNING WARNING WARNING

To display index entry (XE), table of authorities (TA), table of contents (TC), and referenced document (RD) codes, you'll need to display hidden text rather than field codes. Choose Tools ➤ Options to display the Options dialog box, click the View tab, then select the Hidden Text check box or the All check box in the Formatting Marks area. Click the OK button to close the Options dialog box.

Displaying Field Shading

To make things easier when working with documents that include fields, you can turn field shading on and off. Turning it on can not only help you see where all your fields are (again, with the exception of the XE, TA, TC, and RD fields), but also prevent you from deleting fields while under the impression that they're just text. At other times, though, field shading can be distracting, and you may want to turn it off so you can treat the field results as regular text.

> The following is a date field with shading: Monday, March 08, 1999

To turn field shading on and off, choose Tools ➤ Options to display the Options dialog box. On the View tab, choose the appropriate option from the Field Shading drop-down list: Never, Always, or When Selected (the latter displays field shading when the insertion point is anywhere in the field, not just when the whole field is selected). Click the OK button to close the Options dialog box and implement your choice.

NOTE NOTE NOTE NOTE NOTE NOTE NOTE NOTE NOTE NOTE NOTE NOTE NOTE NOTE NOTE

Field shading is just a visual aid for working on screen—it does not print under any circumstances.

Updating Fields

For your fields to be most useful, you'll need to update them so the information is current. You can update fields one at a time manually, all at once manually, or have Word update them all for you under certain circumstances.

TIP TIP TIP TIP TIP TIP TIP TIP TIP TIP TIP TIP TIP TIP TIP TIP TIP TIP TIP TIP TIP TIP TIP TIP

If you have fields that you don't want to update, you can lock them or unlink them. See the section titled "Locking Fields" for details.

Updating Fields Manually

To update a single field manually, right-click in it and choose Update Field from the context menu. Alternatively, click anywhere in the field and press the F9 key.

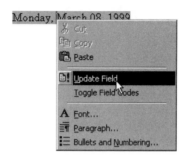

To update several fields at once manually, select the text that contains them, then either right-click and choose Update Field from the context menu or press the F9 key.

To update all the fields in a document at once, choose Edit ➢ Select All, then either right-click and choose Update Field from the context menu or press the F9 key.

Updating Fields Automatically When You Print

By updating fields whenever you print your documents, you can spare yourself the embarrassment of having your printouts contain out-of-date information.

To update fields when you print, choose Tools ➢ Options to display the Options dialog box. On the Print tab, select the Update Fields box in the Printing Options area, then click the OK button to close the Options dialog box. Now every time you print, Word will update all the fields first.

NOTE NOTE NOTE NOTE NOTE NOTE NOTE NOTE NOTE NOTE NOTE NOTE NOTE NOTE NOTE

A side-effect of updating fields automatically when you print is that when you close the document, Word will ask if you want to save changes. This can be confusing if you know you've just opened the document and printed it without making any changes yourself.

Locking Fields

Updating fields is all very good, but sooner or later you'll find yourself with a field that needs to stay the same while all of the other fields in the document get updated. In this case, you can either *lock* the field for the time being to prevent updates (so that you can unlock it later if need be) or *unlink* the field and prevent it from being updated from now until Armageddon.

To lock a field, click in it and press Ctrl+F11; to unlock it, click in the field and press Ctrl+Shift+F11.

TIP TIP TIP TIP TIP TIP TIP TIP TIP TIP TIP TIP TIP TIP TIP TIP TIP TIP TIP TIP TIP TIP TIP

A locked field looks the same as an unlocked field—for example, you'll still see field shading when the insertion point is in it (if field shading is turned on). One way to tell if it's locked is to try to update it—Word will beep if the field is locked. Another way is to right-click it and see if the context menu contains the Update Field item—if the item is grayed out and unavailable, the field is locked.

To unlink a field, click in it and press Ctrl+Shift+F9. (If you do this by accident, you can choose Edit ➤ Undo to undo the action—but make sure you do so straightaway. If you don't catch the mistake in time to undo it, you'll have to re-create the link from scratch.) Once you've unlinked a field, it will appear as regular text—no updating, no shading, nothing special.

Formatting Fields

Formatting fields could hardly be easier—simply format either the field code or the field result by selecting one or the other and using the regular formatting techniques described in Skill 4. Generally speaking, formatting the field results will give you a better idea of how your document will look.

Getting from Field to Field

The easiest way to move from one field to another is by pressing the F11 key to move to the next field (going from the beginning of your document towards the end) and by pressing Shift+F11 to move to the previous field. This option moves you to the next or previous field without discriminating about what kind of field it is.

If you need to move to a field of a particular type—for example, to move to each XE (index entry) field in turn—double-click in the status bar or choose Edit ➤ Go To to display the Go To tab of the Find And Replace dialog box (see Figure 8.10). Choose Field in the Go To What list box and then choose the type of field from the Enter Field Name drop-down list. You can then click the Next button to go to the next instance of that particular type of field (skipping all other intervening fields) or click the Previous button to go to the previous instance of that field. You can enter a + or – value after the field name to skip ahead (or back) a specified number of fields of the same type. For example, to skip ahead five index entry fields, enter **XE+5** and click the Next button.

SKILL
8

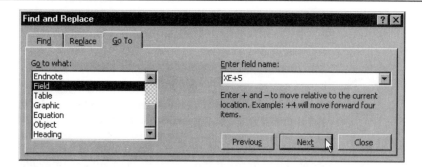

FIGURE 8.10:   Use the Go To tab of the Find And Replace dialog box to move quickly to a particular type of field.

Printing Out Fields

Normally you won't want your field codes to print—but should you ever need to, you can print them by selecting the Field Codes check box in the Include With Document area on the Print tab of the Options dialog box (Tools ➢ Options). Remember to clear this check box the next time you print, or Word will merrily keep printing the field codes rather than the results.

Are You Experienced?

Now You Can...

- ☑ **create and use AutoText entries to enter text and graphics quickly**
- ☑ **create automatic captions on figures, tables, and other document elements**
- ☑ **use bookmarks to identify and access defined areas in your documents**
- ☑ **insert fields containing variable information**
- ☑ **update, lock, and format fields**
- ☑ **move swiftly from field to field**

Working with Tables

- → **Creating and inserting tables**
- → **Navigating and editing in tables**
- → **Formatting tables**
- → **Converting tables to text**
- → **Sorting data in tables**

In this skill, we'll look at how to present tabular data in Word documents without using large numbers of tabs. Word provides a full complement of tools for creating tables made up of rows of cells. Tables can be just about as simple or complex as you need to make them—you can create anything from a single-cell table on up to a multipage monster with a different number of columns in each row and wildly variegated shading.

Word's tables give you a way to present complex information in vertical columns and horizontal rows of cells. Cells can contain text—a single paragraph or multiple paragraphs—or graphics. You can create a table from existing text, or you can create a table first and then enter your text into it. Once you've created a table, you can add further columns or rows, or merge several cells in the same row to make one cell. To embellish your tables, you can use borders, font formatting (bold, italic, underline, highlight, and so on), paragraph formatting (indents, line spacing, and so on), and style formatting—not to mention Word's Table AutoFormat feature.

The Tables And Borders Toolbar

Word provides the Tables And Borders toolbar (see Figure 9.1) for working with tables.

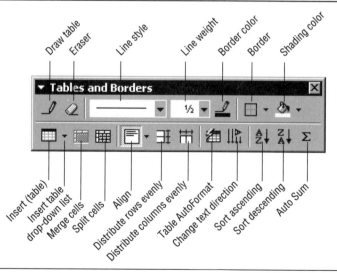

FIGURE 9.1:   The Tables And Borders toolbar

Here's what the buttons on the Tables And Borders toolbar do:

- The Draw Table button turns the mouse pointer into a pen that you can click and drag to draw table cells in a document. Click the button again to restore the mouse pointer.

- The Eraser button turns the mouse pointer into an eraser that you can drag to erase the borders of cells. Click the button again to restore the mouse pointer.

- The Line Style button displays a drop-down list of available line styles. Select one for the cells you're about to draw.

- The Line Weight button displays a drop-down list of available line weights for the current line style.

- The Border Color button displays a palette of available border colors.

- The Border button applies the current border to the selection, or to tables or cells you draw. To change the current border, click the drop-down list button and choose a type of border from the palette.

- The Shading Color button applies the current shading color to the selection. To change the current shading color, click the drop-down list button and choose a color from the palette.

- The Insert Table button displays the Insert Table dialog box for inserting a table. The Insert Table drop-down list button displays a menu of table commands.

- The Merge Cells button merges the contents of selected cells.

- The Split Cells button displays the Split Cells dialog box for splitting the selected cell into two or more cells.

- The Alignment button's drop-down list offers nine choices for the vertical alignment of selected cells.

- The Distribute Rows Evenly button and the Distribute Columns Evenly button adjust row height and column width, respectively, to equal the tallest cell in the row or the widest cell in the column.

- The Table AutoFormat button displays the Table AutoFormat dialog box. We'll look at autoformatting later in this skill.

- The Change Text Direction button toggles the text in the selected cell among horizontal (left to right across the page), vertical down the page, and vertical up the page.

- The Sort Ascending button and the Sort Descending button are for quick sorting.

- The AutoSum button inserts a formula for adding the contents of a row or column.

Drawing a Table with the Draw Table Button

For a quick table of your own design, use the Draw Table feature:

1. Display the Tables And Borders toolbar if it's not displayed: Click the Tables And Borders button on the Standard toolbar, or right-click the menu bar or any displayed toolbar and choose Tables And Borders from the drop-down list of toolbars.

2. Verify the settings in the Line Style and Line Weight drop-down lists and the color on the Line Color button to make sure they're suitable for the table you want to draw.

3. Click the Draw Table button on the Tables And Borders toolbar. (Display the Tables And Borders toolbar if it's not displayed.) The mouse pointer will turn into a pen, and Word will switch the document to Print Layout view if you're using Normal view or Web Layout view.

4. Click and drag in the document to create the shape for the table.

5. Click and drag across the table to create rows and columns, or to create diagonal lines across cells. Click the Draw Table button again when you need to restore the normal mouse pointer to work in the table.

6. To remove extra lines, click the Eraser button and drag the eraser pointer over the line you want to remove. Click the Eraser button again to restore the normal mouse pointer.

Inserting a Table Quickly with the Insert Table Button

The easiest way to insert a table is to click the Insert Table button on the Standard toolbar. Drag the mouse pointer down and to the right—over the grid that appears—to select the table layout (number of rows and columns) you want to create, then release the mouse button. Word will create the table and apply borders to it.

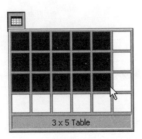

3 x 5 Table

TIP TIP TIP TIP TIP TIP TIP TIP TIP TIP TIP TIP TIP TIP TIP TIP TIP TIP TIP TIP TIP TIP TIP

To create the table from existing text, select the text before clicking the Insert Table button. Word will not display the grid when you click the button, but will convert the text to an appropriate table configuration. For example, if you have three columns laid out with tabs, Word will create a three-column table when you click the Insert Table button.

SKILL
9

Inserting a Table with the Insert Table Command

You can also insert a table at the position of the insertion point by using the Insert Table dialog box:

1. Choose Table ➤ Insert ➤ Table or click the Insert Table button on the Tables And Borders toolbar to display the Insert Table dialog box (see Figure 9.2).

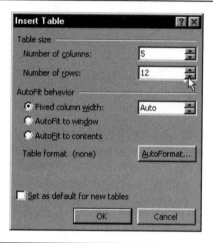

FIGURE 9.2: In the Insert Table dialog box, set up the table you want to create.

2. In the Table Size area, choose the number of columns and the number of rows.

3. In the AutoFit Behavior area, choose how you want the table to behave:

    -   Select the Fixed Column Width option button to create a table with columns all the same width (and whose width does not change automatically). You can specify the column width in the text box or leave the default setting of Auto to have Word size the columns automatically.

    -   Select the AutoFit To Window option button to have Word create a table sized to the Word window. You can resize the columns automatically or manually after that.

    -   Select the AutoFit To Contents option button to have Word create a table with columns that dynamically resize themselves as you enter text in the cells. For many purposes, this will be the best choice.

4. If you want to apply one of Word's table autoformats, click the AutoFormat button to display the Table AutoFormat dialog box (see Figure 9.3).

TIP TIP TIP TIP TIP TIP TIP TIP TIP TIP TIP TIP TIP TIP TIP TIP TIP TIP TIP TIP TIP TIP

If you're not quite sure what shape and layout your table will take on as you create it, you can also apply autoformatting after creating the table. Simply click inside the table and click the Table AutoFormat button on the Tables And Borders toolbar, or right-click in the table and choose Table AutoFormat from the context menu, or choose Table ➢ Table AutoFormat from the menu bar. Alternatively, you can format the table manually, as you'll see in "Formatting a Table" later in this skill.

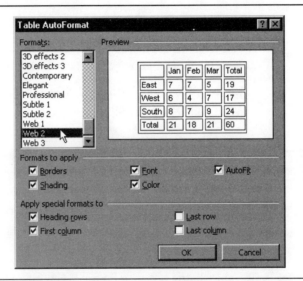

FIGURE 9.3: The Table AutoFormat dialog box offers quick access to a veritable plethora of predefined table formats and options to customize tables.

SKILL
9

- Use the Formats list box and the adjacent Preview box to choose the format that suits your table best. If you're creating a Web page, select one of the Web formats, which are designed to work effectively in HTML, the formatting language of the Web.

- In the Formats To Apply area, choose whether you want Word to apply borders, shading, font, and color formatting to the table by selecting or clearing the appropriate check boxes. Watch the Preview box to see the effects of your changes. The most important of these formatting options is AutoFit, which causes Word to adjust the column width to suit the text in your table rather than blindly allotting a standard (and most likely inappropriate) width to each column.

- In the Apply Special Formats To area, check the boxes to choose which rows and columns you want Word to apply special formatting to: Heading Rows, First Column, Last Row, and Last Column. The last two choices are good for emphasizing totals or conclusions.

TIP TIP TIP TIP TIP TIP TIP TIP TIP TIP TIP TIP TIP TIP TIP TIP TIP TIP TIP TIP TIP TIP TIP

To remove AutoFormat from a table, select None in the Formats list box in the Table AutoFormat dialog box.

- Click the OK button to return to the Insert Table dialog box.

5. If you want all the tables you create in the future to use the parameters you just set for this table, select the Set As Default For New Tables check box.

6. Click the OK button. Word will close the Insert Table dialog box and will insert the table you specified.

Converting Existing Text to a Table

If you've already got the material for a table in a Word document, but it's laid out with tabs, paragraphs, commas, or the like, you can quickly convert it to a table.

1. Select the text.

2. Choose Table ➤ Convert Text To Table. Word will display the Convert Text To Table dialog box (see Figure 9.4) with its best guess about how you want to separate the text into table cells.

    - If the selected text consists of apparently regular paragraphs of text, Word will suggest separating it at the paragraph marks—each paragraph will then go into a separate cell.

    - If the selected text appears to contain tabbed columns, Word will suggest separating it at each tab so that each tabbed column will become a table column.

FIGURE 9.4: In the Convert Text To Table dialog box, choose the options for converting existing text into a Word table.

- If the selected text appears to have commas at regular intervals in each paragraph—as in a list of names and addresses, for example—Word will suggest separating the text at each comma. This is good for database-output information (such as names and addresses) separated by commas.

- If the selected text appears to be divided by other characters (such as hyphens), Word will suggest dividing it at each hyphen.

3. If necessary, change the setting in the Separate Text At box. This may change the number of columns and rows that Word has suggested. If you choose Other, enter the separator character in the Other box. This can be any character or any letter.

4. If necessary, manually adjust the number of columns and rows by entering the appropriate number in the Number Of Columns. (For example, you might want to add an extra column at the right-hand side of the table and enter text in it later.) The setting in the Number Of Columns box automatically adjusts the setting in the Number Of Rows box to match the possible configurations of the table based on the setting in the Separate Text At group box.

5. Choose a setting in the AutoFit Behavior area, as described in step 3 in the previous section.

**SKILL
9**

6. If you want to autoformat the table, click the AutoFormat button and choose autoformatting as described in step 4 in the previous section. Otherwise, click the OK button to convert the text to a table.

Selecting Parts of a Table

When manipulating your tables, first you need to select the parts you want to manipulate. While you can just click and drag with the mouse (or use the keyboard or the Shift-click technique discussed in Skill 2), Word also offers shortcuts for selecting parts of tables.

TIP TIP TIP TIP TIP TIP TIP TIP TIP TIP TIP TIP TIP TIP TIP TIP TIP TIP TIP TIP TIP TIP TIP TIP TIP

One of the keys to understanding how Word selects cells is the hidden end-of-cell marker that each cell contains. Once you drag past this to another cell, you've selected both that cell and the other. The end-of-cell marker is a little circle with pointy corners, inescapably reminiscent of the original *Space Invaders* that transformed school life in the late 1970s. To display end-of-cell markers, choose Tools ➢ Options and select the Paragraphs check box in the Nonprinting Characters area on the View tab in the Options dialog box, or click the Show/Hide ¶ button on the Standard toolbar.

Here's how to select parts of tables:

- To select one cell, move the mouse pointer into the thin cell-selection bar at the left edge of the cell. You'll know when it's in the right place because the insertion point will change to a fat, black arrow pointing north-northeast. Then click once to select the cell (including its end-of-cell marker).

- To select a row, move the mouse pointer into the table-selection bar to the left of the row and then click. Alternatively, double-click in the cell-selection bar at the left edge of any cell in the row.

- To select multiple rows, click in the table-selection bar and drag up or down.

- To select a column, Alt-click in it. Alternatively, move the mouse pointer to just above the topmost row of the column, where it turns into a fat black arrow pointing straight down, and then click.

- To select multiple columns, click just above the topmost row of any column and drag left or right.

- To select the whole table, Alt + double-click anywhere in it.

Word also offers menu options for selecting parts of tables. Place the insertion point in the appropriate row or column (or drag through the rows or columns to select cells in multiple rows or columns) and then do the following:

To Select	Choose
A cell	Table ➤ Select ➤ Cell
A column	Table ➤ Select ➤ Column
A row	Table ➤ Select ➤ Row
The whole table	Table ➤ Select ➤ Table

Navigating in Tables

You can move easily through tables using the mouse, the arrow keys, or the Tab key. The ← moves you backward through the contents of a cell, character by character, and then to the end of the previous cell; → moves you forward and then to the start of the next cell; ↑ moves you up through the lines and paragraphs in a cell and then up to the next row; and ↓ moves you down. Tab moves you to the next cell, selecting any contents in the process; Shift+Tab moves you to the previous cell and also selects any contents in the cell.

Editing Text in a Table

Once the insertion point is inside a cell, you can enter and edit text (and other elements) as in any Word document, except for entering tabs, for which you need to press Ctrl+Tab.

Row height adjusts automatically as you add more text to a cell or as you increase the height of the text. You can also adjust the row height manually, as you'll see in a moment.

SKILL
9

Adding and Deleting Cells, Rows, and Columns

Often, you'll need to change the layout of your table after you create it—for example, you might need to add a column or two, or delete several rows, so that it presents your information most effectively.

Word distinguishes between deleting the *contents* of a cell, row, or column and deleting the cell, row, or column itself. When you delete the contents of a cell, row, or column, the cell, row, or column remains in place; but when you delete the cell, row, or column, both it and its contents disappear. To delete just the contents of a cell, row, or column, select your victim and press the Delete key.

Deleting Cells

To delete cells and their contents from a table, select the cells, right-click, and choose Delete Cells from the context menu, or choose Table ➤ Delete ➤ Cells. If your selection includes an entire row or an entire column, this command will be displayed as Delete Rows or Delete Columns (see the Deleting Rows and Deleting Columns sections a little later in this skill). Otherwise, Word will display the Delete Cells dialog box. This dialog box offers to move the remaining cells up or to the left to fill the space left by the cells you're deleting. It also offers to delete the entire row or column that the selected cells occupy. Make your choice and then click the OK button.

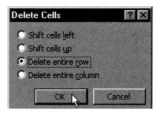

Adding Cells

To add cells to a table, select the cells above which, or to the right of which, you want to insert the new cells. Then click the Insert Table drop-down list button and choose Insert Cells from the menu, or choose Table ➤ Insert ➤ Cells, to display the Insert Cells dialog box. Choose the Shift Cells Right option button or the Shift Cells Down option button, or choose Insert Entire Row or Insert Entire Column, to specify how the selected cells should move. Then click the OK button.

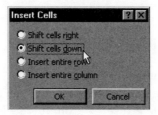

Adding Rows

To add a row to the end of a table quickly, position the insertion point in the last cell (the lower-right cell) of the table and press Tab.

To add a row to a table, click in the row above or below which you want to add the new row, then click the Insert Table drop-down list button and choose Insert Rows Above or Insert Rows Below, as appropriate. Alternatively, choose Table ➤ Insert ➤ Rows Above or Table ➤ Insert ➤ Rows Below, as appropriate.

- To insert multiple rows, select the same number of existing rows, then click the Insert Table drop-down list button and choose Insert Rows Above or Insert Rows Below, as appropriate. Alternatively, choose Table ➤ Insert ➤ Rows Above or Table ➤ Insert Rows ➤ Below. For example, to add three rows, select three rows. The new rows will appear above (or below) the rows you selected. (If you need to insert more new rows than the number of rows the table currently contains, you'll need to add them in stages.)

- Alternatively, after selecting a cell, or cells in a number of rows, choose Table ➤ Insert ➤ Cells, select the Insert Entire Row option in the Insert Cells dialog box, and then click OK.

Skill
9

Deleting Rows

To delete one or more rows of cells from a table, click in the row (or drag through the rows) and choose Table ➤ Delete ➤ Rows. Alternatively, select the row or rows you want to delete, then right-click and choose Delete Rows from the context menu.

Adding Columns

To add a column to a table, select the column to the left or right of which you want the new column to appear, then choose Table ➤ Insert ➤ Columns To The Left or Table ➤ Insert ➤ Columns To The Right, as appropriate. Alternatively, click the Insert Table drop-down list button and choose Insert Columns To The Left or Insert Columns To The Right, as appropriate.

To insert multiple columns, select the same number of existing columns before issuing the command. For example, to add three columns, select three columns.

Deleting Columns

To delete one or more columns of cells from a table, place the insertion point in the column (or drag through cells in multiple columns) and choose Table ➤ Delete ➤ Columns. Alternatively, select the column or columns, right-click in the selection, and choose Delete Columns from the context menu.

Deleting an Entire Table

To delete an entire table, click anywhere in the table and choose Table ➤ Delete ➤ Table.

Formatting a Table

As with editing a table, you can use the regular Word formatting features—from the toolbars, the Font and Paragraph dialog boxes, and so on—to format your tables. However, there are a couple of exceptions worth mentioning: alignment and indents.

Setting Alignment and Text Wrapping in Tables

Alignment in tables is very straightforward once you know that not only can any row of the table be left-aligned, right-aligned, or centered (all relative to the margins set for the page), but also, within those rows, the text in each cell can be left-aligned, right-aligned, centered, or justified, relative to the column it's in. If that's not enough, the contents of any cell can be aligned top or bottom, or centered vertically.

To set horizontal and vertical alignment within any cell, right-click in the cell, choose the right-arrow button to the right of the Cell Alignment item from the context menu, and choose one of the nine alignment options from the pop-up panel. Use the Cell Alignment item on the context menu to apply the currently selected alignment without opening the pop-up panel.

TIP TIP TIP TIP TIP TIP TIP TIP TIP TIP TIP TIP TIP TIP TIP TIP TIP TIP TIP TIP TIP TIP TIP TIP

To set horizontal alignment only, you can also use the alignment buttons on the Formatting toolbar, the keyboard shortcuts, or the Paragraph dialog box.

To set alignment for the whole table, right-click in the table and choose Table Properties from the context menu, or choose Table ➤ Table Properties, to display the Table Properties dialog box (see Figure 9.5). Display the Table tab if it's not already displayed, then choose an alignment option (Left, Center, or Right) in the Alignment area. If you want the table to be wrapped into the text on the page, select the Around option in the Text Wrapping area; otherwise, leave the None option selected. Click the OK button to close the Table Properties dialog box.

Setting Indents in Tables

As with alignment, you can indent the entire table or the contents within each cell. By understanding the difference, you can position your tables precisely where you want them on the page and lay out the table text using suitable indents.

To set indentation for a table, right-click in the table and choose Table Properties from the context menu, or choose Table ➤ Table Properties, to display the Table Properties dialog box. On the Table tab, set the indentation in the Indent From Left text box, then click the OK button.

To set indentation for the text in the current cell, use the methods you learned in Skill 4—drag the indentation markers on the ruler or change the settings in the Indentation area on the Indents And Spacing tab of the Paragraph dialog box.

SKILL
9

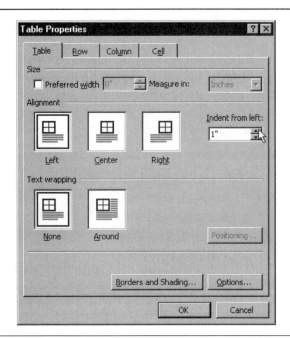

FIGURE 9.5: Use the Table tab of the Table Properties dialog box to set indentation for a table.

Changing Column Width

The easiest way to change column width is to move the mouse pointer over a column's right-hand border so that the insertion point changes into a two-headed arrow pointing left and right. Then click and drag the column border to a suitable position. (You can also click in the column division mark in the horizontal ruler and drag that instead.) If there is a column to the right of the border you're dragging, Word will resize it accordingly. If you want to change only the column whose right-hand border you're dragging, hold down Shift as you drag. Word will increase or decrease the width of the table to allow for the increase or decrease in the width of the column you adjust.

To change column width more precisely:

1. Right-click in the column you want to change and choose Table Properties from the context menu, or position the insertion point in the column and then choose Table ➢ Table Properties, to display the Table Properties dialog box.

2.   Click the Column tab to display it.

3.   Select the Specify Width check box if it isn't already selected.

4.   Enter the width in the text box.

5.   To set the width for one or more other columns, use the Previous Column button or Next Column button to navigate to the column, then set the width as described in the previous step.

6.   Click the OK button to close the Table Properties dialog box.

TIP TIP TIP TIP TIP TIP TIP TIP TIP TIP TIP TIP TIP TIP TIP TIP TIP TIP TIP TIP TIP TIP

To share available space evenly among columns, select the columns (or the whole table), right-click, and choose Distribute Columns Evenly from the context menu. Unless your data is very short or very regular, this is not usually a good idea.

Changing Row Height

Word sets row height automatically as you add text to (or remove text from) the cells in any row or adjust the height of the contents of the cells. But you can also set the height of a row manually as follows:

1.   Right-click in the row you want to change and choose Table Properties from the context menu, or position the insertion point in the row and then choose Table ➤ Table Properties, to display the Table Properties dialog box.

2.   Click the Row tab to display it.

3.   Select the Specify Height check box if it isn't already selected.

4.   Enter the width in the text box.

5.   To set the height for one or more other columns, use the Previous Row button or Next Row button to navigate to the row, then set the height as described in the previous step.

6.   Click the OK button to close the Table Properties dialog box.

SKILL
9

TIP TIP TIP TIP TIP TIP TIP TIP TIP TIP TIP TIP TIP TIP TIP TIP TIP TIP TIP TIP TIP TIP

To make a number of rows the same height as the row that contains the tallest cells, select the rows, right-click in them, and choose Distribute Rows Evenly from the context menu. In contrast to Distribute Columns Evenly, this usually produces good results.

NOTE NOTE NOTE NOTE NOTE NOTE NOTE NOTE NOTE NOTE NOTE NOTE NOTE NOTE NOTE

You can also change row height in Print Layout view or Print Preview by clicking and dragging a row-break mark on the vertical ruler or dragging any horizontal border (except the top one) in a table.

Adding Borders and Shading to Your Tables

Adding borders and shading to your tables is a little more complex than you might expect. Because Word lets you add borders and shading to the paragraphs inside the table, to any given cell, or to the whole table, you have to be a little careful about what you select.

TIP TIP TIP TIP TIP TIP TIP TIP TIP TIP TIP TIP TIP TIP TIP TIP TIP TIP TIP TIP TIP TIP TIP

The quickest way to add borders and shading to a table is to use the Table Auto-Format command, discussed earlier in "Inserting a Table with the Insert Table Command." If you want more information, read on. You can also experiment by using the Border button and Shading button on the Tables And Borders toolbar.

Adding Borders and Shading to the Whole Table

To add borders and shading to the whole table, right-click anywhere in it and choose Borders And Shading from the context menu to display the Borders And Shading dialog box. Make sure the Apply To drop-down list shows Table, choose the border options you want on the Borders tab and the shading options you want on the Shading tab, then click the OK button to apply them.

Adding Borders and Shading to Selected Cells

To add borders and shading to selected cells in a table, select the cells by dragging through them or by using the keyboard. (If you're selecting just one cell, make sure you select its end-of-cell mark as well, so that the whole cell is highlighted, not just part of the text.) Then right-click in the cell and choose Borders And Shading from the context menu to display the Borders And Shading dialog box. Make sure the Apply To drop-down list shows Cell rather than Table, Paragraph, or Text. Again, choose the border options you want on the Borders tab and the shading options you want on the Shading tab, then click the OK button to apply them.

Adding Borders and Shading to Paragraphs within Cells

To add borders and shading to paragraphs within a cell, select the text you want
to format in the cell but don't select the end-of-cell mark. Then right-click in the
selection and choose Borders And Shading from the context menu to display the
Borders And Shading dialog box. This time, make sure that the Apply To drop-
down list shows Text (for less than a paragraph) or Paragraph (for more than one
paragraph). Choose the border and shading options you want, then click the OK
button to apply them.

NOTE NOTE NOTE NOTE NOTE NOTE NOTE NOTE NOTE NOTE NOTE NOTE NOTE NOTE NOTE

**If you've selected a complete paragraph, you can adjust the placement of the
borders from the text. In the Apply To drop-down list in the Borders And Shading dialog box, Paragraph will be selected. Click the Options button to display
the Border And Shading Options dialog box, then set the placement in the Top,
Bottom, Left, and Right boxes in the From Text area and click OK.**

Merging Cells

Once you've set up your table, you can create special layout effects by merging
cells—i.e., converting two or more cells into a single cell. To merge cells, select the
cells to merge, then click the Merge Cells button on the Tables And Borders toolbar;
or right-click and choose Merge Cells from the context menu; or choose Table ➤
Merge Cells. Word will combine the cells into one, putting the contents of each in
a separate paragraph in the merged cell. You can then remove the paragraph
marks to reduce them to one paragraph if necessary.

Merged cells are especially useful for effects such as table spanner heads. In the
example shown here, the headings *Western Region Results* and *Eastern Seaboard
Results* occupy merged cells that span the whole table:

1995	1996	1997	1998	1999	2000	2001
Western Region Results						
15	32	46	30	50	54	67
Eastern Seaboard Results						
26	25	32	40	38	45	47

Table Headings

If you're working with tables too long to fit on a single page, you'll probably want to set table headings that repeat automatically on the second page and subsequent pages. To do so, select the row or rows that form the headings and then choose Table ➤ Heading Row Repeat. Word will place a check mark by the Heading Rows Repeat item in the Table menu.

Word will repeat these headings automatically if the table is broken with an automatic page break, but not if you insert a manual page break. Word displays the repeated headings only in Print Layout view and Print Preview, so don't expect to see them in Normal view.

To remove table headings, select the row and choose Table ➤ Heading Rows Repeat again. Word will remove the check mark from the Heading Rows Repeat item in the Table menu.

Table Formulas

If you're using tables for numbers—sales targets, net profits, expense reports, etc.—you may want to use Word's table formulas, for which you use the Table ➤ Formula command to display the Formula dialog box. These include a variety of mathematical functions, including rounding and averaging, that you may want to get into on your own but which go beyond the scope of this book.

The most useful formula for everyday purposes is the SUM formula. To add the numbers in a row or column of cells, click the AutoSum button on the Tables And Borders toolbar.

TIP TIP TIP TIP TIP TIP TIP TIP TIP TIP TIP TIP TIP TIP TIP TIP TIP TIP TIP TIP TIP TIP TIP
Using table formulas is a bit like building a mini-spreadsheet in Word. If table formulas aren't enough to satisfy you, and you need to create a full-fledged spreadsheet in Word, look ahead to Skill 17, in which we'll look at how you can embed an Excel spreadsheet in a Word document.

Copying and Moving within Tables

To copy or move material within a table, use the methods discussed in Skill 2—either use the mouse and drag to move the selection (or Ctrl-drag to copy it), or use the Cut, Copy, and Paste commands via the Standard toolbar, the Edit menu, or the keyboard shortcuts.

Converting a Table to Text

Sooner or later you're going to need to convert a table back to text. To do so, simply select the table by choosing Table ➤ Select ➤ Table or by Alt + double-clicking inside it, and then choose Table ➤ Convert ➤ Table To Text. Word will display the Convert Table To Text dialog box with its best guess (based on the contents of the table) at how it should divide the cells when it converts it: with paragraphs, with tabs, with commas, or with another character of your choice. Correct the Separate Text With setting if it's inappropriate, and then click the OK button.

Sorting Information in Tables

Once you've created tables of information or even multicolumn lists formatted using tabs, you'll probably need to sort the information.

Word's sorting feature lets you sort data by up to three types of information at once, such as last name, street name, and zip code. If that doesn't produce fine enough results, you can then sort the same data again using different types of information, such as first name and age—and again, if need be.

We'll look first at how Word sorts information, so you can make full use of the sorting feature. Then we'll look at how to arrange information in your documents, so you can sort the data effectively at a moment's notice. Then you'll perform a multilevel sort.

SKILL
9

TIP TIP TIP TIP TIP TIP TIP TIP TIP TIP TIP TIP TIP TIP TIP TIP TIP TIP TIP TIP TIP TIP TIP TIP
You can sort paragraphs of text as well as tables by using the techniques described in this section.

How Word Sorts

Word sorts by records and fields, two familiar words that carry quite different meanings in computing. A *record* will typically make up one of the items you want to sort and will consist of a number of *fields*, each of which contains one piece of the information that makes up a record. For example, in a mailing database containing name and address information, each customer and their associated set of data would form a record; that record would consist of a number of fields such as the customer's first name, middle initial, last name, street address, city, state, zip code, area code, phone number, etc. In Word, this record could be entered in a table (with one field per cell) or as a paragraph, with the fields separated by tabs, commas, or a character of your choice.

Next, you need to know what order Word sorts things in. Here are the details:

- Word can sort by letter, by number, or by date (in a variety of date formats).

- Word can sort in ascending order—from *A* to *Z*, from *0* to *9*, from early dates to later dates—or in descending order (the opposite).

- When sorting alphabetically, Word sorts punctuation marks and symbols (e.g., &, !) first, then numbers, and finally letters. When sorting numerically, Word sorts symbols first, then letters, then punctuation marks, and finally numbers. If two items start with the same letter, Word goes on to the next letter and sorts by that, and so on; if two fields are the same, Word sorts using the next field, etc.

Arranging Your Data for Sorting

If you've already entered all the data in your document or table and are raring to go ahead and sort it, skip to the next section, "Performing a Multilevel Sort." If you're still in the process of entering your data, or haven't yet started, read on.

The first key to successful sorting is to divide up your records into as many fields as you might possibly want to sort by. For example, it's usually best to put first names and last names in separate fields so that you can sort by either; likewise, you'll usually want to break addresses down into street, city, state, and zip code so that you can sort your data by any one of them. If you need to be able to target customers street by street, you might even break up the street address into the number and the street name, so that you can produce a list of customers on Green Street, say, or Hesperian Avenue.

Use a table for complex data or for data that won't all fit on one line of a tabbed document. (You can carry over tabs from the first line of a paragraph onto the second and subsequent lines, but it's visually confusing and rarely worth the effort when table cells can wrap text and keep it visually clear.)

TIP TIP TIP TIP TIP TIP TIP TIP TIP TIP TIP TIP TIP TIP TIP TIP TIP TIP TIP TIP TIP TIP TIP

Above all, before running any complex sorts, save your data and make a backup of it—or even run a practice sort on a spare copy of the data.

Performing a Multilevel Sort

For finer results, you can perform a multilevel sort as follows:

1. Select the part of the table you want to sort. To sort the whole table, just click anywhere inside the table; Word will select the whole table for you automatically when you choose Table ➤ Sort.

TIP TIP TIP TIP TIP TIP TIP TIP TIP TIP TIP TIP TIP TIP TIP TIP TIP TIP TIP TIP TIP TIP

Word sorts tables by rows, treating each row as a unit, unless you tell it otherwise. For example, if you select only cells in the first two columns of a four-column table and run a sort operation, Word will also rearrange the third and fourth columns according to the sort criteria you chose for the first two columns. To sort columns without sorting entire rows, see the section titled "Using Sort Options" later in this skill.

2. Choose Table ➤ Sort to display the Sort dialog box (see Figure 9.6).

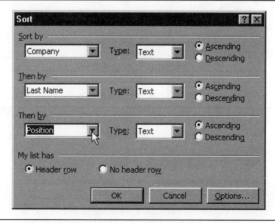

**SKILL
9**

FIGURE 9.6: Choose options for sorting tables in the Sort dialog box.

3. Look at the My List Has area at the bottom of the dialog box and ensure that Word has correctly identified any header row (i.e., row of headings) at the top of the table or of the rows you're sorting. Word omits the header row from the sort, figuring that you'll still want it at the top of the table. If the text has a header row, make sure the Header Row option button has been selected—otherwise, Word will treat the header row as text and sort it along with everything else. You will need to select at least three rows to persuade Word that the rows have a header row.

    •   If you've set table headings by using the Table ≻ Headings command, you don't need to worry about the My List Has box—Word knows that the table has headings and dims the options in the My List Has box.

4. In the Sort By group box, choose the column (i.e., the field) by which to sort the rows of cells first.

    •   If your table (or your selected rows) has a header row, Word will display the names of the headings (abbreviated if necessary) in the drop-down list to help you identify the sort key you want. If your text has no header row, Word will display Column 1, Column 2, and so on.

5. In the Type box, make sure that Word has chosen the appropriate option: Text, Number, or Date.

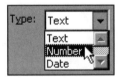

6. Choose Ascending or Descending for the order in which to sort the rows.

7. If necessary, specify a second sort key in the first Then By box. Again, choose the field by which to sort, verify the Type, and choose Ascending or Descending.

8. To sort by a third sort key and produce a finer sort, repeat step 7 for the second Then By box.

9. Click the OK button to perform the sort and close the Sort dialog box.

Word will leave the table (or the selection of rows) highlighted, so if you want to run another sort to get your data into a more precise order, simply repeat steps 2–9.

Using Sort Options

To allow you to direct its sorting capabilities even more precisely, Word offers five sort options in the Sort Options dialog box (see Figure 9.7). Some of these options are available only for particular types of sorts.

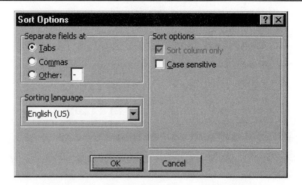

FIGURE 9.7: The Sort Options dialog box provides ways of refining the sort process even further.

To choose sort options, click the Options button in the Sort Text dialog box or the Sort dialog box.

The Sort Options group box in the Sort Options dialog box offers the following options:

Sort Column Only   Sorts only the selected columns of a table or the selected columns of characters in regular text or in a tabbed list (selected by Alt-dragging). This option is not available if you've selected entire paragraphs or rows.

Case Sensitive   Sorts (in ascending order) lowercase before uppercase, sentence case before title case, and title case before all capitals.

SKILL 9

The Separate Fields At group box lets you specify which character separates the different fields of text when sorting paragraphs: Tabs, Commas, or Other. Word can usually identify fields separated by tabs or commas, or even with conventional separators such as hyphens, but if your boss has used something unorthodox (such as em dashes) as separators, you'll need to specify that in the Other box.

The Sorting Language group box allows you to specify that your text be sorted in a different language. This will change the sort order to follow the alphabet and sorting rules of that language.

Once you've made your choices in the Sort Options dialog box, click the OK button to return to the Sort Text dialog box or Sort dialog box.

Are You Experienced?

Now you can...

- ☑ **create simple and complex tables**
- ☑ **enter text and graphics in a table**
- ☑ **navigate and edit in tables**
- ☑ **format a table**
- ☑ **convert text to a table**
- ☑ **convert a table to text**
- ☑ **sort data in tables**

Using Graphical Elements and Text Boxes

- ➔ Inserting a picture or other graphical object in a document
- ➔ Positioning and resizing a graphical object
- ➔ Adding clips to the Clip Gallery
- ➔ Inserting a chart
- ➔ Creating and using AutoShapes
- ➔ Creating and using text boxes

In this skill, you'll learn how to use graphical elements and text boxes in your documents. Graphical elements include pictures and videos (as you might imagine), and Office's AutoShapes, which are graphical objects that you create using Word's drawing tools.

A text box is a box that you can place anywhere you choose on a page, rather than being constrained by the margin settings for the page. Despite their name, text boxes can contain not only text but also graphics and other objects.

Along the way, I'll discuss how to work with the Clip Gallery, Microsoft's repository of clip art, sound clips, and video clips.

Inserting, Sizing, and Positioning Graphical Objects

You can easily insert graphical objects of various types into Word documents. Once you've inserted them, you can resize them, move them, and crop them as necessary. In this section, I'll discuss graphical objects using pictures as the examples, but the techniques apply to other graphical objects (such as shapes and video clips) as well. The inserting and positioning skills even apply to sound clips, which you can also insert in your documents and position where you need them to appear.

Inserting a Picture

To insert a picture at the insertion point:

1. Choose Insert ➤ Picture to display the Picture submenu.

2. Choose from the six options for inserting a picture: Clip Art, From File, AutoShapes, WordArt, From Scanner Or Camera, or Chart. The process is a little different for each of the options. In this example, choose Clip Art, because it's the one you're most likely to want to use first; it demonstrates the Microsoft Clip Gallery and also shows some of the other items you may want to insert in your documents. Word starts the Microsoft Clip Gallery application, which manifests itself as the Insert ClipArt window (see Figure 10.1).

3. On the Pictures tab, select the category of clip you want to insert in the document. Scroll down to see categories of clips beyond those that fit in the dialog box. In this example, choose Animals. The Pictures tab will change to show the clips available in that category (see Figure 10.2). Again, scroll to see more clips than those that initially appear in the window.

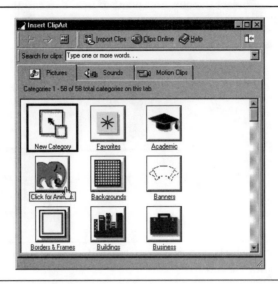

FIGURE 10.1: In the Insert ClipArt window, choose the category of clip you want to insert.

FIGURE 10.2: Next, choose the clip you're interested in.

4. Select the clip you want to use. You can then choose from the following options on the context menu that the clip displays (see Figure 10.3):

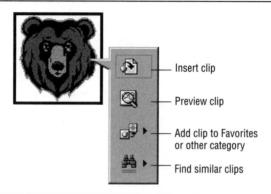

Insert clip

Preview clip

Add clip to Favorites or other category

Find similar clips

FIGURE 10.3: Use the clip's context menu to tell Word what you want to do with the clip.

- Click the Insert Clip button to insert the clip in the document.

- Click the Preview Clip button to display a preview window that shows an enlarged version of the clip.

- Click the Add Clip To Favorites Or Other Category button to display a pop-out panel with a drop-down list of the categories. Select the category and click the OK button.

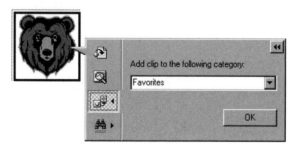

- Click the Find Similar Clips button to display a pop-out panel that you can use to search for best-matching clips or for clips with keywords associated with the current clip's keywords.

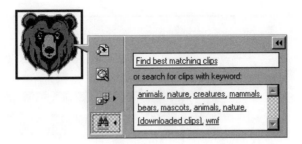

TIP TIP TIP TIP TIP TIP TIP TIP TIP TIP TIP TIP TIP TIP TIP TIP TIP TIP TIP TIP TIP TIP TIP TIP TIP

Use the Back button and the Forward button at the top of the Insert ClipArt window to move backward and forward as you navigate through the categories of clips and the clips themselves. Click the All Categories button to return to the topmost level of categories (the categories you see when you initially display the Insert ClipArt dialog box).

5. Insert further clips as necessary. Then click the Close button to close the Insert ClipArt application, or click in the Word window to continue working in Word while leaving the Insert ClipArt application running so that you can insert further pictures or objects easily.

Resizing and Cropping a Picture

To resize a picture quickly, first click it to select it. Word will display the Picture toolbar (see Figure 10.4) and an outline around the picture with eight handles, one at each corner and one in the middle of each side. Drag a corner handle to resize the image proportionally; drag a side handle to resize the image only in that dimension (horizontally or vertically).

To crop a picture quickly (cutting off part of it), click the picture to select it, then click the Crop button to select the cropping tool. The mouse pointer will change into cropping handles. Move the mouse pointer over one of the picture's handles, then drag inward or outward to crop the picture.

To resize or crop a picture more precisely:

1. Click the picture to display the outline and handles around it.

2. Click the Format Picture button, double-click the picture, right-click and choose Format Picture from the context menu, or choose Format ➤ Picture. Word will display the Format Picture dialog box (see Figure 10.5).

SKILL
10

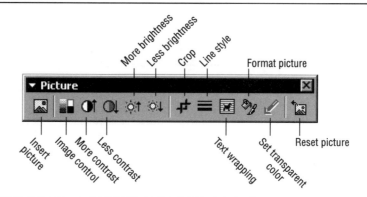

FIGURE 10.4:   The Picture toolbar contains buttons for manipulating pictures quickly.

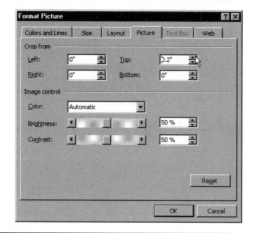

FIGURE 10.5:   The Format Picture dialog box lets you resize and crop pictures precisely.

3.   To crop a picture, make sure the Picture tab is displayed (click it if it isn't). Enter the amount you want to crop in the Left, Right, Top, and Bottom boxes in the Crop From area.

4.   To resize the picture, click the Size tab to display it. Then either set Width and Height percentages in the Scale area, or enter the desired width and height, such as 1.46" by 1.74", in the Width and Height boxes in the Size And Rotate area.

TIP TIP TIP TIP TIP TIP TIP TIP TIP TIP TIP TIP TIP TIP TIP TIP TIP TIP TIP TIP TIP TIP

The Lock Aspect Ratio check box in the Scale area of the Size tab controls whether the Height and Width boxes act in concert or independently.

5. Click the OK button to close the Picture dialog box and apply your changes.

To reset a picture to its original size, click the Reset button on the Size tab of the Format Picture dialog box. To reset a picture to its original coloring, click the Reset button on the Picture tab of the Format Picture dialog box. To reset a picture to both its original size and its original coloring, click the Reset button on the Picture toolbar.

Positioning a Picture

Once you've inserted a picture, you can position it exactly where you want it to appear. To position a picture effectively, you need to understand how pictures (and other objects) can be positioned in relation to the text on the page.

The text in a Word document is contained in the main layer of the document, the *text layer*. You can place pictures in the text layer, either inline with the text (as if they were just another character) or with the text wrapping around them. For greater freedom of placement, you can also place pictures behind the text layer (so that any text that occupies the same space appears superimposed on the picture) or in front of the text layer, where the picture will block out anything that is positioned behind it.

Each graphical object that is not inline in a Word document is secured by an *anchor*, which represents the point in the text to which the object is attached (as shown here). Anchors are normally hidden, but you can display them by choosing Tools ➢ Options, selecting the View tab of the Options dialog box, and selecting the Object Anchors check box in the Print and Web Layout Options area.

To position a picture, click it to select it, then click the Text Wrapping button on the Picture toolbar to display the context menu of wrapping choices. Select the appropriate choice: Square (with text around it), Tight (with text tight around it),

Behind Text, In Front Of Text, Top And Bottom (no text alongside the picture), or Through (text fills in white space in the picture). Then click the picture and drag it vertically to where you want it to appear in the document.

To change the wrapping and horizontal alignment of a picture:

1. Right-click the picture and choose Format Picture from the context menu, or select the picture and click the Format Picture button on the Picture toolbar, to display the Format Picture dialog box.

2. Click the Layout tab to display it (see Figure 10.6).

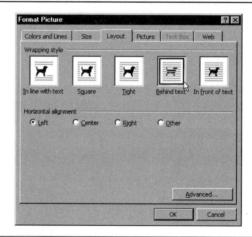

FIGURE 10.6: Use the Layout tab of the Format Picture dialog box to set layout and horizontal alignment for a picture.

3. In the Wrapping Style area, choose the wrapping option for the picture.

4. In the Horizontal Alignment area, select the horizontal alignment for the picture: Left, Center, Right, or Other.

5. For more alignment options, click the Advanced button to display the Advanced Layout dialog box (see Figure 10.7).

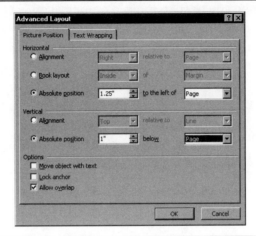

FIGURE 10.7: Use the Advanced Layout dialog box to specify advanced alignment options for a picture.

*   On the Picture Position tab, you can specify horizontal and vertical alignment options. One of the most useful capabilities here is to specify an absolute position (horizontal, vertical, or both) for a picture relative to the page. The Move Object With Text check box controls whether the picture can move along with the text to which it is anchored. The Lock Anchor check box controls whether the anchor for the picture can be moved; once you've positioned a picture carefully, you can lock the anchor to make sure no one moves the picture by accident. The Allow Overlap check box controls whether the picture can be overlapped by other pictures.

*   On the Text Wrapping tab, select a wrapping style in the Wrapping Styles area. In the Wrap Text area, select how to wrap the text: Both Sides, Left Only, Right Only, or Largest Only. Finally, you can specify the distance between the picture and the text that wraps around it by entering values in the Top, Bottom, Left, and Right text boxes in the Distance From Text area. Click the OK button when you've finished.

6. Click the OK button to apply the wrapping and alignment to the picture.

SKILL
10

FINER MOVEMENTS: NUDGING A GRAPHICAL OBJECT INTO PLACE

When you need to move a graphical object only a small amount, it can be difficult to achieve the necessary precision with the mouse, particularly if you've had too much coffee. Word provides a Nudge tool for moving an object a little at a time.

The easiest way to nudge an object is with the keyboard. Select the object, then press the appropriate arrow key to move the object just a fraction.

You can also nudge a graphical object with the mouse, but the process is a little more protracted. Select the object, then choose Draw ➤ Nudge from the Drawing toolbar to display the Nudge submenu. Choose the direction in which to nudge the object (Up, Down, Left, or Right).

Importing Clips into the Clip Gallery

You can add to the clips in the Clip Gallery by either downloading clips from the Microsoft Web site or by importing clips stored elsewhere (for example, on a local hard drive or on a network).

Downloading Clips Online

To download clips from the Microsoft Web site:

1. Choose Insert ➤ Picture ➤ Clip Art to display the Insert ClipArt application window (if it isn't already displayed).

2. Click the Clips Online button. The Clip Gallery will display the Connect To Web For More ClipArt, Photos, Sounds dialog box.

3. Select the Don't Show This Message Again check box to suppress future appearances of this dialog box, then click the OK button. The Clip Gallery will start Internet Explorer, fire up your Internet connection, and display the Microsoft Clip Gallery Live Site. Read the End User License agreement, and click the Accept button if you agree to be bound by its terms.

4. Navigate to the category of clips you want and download the clips. The Clip Gallery will add them to its repertoire.

Importing Clips from Other Locations

To import clips into the Clip Gallery:

1. Choose Insert ➤ Picture ➤ Clip Art to display the Insert ClipArt window (if it isn't already displayed).

2. Select the tab containing the type of clip you want to import. For example, if you want to import video clips, select the Motion Clips tab.

3. Click the Import Clips button to display the Add Clip To Clip Gallery dialog box (see Figure 10.8).

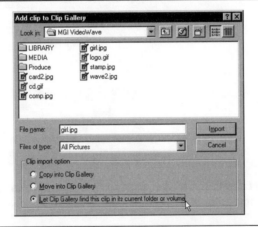

FIGURE 10.8: In the Add Clip To Clip Gallery dialog box, choose which clips to import into the Clip Gallery and how to import them.

4. Navigate to the clips using the usual Windows techniques and select the clips.

5. In the Clip Import Option group box, choose how to import the clips:

    *   Choose the Copy Into Clip Gallery option button (the default) to copy the clips to the Clip Gallery. It's best not to use this option if the files are on your computer's hard drive, as it will make them take up twice as much space as they need.

    *   Choose the Move Into Clip Gallery option button (if it's available) to move the clips. Use this option if the clips are on your computer's hard drive and you want to manage all your clips through the Clip Gallery.

SKILL
10

- Choose the Let Clip Gallery Find This Clip In Its Current Folder Or Volume option button if you prefer to leave the clips where they are but let the Clip Gallery learn about their location.

6. Click the Import button to import the clips. The Clip Gallery will then display the Clip Properties dialog box (see Figure 10.9) for each clip in turn. Enter a description on the Description tab, choose one or more categories on the Categories tab, and select one or more keywords on the Keywords tab if you want. Select the Mark All Clips With The Same Properties check box if you want to give the same properties to each of the clips you're importing.

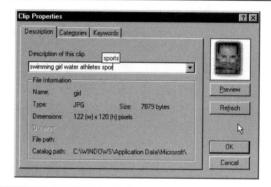

FIGURE 10.9: In the Clip Properties dialog box, add a description, choose categories, and select keywords for the clips you're importing.

7. Click the OK button to import the clip. The Clip Gallery will display the Clip Properties dialog box for the next clip (if there is one); if not, it will return you to the Insert ClipArt window, which will show the clips you imported.

Inserting a Chart

To insert a chart in a document:

1. If you have columnar text or a table from which you want to create the chart, select it. Otherwise, place the insertion point where you want the chart to appear.

2. Choose Insert ➤ Picture ➤ Chart to start the Microsoft Graph charting application. Word will add a prototype column chart to the document,

together with a datasheet for entering information for the chart (see Figure 10.10). If you chose data in step 1, the datasheet and the chart will reflect your data; otherwise, they will show sample information.

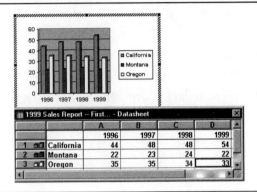

FIGURE 10.10: Enter the data for the chart in the Microsoft Graph datasheet.

3. Enter your data in the datasheet, or adjust your data as necessary. The chart will show the data you enter in the datasheet.

4. Right-click the chart and choose Chart Type from the context menu to display the Chart Type dialog box (see Figure 10.11).

FIGURE 10.11: Choose an appropriate type of chart in the Chart Type dialog box.

5. To create a standard type of chart, select the type of chart in the Chart Type list box on the Standard Types tab, then select a suitable subtype in the Chart Sub-Type list box. To see a sample of how the chart will look with the data in your datasheet, click the Click And Hold To View Sample button and hold the mouse button down until the sample appears in place of the chart sub-types.

6. To create a custom chart, select the Custom Types tab. Select the chart type in the Chart Type list box.

7. If you want to create this type of chart regularly, click the Set As Default Chart button.

8. Click the OK button to apply your choice of chart type to the chart.

You can now size and position the chart using the techniques described for pictures earlier in this skill.

Changing the Background of a Document

For most of the documents you print, you'll want to keep the default white background that Word uses in most of its templates. But for online documents and Web pages, you might want to apply a colored background or a fill effect.

You can change the background of a document by choosing Format ➢ Background and selecting a fill color from the color panel that appears. If none of the colors appeals to you, select the More Colors item to display the Colors dialog box. Select the color you want on either the Standard tab or the Custom tab and choose the OK button to apply it.

To apply a fill effect to the background of a document, choose Format ➢ Background ➢ Fill Effects to display the Fill Effects dialog box. Select a suitable fill effect on either the Gradient tab, the Texture tab, the Pattern tab, or the Picture tab, and click the OK button to apply it to the document.

TIP TIP TIP TIP TIP TIP TIP TIP TIP TIP TIP TIP TIP TIP TIP TIP TIP TIP TIP TIP TIP TIP TIP TIP

One of the easiest ways of changing the background of a document is to apply a different theme to the document, as discussed in Skill 5.

Working with the Drawing Tools

Word provides a full set of drawing tools for creating drawing objects in your documents, annotating the documents, and so on. To access the drawing tools, display the Drawing toolbar (see Figure 10.12) by clicking the Drawing button on the Standard toolbar, or by right-clicking the menu bar or any displayed toolbar and choosing Drawing from the context menu of toolbars.

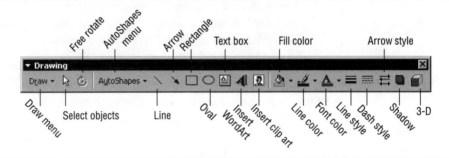

FIGURE 10.12: The Drawing toolbar provides you with the means of adding drawings, lines, and shapes to your documents.

The drawing tools are largely self-explanatory. For example, to create a rectangle, you click the Rectangle button, then click where you want one corner of the rectangle to be, and drag until the rectangle is the size you want it. To change the lines of the rectangle to red, select the rectangle, click the Line Color drop-down list button, and choose the color you want from the color palette. To apply 3-D effects to the rectangle, select the rectangle, click the 3-D button, and choose a suitable effect from the drop-down panel.

That said, there are a number of techniques that are less immediately apparent:

- Click the Select Objects button, then click and drag to select multiple objects.

- Hold down Shift as you drag to constrain a rectangle to a square and an oval to a circle.

- Hold down Ctrl as you drag to center the object you create on the point at which you started to drag.

- Hold down Ctrl and Shift as you drag to create a square or a circle centered on the point at which you started to drag.

SKILL 10

- Use the commands on the Draw ➤ Order submenu to rearrange layers of objects: Bring To Front, Send To Back, Bring Forward, Send Backward, Bring In Front Of Text, and Send Behind Text.

- Word places drawing objects according to an underlying grid that is normally invisible. You can display the grid, or adjust it, by choosing Draw ➤ Grid and selecting settings in the Drawing Grid dialog box. To adjust the grid, choose horizontal and vertical spacing in the Grid Settings area. To display the grid on screen (which makes it easier to place objects precisely but makes your documents look like graph paper), select the Display Gridlines On Screen check box and the Horizontal Every check box, and set the number of units (whose measurements are defined in the Grid Settings area) in the Horizontal Every and Vertical Every text boxes. Click the OK button to apply your choices.

Two of the more complex and useful drawing elements are AutoShapes and text boxes. We'll look at how to use these in the upcoming sections.

Working with AutoShapes

An AutoShape is any of a number of regular or semi-regular shapes that Word provides. AutoShapes include circles, rectangles, stars, and speech balloons. As with other graphical objects, you can format AutoShapes to your heart's content. You can also add text to AutoShapes.

Inserting an AutoShape

To insert an AutoShape:

1. Click the AutoShapes drop-down menu on the Drawing toolbar to display the AutoShapes drop-down menu.

2. Choose one of the categories of shapes—Lines, Basic Shapes, Block Arrows, Flowchart, Stars And Banners, or Callouts—to display a submenu of shapes.

3. Click the shape you want. Word will change the mouse pointer to a cross and the view to Print Layout view if it is not currently in Print Layout view.

4. Click in the document at the point where you want one extreme of the AutoShape to appear, then drag to create the size of shape you want.

Now that you've inserted the AutoShape, you can format it by using the formatting options on the Drawing toolbar, as discussed earlier in this skill.

Adding Text to an AutoShape

To add text to an AutoShape, right-click the AutoShape and choose Add Text from the context menu. Word will select the AutoShape and will position the insertion point inside it. Type the text you want the AutoShape to have. You can then select the text and choose Format ➤ Font to display the Font dialog box or Format ➤ Paragraph to display the Paragraph dialog box. Then apply font or paragraph formatting as discussed in Skill 4.

Changing an AutoShape to a Different Type

You can change an AutoShape you've created to another type of AutoShape. Click the AutoShape to select it, then choose Draw ➤ Change AutoShape from the Drawing toolbar to display the submenu of shape categories. Select the category of shape you want and then select the shape from the submenu that appears.

Inserting, Positioning, and Formatting Text Boxes

To precisely position text or a picture in a document, use a text box. A *text box* is a container that Word uses to position items (pictures, text, etc.) in an exact place on the page; you can use text boxes for positioning text such as sidebars in a newspaper layout or captions (also known as *callouts*) in an annotated figure.

You can position a text box relative to a paragraph (so that it moves with the text when the paragraph moves) or relative to the margin or page (so that it remains in place even if the paragraph moves). The advantage of positioning a text box relative to the page rather than relative to one of the margins is that you can adjust the margins without the text box moving. Text boxes are held in place by anchors.

Inserting a Text Box

To insert a text box:

1. Choose Insert ➤ Text Box. Word will change the insertion point to a large + sign and, if you are in Normal view or Outline view, will switch to Print Layout view.

2. Click and drag in the document to create a text box of the size you want, as shown here. The text box will appear with a thick shaded border, and Word will display the Text Box toolbar.

Now you can click inside the text box and either enter text in it or insert a picture in it as described earlier in this skill.

Sizing and Positioning a Text Box

To resize a text box quickly, click in it to display the text box border and then drag one of the sizing handles.

To position a text box quickly:

1. Click inside the text box to display the text box border and handles. Make sure that you've selected the text box rather than any picture in it.

2. Move the mouse pointer onto the shaded border of the text box so that the pointer becomes a four-headed arrow attached to the normal mouse-pointer arrow.

3. Click and drag the text box to wherever you want to place it on the page. Here, I'm dragging a text box and its contents.

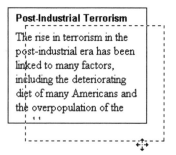

To resize and position a text box exactly:

1. Right-click the border of the text box and choose Format Text Box from the context menu to display the Format Text Box dialog box (see Figure 10.13).

FIGURE 10.13: Choose the text box's position on the page in the Format Text Box dialog box.

2. To resize the text box, click the Size tab to display it. You can then set the height and width either by entering measurements in the Height and Width boxes in the Size And Rotate area or by entering percentages in the Height and Width boxes in the Scale area. To resize the image proportionally, select the Lock Aspect Ratio check box; to resize the image differently in each dimension, clear the check box.

3. To reposition the text box, click the Layout tab to display it. Choose the wrapping style for the text box in the Wrapping Style area, then choose the horizontal alignment of the text box in the Horizontal Alignment area. To specify a more precise position for the text box, click the Advanced button to display the Advanced Layout dialog box. On the Picture Position tab, specify the position for the text box using the techniques discussed for the Format Picture dialog box earlier in this skill.

    •   To allow the text box to move when the text it is attached to moves, select the Move Object With Text check box. For example, if you position a text box relative to a paragraph, select this check box; if you position a text box relative to the page, clear this check box.

    •   To lock the text box to the paragraph it belongs with (so you can't move it by accident to another paragraph), select the Lock Anchor check box.

    •   To allow the text box to be overlapped by another text box or a graphical object, select the Allow Overlap check box.

Skill
10

4. Click the OK button to apply your choices to the text box.

Linking Text Boxes

If you're presenting text in a series of text boxes, you can link the text boxes together so that text flows from the end of the first to the beginning of the next. This is much easier than dividing your text into separate chunks for each text box.

To create a text box link, right-click the first text box and choose Create Text Box Link from the context menu. The mouse pointer will change to a pitcher of text, as shown here. Click this pitcher-pointer on the next text box to pour the text into it. To link this text box to another text box, repeat the procedure.

To move from one linked text box to another, right-click the border of the current text box and choose Next Text Box or Previous Text Box from the context menu, as appropriate.

To remove a text box link, right-click the border of the text box and select Break Forward Link from the context menu.

Removing a Text Box

To delete a text box, select it by clicking its border, then press the Delete button. This deletes both the text box and any contents it has. To preserve the contents of the text box, copy and paste them into the document before deleting the text box.

Are You Experienced?

Now you can...

- ☑ **insert pictures and graphical objects in your documents**
- ☑ **position and format pictures and graphical objects**
- ☑ **import clips into the Clip Gallery**
- ☑ **insert a chart in a Word document**
- ☑ **change the background color or fill of a document**
- ☑ **use Word's drawing tools to add drawings, lines, and arrows to documents**
- ☑ **create AutoShapes, format them, and enter text in them**
- ☑ **create, use, and delete text boxes**

Creating Headers, Footers, and Watermarks

- ➔ Creating simple headers and footers
- ➔ Inserting the date and time in headers and footers
- ➔ Formatting headers and footers
- ➔ Creating complex headers and footers
- ➔ Creating watermarks

Headers and footers give you an easy way to repeat identifying information on each page of your document. For example, in a header (text placed at the top of each page) you might include the title of a document and the name of the author, while in a footer (text placed at the bottom of each page) you might include the filename, the date, and the page number out of the total number of pages in the document (e.g., *Page 1 of 9*).

You can repeat the same header and footer throughout all the pages of your document or you can vary them from page to page. For example, if a proposal has two different authors, you might want to identify in the header which author wrote a particular part of the proposal; or if you want to identify in the header the different part titles, you can easily arrange that, too. You can also arrange for odd pages to have different headers and footers from those on even pages, or for the first page in a document to have a different header and footer than subsequent pages.

Setting Headers and Footers

To include a header in your document:

1. Choose View ➢ Header And Footer. Word will display the page in Page Layout view and will display the Header And Footer toolbar (see Figure 11.1).

NOTE NOTE NOTE NOTE NOTE NOTE NOTE NOTE NOTE NOTE NOTE NOTE NOTE NOTE NOTE

You can work with headers and footers only in Print Layout view and Print Preview. If you choose View ➢ Header And Footer from Normal view, Web Layout view, or Outline view, Word will switch you to Page Layout view. When you leave the Header or Footer area, Word will return you to the view you were in before.

2. Enter the text (and graphics, if you like) for the header in the Header area at the top of the page. Use the buttons on the Header And Footer toolbar to speed your work:

    - Insert AutoText provides a drop-down menu of predefined header and footer text, including the filename and path and *page X of Y* (e.g., Page 3 of 34).

    - Insert Page Number inserts a field code for the current page number at the insertion point.

    - Insert Number Of Pages inserts a field code for the number of pages in the document.

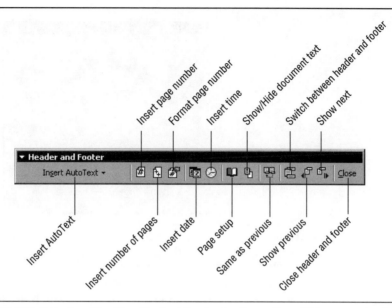

FIGURE 11.1: The Header And Footer toolbar offers 13 buttons that help you produce headers and footers quickly and easily, including a Close Header And Footer button to get you out of the header or footer.

- Format Page Number displays the Page Number Format dialog box (see Figure 11.2). In the Number Format drop-down list, choose the type of numbering you want: 1, 2, 3; a, b, c; etc. If you want to include chapter numbers in the page numbering, select the Include Chapter Number check box. Then, in the Chapter Starts With Style drop-down list, choose the Heading style with which each chapter in the document starts. In the Use Separator drop-down list, choose a separator character for the numbering. Finally, in the Page Numbering area, choose whether to continue the page numbering from the previous section of the document (if there is a previous section) or to start at a number of your choosing. Click the OK button when you've made your selections.

- Insert Date inserts a code for the current date in the document.

- Insert Time inserts a code for the current time in the document.

- Page Setup displays the Page Setup dialog box with the Layout tab at the front.

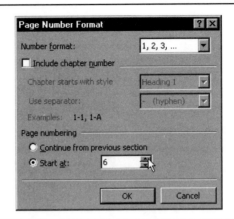

FIGURE 11.2: In the Page Number Format dialog box, choose formatting and numbering options for the page numbers.

- Show/Hide Document Text displays and hides the document text. Its purpose is a little esoteric: You probably won't want to hide your document's text unless you're trying to place a header or footer behind the text. For example, you might want to add a watermark behind the text on a business letter or a brochure. (For information on creating a watermark, see the section titled "Creating a Watermark" a little later in the skill.)

WARNING WARNING WARNING WARNING WARNING WARNING WARNING WARNING

Unwittingly clicking the Show/Hide Document Text button can lead you to think you've lost all the text in your document. If your text suddenly disappears under suspicious circumstances, check to see if the Show/Hide Document Text button is selected. If it is, restore the display of the document text by clicking the Show/Hide Document Text button again. If the Show/Hide Document Text button isn't the culprit and your text has really vanished, try undoing the last action by choosing Edit ≻ Undo or pressing Ctrl+Z. You can also try closing the document without saving changes.

- Same As Previous makes the current header or footer the same as the header or footer in the previous section (if there is a previous section) or page (if you're using a different header and footer on the first page). If there is no previous section, this button will not be available (we'll look at headers and footers in relation to sections in a moment).

- Switch Between Header And Footer moves the insertion point between header and footer. Alternatively, you can use the up and down arrow keys to move between the two.

- Show Previous moves the insertion point to the header or footer in the previous section (if there is a previous section) or page (if you're using different headers and footers on the first page, or different headers and footers for odd and even pages).

- Show Next moves the insertion point to the header or footer in the next section (if there is a next section) or page (if you're using a different header and footer on the first page).

- Close Header And Footer hides the Header And Footer toolbar, closes the header and footer panes, and returns you to whichever view you were using before.

3. To return to your document, click the Close Header And Footer button or choose View ➤ Header And Footer again. You can also double-click anywhere in the main document as long as the Show/Hide Document Text button is not selected.

Formatting Headers and Footers

Despite their special position on the page, headers and footers can contain regular Word elements (text, graphics, text boxes, and so on), and you work with them as described in the previous skills.

By default, Word starts you off with the Header style in the Header area and the Footer style in the Footer area. You can modify these styles (as described earlier in this skill), choose other styles (including Header First, Header Even, and Header Odd—which Word provides in some templates) from the Styles dropdown list on the Formatting toolbar (or by choosing Format ➤ Style and using the Styles dialog box), or apply extra formatting.

TIP TIP TIP TIP TIP TIP TIP TIP TIP TIP TIP TIP TIP TIP TIP TIP TIP TIP TIP TIP TIP TIP TIP TIP

Headers and footers aren't restricted to the Header and Footer areas that appear on your screen. You can use headers and footers to place repeating text anywhere on your page. While in the Header or Footer area, you can insert a text box at a suitable location on the page, then insert text, graphics, and so on inside the text box.

Producing Different Headers and Footers for Different Sections

Often you'll want different headers and footers on different pages of your documents. Word gives you three options:

- A header and footer on the first page of a document that is different from the header and footer on subsequent pages

- A header and footer on odd pages that is different from the header and footer on even pages (combined, if you like, with a header and footer on the first page that is different from the header and footer on subsequent pages)

- A different header and footer for different sections (combined, if you like, with the two previous options)

Different First Page Headers and Footers

To produce a header and footer on the first page of a document that is different from the header and footer on subsequent pages:

1. Choose File ➤ Page Setup to display the Page Setup dialog box, then click the Layout tab to bring it to the front. If you have headers or footers displayed already, you can click the Page Setup button on the Headers And Footers toolbar instead.

2. In the Headers And Footers group box, select the Different First Page check box.

3. Click the OK button to close the Page Setup dialog box.

After setting up your header and footer for the first page of the document, move to the second page and set up the header and footer for that page and subsequent pages.

Different Headers and Footers on Odd and Even Pages

To create a header and footer on odd pages that is different from the header and footer on even pages, select the Different Odd And Even check box in the Headers And Footers box on the Layout tab of the Page Setup dialog box (File ➤ Page Setup). Move the insertion point to an odd page and set its header and footer, then move to an even page and set its header and footer.

Different Headers and Footers in Different Sections

To set different headers and footers in different sections of a document, create the document and divide it into sections as described in "Section Formatting" in Skill 5. To adjust the header or footer for any section, click in that section and choose View ➤ Header And Footer to display the Header area of the document.

By default, when a document consists of more than one section, Word sets the header and footer for each section after the first to be the same as the header and footer in the previous section; so the Same As Previous button on the Header And Footer toolbar will appear pushed in, and the legend Same As Previous will appear at the top right corner of the header or footer area. To change this, click the Same As Previous button on the Header And Footer toolbar and then enter the new header or footer in the Header or Footer area.

To move through the headers or footers in the various sections of your document, click the Show Previous and Show Next buttons on the Header And Footer toolbar.

Creating a Watermark

A useful but little-used capability of Word is creating watermarks—text or graphics that appear behind or in front of the main text in a document. For example, you might want to stamp DRAFT across a report you were creating.

To create a watermark, you work with the header or footer for the appropriate page or section of a document. The header or footer is the mechanism that Word uses for creating the watermark so that it appears on each page, but the watermark can appear anywhere on the page: It's not limited to the Header area or the Footer area.

To create a watermark:

1. Choose View ➤ Header And Footer to display the Header area of the current page.

2. Insert a picture (or an AutoShape or a piece of WordArt) or a text box and position it where you want it to appear on the page. If you created a text box, enter the text in it.

TIP TIP TIP TIP TIP TIP TIP TIP TIP TIP TIP TIP TIP TIP TIP TIP TIP TIP TIP TIP TIP TIP TIP TIP TIP TIP

To clear the screen so that you can better see what you're doing, click the Show/Hide Document Text button on the Header And Footer toolbar to hide the document text.

3.   Format the item as appropriate. For example, if you place a drawing object behind the main text of a document, you may want to color it gray so that it shows faintly through the text rather than obscuring it completely. To lighten a picture, right-click it and choose Format Picture to display the Format Picture dialog box. Click the Picture tab to display it, then choose Watermark in the Color drop-down list in the Image Control area; alternatively, adjust the Brightness and Contrast sliders until the picture takes on a suitable hue. Then click the Layout tab and choose the Behind Text option or the In Front Of Text option in the Wrapping style area, as appropriate. Click the OK button to apply the effect.

4.   Click the Close button on the Header And Footer toolbar (or choose View ➤ Header And Footer, or press Alt+Shift+C) to close the header and footer.

Are You Experienced?

Now you can...

- ☑ **create headers and footers that repeat on every page of a document**
- ☑ **insert the date and time in headers and footers**
- ☑ **format headers and footers**
- ☑ **create a different header for the first page of a document**
- ☑ **create different headers for the odd pages and even pages of a document**
- ☑ **use different headers and footers in different sections of a document**
- ☑ **create watermarks**

SKILL 12

Creating Web Pages

- ➔ Understanding Word's Web tools
- ➔ Understanding Web pages and Web sites
- ➔ Opening a document on a Web server
- ➔ Creating a Web site with the Web Page Wizard
- ➔ Creating new Web pages
- ➔ Creating Web pages from Word documents

Over the last few years, the surge in popularity of the World Wide Web, and of internal corporate webs or *intranets*, has left many people wishing for an easy way to create Web pages from inside their word processor. Word 2000 not only provides those capabilities, and a Wizard for building a complete Web site of your own, but also enables you to open Web pages (on the Web or on an intranet) in Word, alter them, and (if you have the necessary rights) save the changes to the page on the intranet site or Web site.

In the Web component for this skill, I cover two other features of Word: First, its ability to open documents on an FTP server and save documents on an FTP server; and second, its ability to work as an enhanced e-mail editor inside the Exchange client or the Outlook client. You'll find this coverage on the Sybex Web site, `www.sybex.com`.

At the risk of stating the obvious, to use the features described in this skill, you need to have either an Internet connection, a network connection, or both. Also, you need to have Internet Explorer installed to make the most of Office's Web features, because Word (and the other Office applications) integrates with Internet Explorer for viewing Web pages.

NOTE NOTE NOTE NOTE NOTE NOTE NOTE NOTE NOTE NOTE NOTE NOTE NOTE NOTE NOTE

For you to use Office's Web features successfully on a Web server, the server in question needs to be running the Office Server Extensions. Consult your network administrator, Webmaster, or Internet service provider to check that the server in question is running the extensions.

What Is a Web Page?

Essentially, a Web page is a document, stored on a Web server, that you can access using a browser such as Microsoft's Internet Explorer, Netscape's Navigator, or Opera Software's Opera. The Web server can be either on an intranet or on the World Wide Web. You can also choose to store Web pages on your local hard drive, but unless you are using a Web server tool such as Microsoft's Personal Web Server (for Windows 95, Windows 98, and Windows NT Workstation) or Internet Information Server (for Windows NT Server), you don't gain much benefit from doing so.

Web pages are formatted using the Hypertext Markup Language, or HTML, which consists of large numbers of ugly codes within angle brackets. Previous versions of Word were able to convert Word documents to HTML-formatted Web pages, but at the cost of much of the extra information that Word stores within a document—information describing styles, for example, or bookmarks. Word 2000 improves greatly upon this by using another markup language, Extensible Markup Language (XML), to retain this information and indicate which part of a document is which. You can now save all the contents of a Word document as a Web page to a Web server. When someone else opens that Web page in Word, they will see the document as you created it. If they want, they can save the Web page as a Word document, and it will have lost none of its information.

HTML and XML codes are complex and confusing until you've spent a considerable amount of time working with them. The best part of the Office Web features is that Word (and the other Office applications) handles the translation of documents to Web pages seamlessly. If you don't want to see the HTML and XML codes, you don't need to. On the other hand, if you do want to examine or edit the HTML and XML codes, you can use the Microsoft Script Editor application that comes with Office to view the code behind the Web page and adjust it.

What Is a Web Site?

A Web site is a collection of linked Web pages stored on a Web server. (Actually, that's not exactly true: A site *can* be just one page, but there's little point in having so simple a site.)

Each Web site includes a *home page*, the page that appears when you enter the address of the site in your Web browser. For example, if you enter `http://www.sybex.com` in Internet Explorer, it will display the home page of the Sybex Web site. From the home page, links lead to other pages, from which further links lead to yet more pages.

Many sites use *frames*, separate areas of the page that can either display a separate set of information or remain more or less constant. Many sites use a frame at either the top of the page or at the left side of the page to contain links, so that they're always easy to find.

Web Folders and the Web Toolbar

Most of Word's (in fact, Office's) Web tools work in the background, so you see the effects of their work rather than the tools themselves. Two tools that you will see are the Web Folders feature and the Web toolbar. I'll discuss these briefly in this section. After that, you'll put the Web Folders feature into action later in the skill, opening documents from and saving document to Web servers. The Web toolbar you can explore for yourself.

Web Folders, as its name suggests, is a collection of the Web folders that you set up to use with the Office applications. Web Folders is the means by which Office enables you to work with files directly on a Web server: You can create a file and save it to a Web server; you can view a file on a Web server; and you can open and edit a file on a Web server. Beyond this, and more obviously, Web Folders provides an easy way to keep track of all the Web folders you work with.

Word's Web toolbar (see Figure 12.1) provides a means for accessing Web pages from Word. For browsing Web pages, Word relies largely on Internet Explorer, so many of the actions you take on the Web toolbar end up displaying Internet Explorer rather than opening the Web page in question in Word.

To display the Web toolbar, right-click the menu bar or any displayed toolbar and choose Web from the context menu of toolbars.

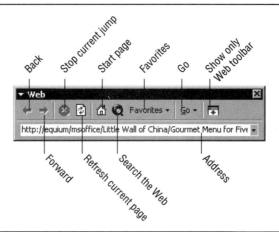

FIGURE 12.1:   Use the Web toolbar for browsing intranets and the Web.

If you've used a Web browser before, you'll find this straightforward; if you've used Microsoft's Internet Explorer, you'll find that Word's Web-browsing features look very familiar indeed. Here's what the buttons on the Web toolbar do:

- Back moves to the previous page you were on.

- Forward moves forward again to the page you were on before you clicked the Back button.

- Stop Current Jump stops Word from pursuing a jump that's in progress. (You might want to click this button if a jump has stalled or if a page is dreadfully slow in loading.)

- Refresh Current Page makes Word reload the current page. You may want to do this if part of the page fails to transfer properly or if you've had the page open for a while and you suspect it may have been updated in the interim.

- Start Page displays Internet Explorer, starting it if it was not already running, and jumps to your *start page* (the Web location your Web browser heads to when you start it; also known as your *home page* to Internet Explorer).

- Search the Web displays your chosen Web search tool in Internet Explorer.

- Favorites displays the Favorites menu. *Favorites* are pages whose address you tell Windows to store so you can return to them quickly; other browsers call them *bookmarks*. To add the current page to your list of favorites, choose Add To Favorites, enter the name you want for the favorite in the File Name text box in the Add To Favorites dialog box, and click the Add button. To open a favorite Web page, either choose it from the list of favorites on the Favorites menu or choose Open Favorites, select the favorite in the Favorites dialog box, and click the Open button to jump to it.

- Go displays a menu of actions and jumps you can make from the current page:

    Open Displays the Open Internet Address dialog box, where you can enter a Web address to go to or click the Browse button to open a file or an address by using the Browse dialog box. Select the Open in New Window check box in the Open Internet Address dialog box if you want to open the page in a new window rather than using the same window and leaving the current page.

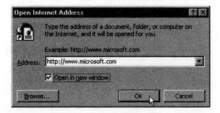

    Back/Forward Move you back and forward through the series of pages you've visited.

Start Page   Takes you to your start page in Internet Explorer.

Search The Web   Displays your Web search tool in Internet Explorer.

Set Start Page   Offers to set your start page to the page currently displayed. Click the Yes button to accept the offer.

Set Search Page   Offers to set your search page to the page currently displayed. Again, click the Yes button to accept.

The bottom of the Go menu provides a list of jumps you can take from the current page.

Show Only Web Toolbar   Toggles on and off the display of all displayed toolbars other than the Web toolbar. This is good for quickly freeing up screen real estate so that you can better view Web pages—and, when you need them again, for restoring the toolbars you were using before.

Address   Where you can enter an address to go to in Internet Explorer or choose an address from the drop-down list of addresses you've previously visited.

Opening a Document on a Web or Intranet

To open a document on an intranet or on a Web server:

1.   Click the Open button on the Standard toolbar, or choose File ➤ Open, to display the Open dialog box.

2.   Navigate to the folder that contains the document:

   •   For a local folder, navigate to it by using the Look In drop-down list and Look In list box as usual.

   •   For an existing Web folder, click the Web Folders button in the Places panel at the left-hand side of the Open dialog box to display your list of Web folders. (Alternatively, you can choose Web Folders from the Look In drop-down list.) Double-click the folder in the Look In list box to open it.

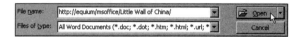

- To create a new Web folder and open a document from it, enter the path to the folder in the File Name text box, then click the Open button. Word will display the contents of the folder and will add the location to your Web Folders list. Double-click the folder in the Look In list box to open it. The first time you connect to a Web server, you may need to enter your username and password in the Enter Network Password dialog box (see Figure 12.2). If you want Word to remember the password for you, select the Save This Password In Your Password List check box. Be warned that saving the password means that anybody logged on to the computer in your name will now be able to access this Web server as you.

SKILL 12

FIGURE 12.2: In the Enter Network Password dialog box, enter your username and password. Select the Save This Password In Your Password List check box if you want Word to remember the password for you.

3. Select the document you want to open.

TIP TIP TIP TIP TIP TIP TIP TIP TIP TIP TIP TIP TIP TIP TIP TIP TIP TIP TIP TIP TIP TIP TIP TIP

When you're opening a document over a slow connection, such as a dial-up connection to the Web, use List view in the Open dialog box rather than Details view, Properties view, or Preview. List view needs to retrieve only the names of the documents in the folder, making it quicker than Details view, Properties view, and Preview, which all need to retrieve information about the current document selected as well. (Over a local area network, such as when you're connecting to an intranet, speed is much less of a problem.)

4. Click the Open button to open the document.

Creating a Web Site with the Web Page Wizard

If you want to create a Web site of your own, the Web Page Wizard is the place to start. The Web Page Wizard takes you through the process of creating a site, letting you specify the site and its title, which pages you want in it, how the pages should be linked to each other, and what the theme of the pages should be. Once you've made your choices and the Wizard has created your site, you enter your own text and graphics in the pages. You can also add further pages and links to the site as needed.

To create a Web site with the Web Page Wizard:

1. Choose File ➤ New to display the New dialog box.

2. Click the Web Pages tab to display it at the front of the dialog box. (If you don't see a Web Pages tab in the New dialog box, whoever installed Word on your computer probably didn't install the Web templates. See the Appendix for instructions for installing Word components.)

3. Click the Web Page Wizard icon, then click the OK button. Word will start the Web Page Wizard and display the first Web Page Wizard dialog box.

TIP TIP TIP TIP TIP TIP TIP TIP TIP TIP TIP TIP TIP TIP TIP TIP TIP TIP TIP TIP TIP TIP TIP

While specifying the details for your Web site in the Wizard, you can move backward and forward in the Wizard by clicking the Back and Next buttons, or by clicking in the location squares in the location panel on the left of the Wizard's dialog box. You can also click the Finish button at any time to accept the Wizard's default settings for the Web site; usually, though, you'll do best to make choices for each of the options that the Wizard offers.

4. Click the Next button to get things started. Word will display the Title And Location page of the Web Page Wizard (see Figure 12.3).

5. Enter the title for the Web site in the Web Site Title text box. The Wizard will copy the title into the subfolder part of the Web Site Location text box below. For example, if you enter **Great American Industrials** in the Web Site Title text box when c:\My Documents is in the Web Site Location text box, the Wizard will read c:\My Documents\Great American Industrials\Default.htm in the Web Site Location text box.

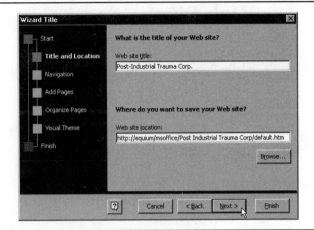

FIGURE 12.3: On the Title And Location page of the Web Page Wizard, enter a title for your Web site and select a location in which to store the files.

6. Enter the location for the Web site in the Web Site Location text box:

    - Either type the location into the Web Site Location text box. This is easy if you need to make a minor adjustment to the default location that Word has suggested.

    - Or click the Browse button to display the Save As dialog box. Select the folder as usual; for example, you might click the Web Folders button to access a Web folder. Then enter the filename in the File Name text box and click the Save button. Word will enter the location you chose in the Web Site Location text box.

7. Click the Next button to proceed to the Navigation stage of the Web Page Wizard.

8. Select the type of navigation you want for the Web site. Your choices are:

    Vertical Frame   An area at the left of the page will contain links for navigation.

    Horizontal Frame   An area at the top of the page will contain links for navigation.

    Separate Page   Each link will lead to a separate page that has links for navigating forward and backward. This design is good for browsers that do not support frames (separate areas of the page), but it means that the user will have to do more clicking to navigate your Web site. (Most modern browsers, such as Internet Explorer and Navigator, support frames.)

9. Click the Next button to proceed to the Add Pages stage of the Web Page Wizard (see Figure 12.4).

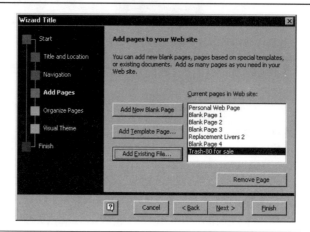

FIGURE 12.4: On the Add Pages page of the Web Page Wizard, select the pages you want to have in your Web site.

10. Choose the pages you want to have in your Web site by adding blank pages, adding pages based on Word's Web page templates, and adding existing files to the list shown in the Current Pages In Web Site list box:

   - Click the Add New Blank Page button to add another blank page to the list. You get to rename these pages later.

   - Click the Add Template Page button to display the Web Page Templates dialog box (see Figure 12.5). Select the type of page from the list box. Word displays the type of page you choose in the document behind the Web Page Templates dialog box, so that you can get a preview of it. Click the OK button to add a page based on the template to your Web site. The page will appear in the list under its template name; for example, if you choose Column With Contents in the Web Page Templates dialog box, the page will appear as Column With Contents in the Current Pages In Web Site list box.

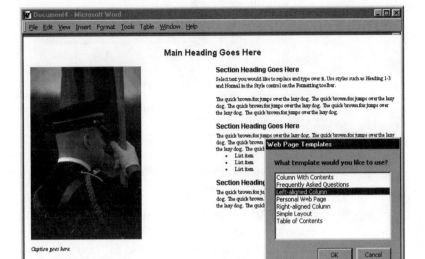

FIGURE 12.5: In the Web Page Templates dialog box, select the template on which to base the page you're adding to your Web site.

- Click the Add Existing File button to display the Open dialog box. Select a file in the usual way and click the Open button to add it to the Current Pages In Web Site list.

- To remove a page from the Web site, select it in the Current Pages In Web Site list box and click the Remove Page button.

11. Click the Next button to move to the Organize Pages page of the Wizard.

12. Change the order of the pages in the Web site by selecting a page that you want to move and then using the Move Up button or Move Down button to move it to where you want it to be.

13. Assign a suitable name to each new page by selecting it in the These Hyperlinks Will Appear As Navigation list box, clicking the Rename button, entering a name in the Rename Hyperlink dialog box (see Figure 12.6), and clicking the OK button. Keep these names relatively short (say, a few words) and as descriptive as possible, because they will appear as navigation links in the Web pages. If they're too long, the navigation frames will be awkwardly big; if they're too short and cryptic, people will have a hard time navigating your site.

FIGURE 12.6: Use the Rename Hyperlink dialog box to assign names to each of the pages in your Web site.

14. Click the Next button to move to the Visual Theme page of the Wizard.

15. Select the visual theme you want to have for the Web site. To use a theme, select the Add A Visual Theme option button and click the Browse Themes button to display the Themes dialog box. Select the theme you want, select choices for the theme (as discussed in "Using Themes" in Skill 5), and click the OK button. (If you don't want to use a theme, select the No Visual Theme option button.)

16. Click the Finish button to have the Wizard create your site. (You can also click the Next button to display the Finish page of the Wizard, and then click the Finish button from there, but there's no point.)

The Wizard will now create the site you specified. Figure 12.7 shows an example of a site created by the Wizard. You'll see that the home page is saved under the name default.htm, Microsoft's name for the home page on a site.

17. Add text to the placeholders in the page by clicking each placeholder and then typing in your text. For example, to add a heading to the Personal Home Page, click in the Insert Heading placeholder and enter the text you want. Rinse and repeat for other heading placeholders in the page, such as any Subheading placeholders.

18. Replace any sample text with suitable text of your own.

19. Edit the page to suit your needs: Add, cut, and edit the text as necessary. Use the hyperlinks to move quickly to a linked part of the page.

20. Save the page when you're finished.

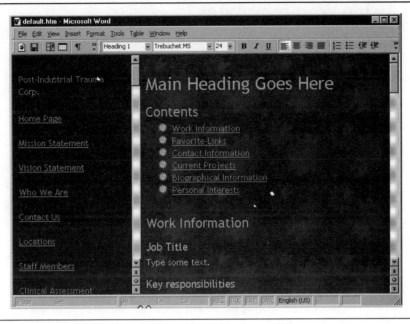

FIGURE 12.7: A site created by the Wizard. You can now customize the contents of each page by replacing the default text and graphics with your own text and graphics.

Creating Web Pages

To add to your Web site, or to add to another site, you can create pages of your own. Word provides two ways of doing so: first, by creating a new document based on one of Word's Web templates; and second, by saving an existing Word document as a Web page. In this section, we'll look at each method in turn.

Which method you choose will typically depend on the type of Web site you work with and what your day-to-day work entails. When you create Web pages for your Web site, it will probably make most sense to start with one of the Web templates. When you are creating a paper document—a report, say—that will later be converted to a Web page and posted to a Web site, you'll do better to create it as a Word document.

Using Web Templates

To start a Web page by using a Web template, select File ➤ New and choose one of the templates on the Web Pages tab of the New dialog box. Word offers such templates as Column With Contents, Frequently Asked Questions, Left-Aligned Column, Right-Aligned Column, and Personal Web Page (these are the same pages that the Web Page Wizard offers). You can download additional Web templates from the Microsoft Web site, `http://www.microsoft.com`.

Enter your text and pictures in the Web page, replacing the default placeholder text and graphics that the templates offer. Then save the Web page as follows:

1. Choose File ➤ Save or File ➤ Save As Web Page to display the Save As dialog box (see Figure 12.8). You'll notice that this Save As dialog box is a little different from the regular Save As dialog box that we've been using so far in the book: There is an item named Page Title below the main list box, and a Change button. You'll also notice that the Save As Type drop-down list at the bottom of the Save As dialog box shows Web Page rather than Word Document. The page title is the text that appears in the title bar of a browser that visits the page. The Web templates supply default text for the page title; you might want to change it.

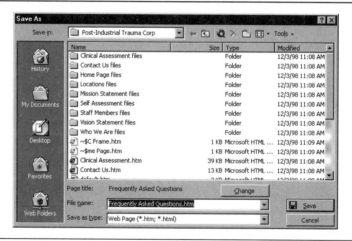

FIGURE 12.8: Word uses a slightly different Save As dialog box for saving Web pages. Note the Page Title label and the Change button below the main list box.

2. Navigate to the folder in which to store the Web page.

3. Enter the name for the file in the File Name text box.

4. To set a different title for the page, click the Change button to the right of the Page Title item. In the Set Page Title dialog box, enter the title you want for the page, then click the OK button.

5. Click the Save button to save the document as a Web page.

Creating a Web Page from a Word Document

Instead of using one of Word's Web templates, you can save a "regular" Word document as a Web page. This is particularly useful for documents created as paper documents that you now need to make available on your intranet or on the Web.

To save a Word document as a Web page, choose File ➤ Save As Web Page, then follow the procedure described in steps 2 through 5 of the previous section.

NOTE NOTE NOTE NOTE NOTE NOTE NOTE NOTE NOTE NOTE NOTE NOTE NOTE NOTE NOTE

If the document has previously been saved as a Word document, the title for the page will be set to the document's name; otherwise, it will be blank.

This technique works well for short documents, but longer documents inevitably produce uncomfortably long Web pages. Often, you'll want to split the document up into several (or many) Web pages, adding hyperlinks (as described in the next section) to link them. You may also want to create a table of contents or a table of figures (both described in Skill 15) as a navigational tool.

WARNING WARNING WARNING WARNING WARNING WARNING WARNING WARNING

When saving a regular Word document as a Web page, you need to be aware that some Word elements do not translate properly to HTML format and may look different or wrong when viewed in a Web browser. These include complex tables, bulleted and numbered lists, and graphics. If you need to include these items in a Web page, you'll probably do best to start with one of Word's Web page templates, which will help you avoid adding items that will not work effectively in a Web page.

SPECIFYING ALTERNATIVE TEXT FOR A TEXT BOX

If you use a text box to position a graphical element in a document and then convert that document to a Web page, it's a good idea to specify alternative text to be displayed while the Web browser is loading the picture or in place of the picture if the picture is missing (or if the user has turned off the display of pictures in their Web browser).

To specify alternative text, right-click the border of the text box and choose Format Text Box from the context menu to display the Format Text Box dialog box. Click the Web tab to display it, enter the text in the Alternative Text text box, and click the OK button.

Creating Hyperlinks

A *hyperlink*, often called simply a *link*, is a jump to another location. This location can be either part of a Web page, part of an Office file (for example, part of a spreadsheet, or of another Word document, or even of the same Word document), an entire Office file (for example, a PowerPoint presentation), or a Web page either on your computer, on a local intranet, or on the World Wide Web. You can mix and match these different types of hyperlinks to suit you.

You can create a hyperlink in any of three ways, as you'll see in the following sections.

Inserting a Hyperlink Manually

To insert a hyperlink:

1. Enter the text or insert the graphical object that you want to have displayed for the hyperlink.

2. Select that text or graphical object.

3. Click the Insert Hyperlink button on the Standard toolbar, or choose Insert ➢ Hyperlink, to display the Insert Hyperlink dialog box (see Figure 12.9).

4. If you chose text, make sure that the Text To Display text box shows the correct text.

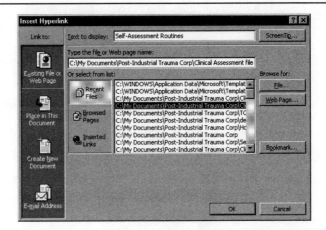

FIGURE 12.9: In the Insert Hyperlink dialog box, specify the details for the hyperlink.

5. To have a ScreenTip appear when the user moves the mouse pointer over the hyperlink, click the ScreenTip button to display the Set Hyperlink ScreenTip dialog box. Enter the text for the ScreenTip, then click the OK button.

6. Enter the information for the hyperlink in the Type The File Or Web Page Name text box in one of the following ways:

   - You can simply type in the URL or the path and the file.

   - You can use the Or Select From List list box to enter the name of a file you've recently used, a page you've recently browsed, or a link you've recently inserted. Click the Recent Files button, the Browsed Pages button, or the Inserted Links button, as appropriate. Then select the entry from the resulting list in the list box.

   - You can click the File button to display the Link To File dialog box and select a file from the Link To File dialog box.

   - You can click the Web Page button to display Internet Explorer, navigate to the URL or page you want, and then activate the Word window again (by clicking on its Taskbar button) to enter the URL in the Type The File Or Web Page Name text box.

   - You can click the Bookmark button to display the Select Place In Document dialog box, choose the bookmark you want, and then click the OK button.

- You can click the Place In This Document button in the Link To panel at the left-hand side of the Insert Hyperlink dialog box to display the Select A Place In This Document list box (see Figure 12.10). Choose the heading or bookmark you want from the list box.

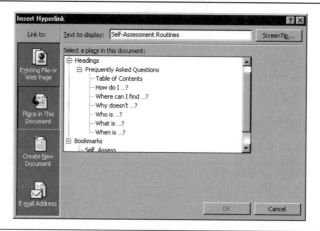

FIGURE 12.10: Use the Select A Place In This Document list box to select a heading or a bookmark for the hyperlink.

- You can click the Create New Document button in the Link To panel to display the Create New Document panel of the dialog box (see Figure 12.11). Enter the name for the new document in the Name Of New Document text box. To change the folder in which the file will be saved, click the Change button to display the Link To File, choose an appropriate folder, and click the OK button. In the When To Edit area, select the Edit The New Document option button if you don't want to work with the document now; otherwise, leave the Edit The New Document Now option button selected, and Word will open the document when you close the Insert Hyperlink dialog box.

- Finally, you can click the E-mail Address button in the Link To panel to display the E-mail Address panel. Enter the e-mail address in the E-mail Address text box, or select the address from the Recently Used E-mail Addresses list box. Then enter a subject for the message in the Subject text box.

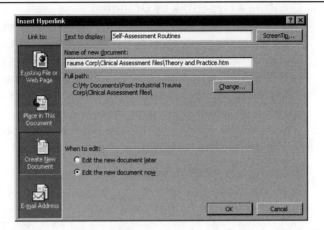

FIGURE 12.11: Use the Create New Document panel of the Insert Hyperlink dialog box to create a new document for the hyperlink.

7.   Click the OK button to insert the hyperlink in your document.

Once you've inserted a hyperlink in a document, you can click the hyperlink to jump to the document or Web page to which it is connected.

Creating Automatic Hyperlinks from Filenames

Word's AutoFormat feature (discussed in Skill 5) can automatically create a hyperlink when you type the name of a file into a Word document. To enable this feature, choose Tools ≻ AutoCorrect to display the AutoCorrect dialog box. Click the AutoFormat As You Type tab and select the Internet And Network Paths With Hyperlinks check box; click the AutoFormat tab, and select the check box there too. Then click the OK button to close the AutoCorrect dialog box. Thereafter, when you type a URL or a network path and filename into a document, Word will automatically format it as a hyperlink.

NOTE NOTE NOTE NOTE NOTE NOTE NOTE NOTE NOTE NOTE NOTE NOTE NOTE NOTE NOTE

To turn URLs and file paths in an existing document into hyperlinks, use the Format ≻ AutoFormat command. Make sure that the Internet And Network Paths With Hyperlinks check box on the AutoFormat tab of the AutoCorrect dialog box is selected as described in the previous paragraph.

Creating a Hyperlink by Dragging

You can also create a hyperlink to an Office document by dragging the object to be linked from the application to the Word document that should receive the hyperlink. For example, you can create a hyperlink from a range of cells in Excel, a slide in PowerPoint, an Access database object, or even part of another Word document.

To create a hyperlink, display Word and the other application (or two windows in Word) on screen at the same time. Then right-click and right-drag the object to where you want it to appear in the Word publication. Word will display a context menu; choose Create Hyperlink Here to create the hyperlink.

Creating a Hyperlink by Copying

To create a hyperlink by copying, select the material in its source application (or in another Word document) and copy it by right-clicking and choosing Copy, clicking the Copy button, or choosing Edit ➤ Copy. Then switch to Word (or to the Word document that will receive the hyperlink), position the insertion point where the hyperlink should go, and choose Edit ➤ Paste As Hyperlink.

Saving a Web Page as a Word Document

You can also save a Web page as a Word document. To do so, choose File ➤ Save As to display the Save As dialog box, then choose Word Document in the Save As Type drop-down list. The Save As dialog box will change from the Web variant (with the Page Title area and the Change button beneath the Save In list box) to the regular Save As dialog box. Specify a name for the document in the Save As dialog box and then click the Save button. Word will save the Web page as a regular Word document.

Viewing the HTML Source Code of a Web Page

To view the source code of a Web page, choose View ➤ HTML Source to display the HTML code for the Web page in the Microsoft Development Environment (see Figure 12.12). When you've finished, choose File ➤ Exit to close the Microsoft Development Environment and return to Word.

TIP TIP TIP TIP TIP TIP TIP TIP TIP TIP TIP TIP TIP TIP TIP TIP TIP TIP TIP TIP TIP TIP TIP

I've made viewing HTML source code sound particularly unappealing—and indeed, you'll probably want to take advantage of Word's ability to create and read HTML to keep your involvement with HTML codes to a minimum. But you can use the View ➤ HTML Source feature as a way of seeing how people create particular effects in HTML. For example, if you run into a Web page that has impressive effects, you could use this feature to sneak a look at the code they're using—and perhaps even try some of the same techniques in your own files.

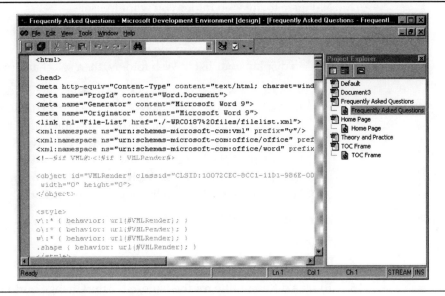

FIGURE 12.12: Use the Microsoft Development Environment to examine the HTML code behind a Web page.

Creating Web Pages with Word

You can create Web pages with Word in three ways: First, you can use the Web Page Wizard to walk you through the steps of creating a Web page. Second, you can use one of Word's Web templates to create a particular type of page. Third, you can convert a regular Word document to a Web page. We'll look at each of these ways in turn. First, though, we need to discuss how you save a document or Web page to a Web folder—either a folder on an intranet or a folder on the World Wide Web itself.

Saving a Word Document to a Web Site or Intranet Site

To save a Word document to a Web site or a folder on an intranet site, you use Office's Web Folders feature as follows:

1.   Choose File ➤ Save As Web Page to display the Save As dialog box.

2. Navigate to the Web folder you want to use:

   - To use an existing Web folder (if you have an existing one), click the Web Folders button in the lower-left corner of the Save As dialog box to display your list of Web folders, then select an appropriate folder.

   - To add a new Web folder, click the Create New Folder button in the toolbar at the top of the Save As dialog box to display the New folder dialog box. Enter the name of the folder into the Name text box, then click the OK button to create the folder. The Save As dialog box will display the list of folders available in that location, and Word will add the current address to the Web Folders list. To open a folder from the list shown in the Save In list box, double-click it.

3. Within the Web folder, select the folder in which you want to save the document.

4. Enter the name for the document in the File Name text box.

5. To set a different title for the page, click the Change button to the right of the Page Title item. In the Set Page Title dialog box (see Figure 12.13), enter the title you want for the page, then click the OK button.

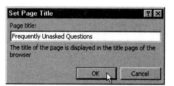

FIGURE 12.13: In the Set Page Title dialog box, enter the title for the Web page.

6. Click the Save button to save the document.

You'll see the Transferring File dialog box (see Figure 12.14), which shows the progress of each piece of the file as it is transferred. For example, if the Web page contains graphics, you'll see the file for each graphic being transferred in turn.

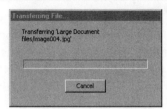

SKILL
12

FIGURE 12.14: The Transferring File dialog box

Choosing Web Options

Word provides a number of Web options that you should know about if you're creating a large number of Web pages. To access the Web options, display the Options dialog box by choosing Tools ➤ Options. Click the General tab to select it, then click the Web Options button to display the Web Options dialog box (see Figure 12.15).

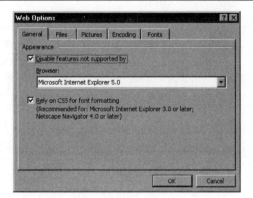

FIGURE 12.15: Use the Web Options dialog box to set options for creating and working with Web pages.

In the following sections, I'll go through the options that the five tabs of the Web Options dialog box provide. I'll recommend the settings that I've found work best for me; be warned that your mileage may vary.

General Tab

Leave the Disable Features Not Supported By check box selected. In the Browser drop-down list, leave Microsoft Internet Explorer 5 selected if you know that all visitors to your Web site (or all readers of your Web pages) will be using Internet Explorer 5; for example, if you're creating pages for an intranet site, and your company has standardized on Internet Explorer, you might be sure of this. Otherwise, select Microsoft Internet Explorer 4 and Netscape Navigator 4 in the Browser drop-down list. This will prevent you from using some of the features that Internet Explorer 5 supports, but will ensure that users of Internet Explorer 4 and Navigator can see your pages.

Leave the Rely On CSS For Font Formatting check box selected. CSS is the abbreviation for *cascading style sheets*, which govern formatting for Web pages.

Files Tab

In the File Names And Locations area, choose the following settings:

- Leave the Organize Supporting Files In A Folder check box selected in order to have Word organize the HTML and XML documents for a Web site into the same folder.

- Leave the Use Long File Names Whenever Possible check box selected to have Word use long filenames for your Web pages whenever possible. (On some servers, you may have to use shortened filenames.)

- Leave the Update Links On Save check box selected if you want Word to update all the links in the document when you save it. Clearing this check box can speed up your save operations a bit.

In the Default Editor area, choose the following settings:

- If you want to use Office (including Word) as the default editor for Web pages created in Office, leave the Check If Office Is The Default Editor For Web Pages Created In Office check box selected. (The Office applications mark Web pages that they have created, so documents are identifiable as having been created by Office applications.)

- If you want to use Word as your default editor for all Web pages, leave the Check If Word Is the Default Editor For All Other Web Pages check box selected. When you choose File ➤ Edit With Microsoft Office 2000 Component from Internet Explorer, the Web page you're viewing will open in Word. If you have a different editor installed, such as FrontPage or PageMill, clear this check box.

Pictures Tab

In the File Formats area, choose the following settings:

- Leave the Rely On VML For Displaying Graphics In Browsers check box cleared unless you're sure that all visitors to your pages will be using Internet Explorer 5. VML is Vector Markup Language, a markup language for describing pictures. Most browsers do not support VML at this writing.

- Leave the Allow PNG As An Output Format check box cleared unless your audience will be using Internet Explorer 5. PNG is a graphics format that other browsers do not support at this writing.

- In the Target Monitor area, choose the minimum screen size you expect most visitors to be using. At this writing, 800 × 600 pixels is the most reasonable size to use. People with monitors set to a higher resolution than the resolution you choose will not have trouble viewing your pages, but people with a lower resolution (e.g., 640 × 480) will have to scroll to see the full page.

- Leave the Pixels Per Inch setting at 96.

Encoding Tab

In the Encoding area, leave both the Reload The Current Document As drop-down list and the Save This Document As drop-down list set to Western European unless you have a good reason for changing them.

Fonts Tab

In the Default Fonts area, leave the Character Set list box set to English/Western European/Other Latin Script.

In the Proportional Font and Fixed-Width Font drop-down lists and Size text boxes, you can choose a proportional font and a fixed width font to be used when the document does not specify a font. Most of the Web pages you create will specify a font, so these fonts will be used only as backup.

NOTE NOTE NOTE NOTE NOTE NOTE NOTE NOTE NOTE NOTE NOTE NOTE NOTE NOTE NOTE
Two other features of Word that you'll probably want to know about are its ability to save files to, and open files on, FTP servers, and its ability to enhance Outlook by acting as an e-mail editor. For coverage of these features, visit the Web component for this book on www.sybex.com.

Are You Experienced?

Now you can...

- ☑ use the Web Folders feature and the Web toolbar
- ☑ open a document on a Web server
- ☑ create a Web site with the Web Page Wizard
- ☑ create new Web pages based on Web templates
- ☑ create Web pages from Word documents

Creating Mail-Merge Documents

- ➔ **Creating the main document**
- ➔ **Creating the data source**
- ➔ **Choosing merge options**
- ➔ **Merging the data**
- ➔ **Merging envelopes and labels**
- ➔ **Using non-Word documents as data sources**

Mail merge strikes terror into the hearts of many office workers. It gained its notoriety quite deservedly in the early days of word processing, when brave souls using WordStar, SuperScripsit, and other pioneering programs fought their way through truly incomprehensible instructions only to produce memorable letters beginning like this:

```
Mr. Dear 8671 Laurel Street
RonaldQGeldofsson     #2
```

You have probably received a few such letters in the past, and from what I can see, Publishers Clearing House is still heroically churning them out. But nowadays you can do better than that with far less effort.

Mail merge in today's word processing applications is, by comparison, friendly and fun. With just a little attention to the details of what you're doing, you can whip together merged letters, forms, envelopes, labels, or catalogs. Word's Mail Merge Helper smoothes out many of the potential speed bumps in the process.

TIP TIP TIP TIP TIP TIP TIP TIP TIP TIP TIP TIP TIP TIP TIP TIP TIP TIP TIP TIP TIP TIP TIP

You can even use data sources from other applications, for example, data from Excel spreadsheets or from Access tables, with zero complications. We'll look at this toward the end of the skill.

While Word's Mail Merge Helper lets you carry out merges in a variety of different orders, in this skill we'll look at the most conventional order of proceeding. Once you see what's what, you can mix and match to produce the variations that suit you best. You'll also find that Mail Merge has a number of different areas, and in some of them, the water gets deep fast—hit a couple of buttons and Word will be expecting you to put together some SQL statements for MS Query to use in torturing a FoxPro database (or worse). I'll show you how to avoid such predicaments and steer a path through the pitfalls of mail merge.

Enough mixed metaphors. Let's look first at creating the main document for the merge.

Creating the Main Document

The *main document* is the file that contains the skeleton into which you fit the variable information from the data file. The skeleton consists of the text that stays the same in each of the letters, catalogs, or whatever, and the *merge fields* that receive the information from the data file. The data file is typically a Word table that contains the information about the recipients of the form letters or the products you're trying to sell them.

First, if you've got a main document that you want to use, open it and make it the active window.

Choose Tools ➢ Mail Merge to start the merging process. Word will respond by displaying the Mail Merge Helper dialog box (see Figure 13.1).

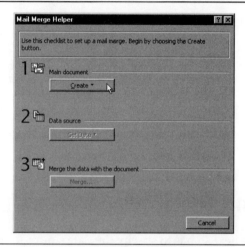

FIGURE 13.1: The first of many appearances for the Mail Merge Helper dialog box. Click the Create button in the Main Document area to get started.

TIP TIP TIP TIP TIP TIP TIP TIP TIP TIP TIP TIP TIP TIP TIP TIP TIP TIP TIP TIP TIP TIP TIP

The Mail Merge Helper dialog box displays increasing amounts of information and instructions about the merge as you go through the process. If you get confused about which stage you've reached and you don't have the Mail Merge Helper dialog box on screen to help you, choose Tools ➢ Mail Merge to display the Mail Merge Helper and then scan the information and instructions it's currently displaying.

Click the Create button in the Main Document area and choose the type of document you want to create: Form Letters, Mailing Labels, Envelopes, or Catalogs.

(For the example, I chose Form Letters because that still seems to be the most popular type of mail merge.)

In the message box that appears, choose whether to use the document in the active document window—the document that was open when you started the Mail Merge Helper—or to create a new main document.

- If you choose to use the active document, Word records its name and path underneath the Create button in the Mail Merge Helper dialog box.

- If you choose to create a new main document, Word opens a new document for you and records its name under the Create button: *Document2* or a similar name.

Specifying the Data Source

The next step is to specify the data source for the mail merge. Click the Get Data button and choose an option from the drop-down list:

- Create Data Source lets you create a new mail merge data source for this merge project.

- Open Data Source lets you open an existing data source (e.g., the one from your last successful mail merge).

- Use Address Book lets you use an existing electronic address book, such as your Outlook address book (if you're using Microsoft Office) or your MAPI Personal Address Book (which you may be using with Exchange), as data for the merge.

- Header Options is a little more esoteric. We won't get into it in detail here, but Header Options lets you run a merge in which the data comes from one source and the header information that controls the data comes from another source. This can be useful if you already have a main document with fields defined and a data source with headers that don't match the fields: Instead of changing the headers in the data source (and perhaps thereby rendering it unsuitable for its regular uses), you can choose Header Options, click the Create button, and set up a new group of headers that will bridge the gap between the main document and the data source.

Creating a New Data Source

To create a new data source, click the Get Data button and choose Create Data Source from the drop-down list. Word will display the Create Data Source dialog box (see Figure 13.2).

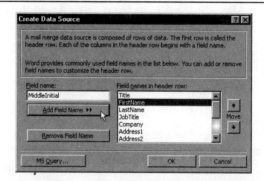

FIGURE 13.2: Creating a new data source in the Create Data Source dialog box.

First, you create the *header row* for the data source—the field names that will head the columns of data and that you will enter into your main document to tell Word where to put the variable information.

Word provides a list of commonly used field names for you to customize: Title, FirstName, LastName, JobTitle, and so on. You'll find these more suitable for some projects than others—for example, for a parts catalog, you'll probably want to customize the list extensively, whereas the list is pretty much on target for a business mailing.

- To add a field name to the list, type it in the Field Name box, then click the Add Field Name button. (The most fields you can have is 31, at which point Word will stop you from adding more.)

Field names can be up to 40 characters long, but you'll usually do better to keep them as short as possible while making them descriptive—ultra-cryptic names can cause confusion later in the merge process. Names can use both letters and numbers, but each name must start with a letter. You can't include spaces in the names, but you can add underscores instead—Career_Prospects, etc.—which helps make them readable.

- To remove a field name from the list, select it in the Field Names In Header Row list box and click the Remove Field Name button.

- To rearrange the field names in the list, click a field name and then click the Move buttons to move it up or down the list.

The list of field names in the Field Names In Header Row list box forms a loop, so you can move the bottom-most field to the top of the list by clicking the down button.

When you have the list of field names to your liking, click the OK button to close the Create Data Source dialog box and save the data source you're creating.

Clicking the MS Query button in the Create Data Source dialog box takes you off into the Twilight Zone of Structured Query Language (SQL, pronounced *sequel* by aficionados, in case you're wondering). I suggest not clicking it unless you're experienced in SQL queries and are happy playing with databases.

Word will now display the Save As dialog box for you to save the data source. Save your document in the usual way.

Once the document is saved, Word will display a message box telling you that the document contains no data—no surprise, as you've just created it—and inviting you to edit it or to edit the main document. For now, choose the Edit Data Source button.

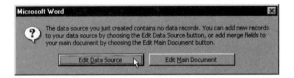

Word will display the Data Form dialog box (see Figure 13.3), which is a custom dialog box built from the field names you entered in the Create Data Source dialog box.

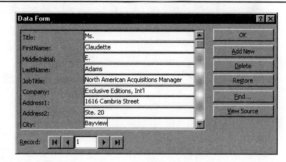

FIGURE 13.3: In the Data Form dialog box, enter records for the data source you just created.

Add data to the data source: Type information into the fields in the dialog box. Press Enter or Tab to move between fields.

- Click the Add New button to begin a new record after entering the first one.

- Click the Delete button to delete the current record. This gets rid of the record completely, and you cannot recover it from the Data Form dialog box. (You may be able to recover it by closing the Data Form dialog box and closing the document without saving changes, but you will then lose any other changes you have made to the document.) Once you've deleted a record, Word displays the next record if there is one; if you delete the last record in the list, Word displays the previous record.

- Click the Restore button to restore the record to its previous condition (the information it contained before any changes you just made on screen). The Restore button will not restore a record you have deleted, because the record is no longer there to be restored.

- Click the View Source button to see the kind of data source you're working with in Word. Usually this means that Word will display a table containing the records that you've entered, together with the Database toolbar (see Figure 13.4). Click the Data Form button (the leftmost button on the Database toolbar) to display the Data Form dialog box again so that you can continue creating or editing your data source.

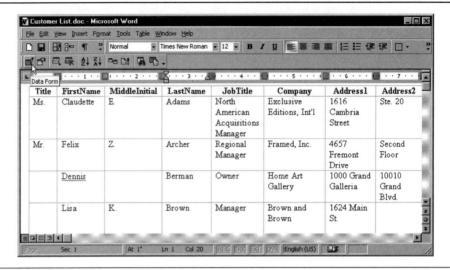

FIGURE 13.4: You can click the View Source button from the Data Form dialog box to display the data source you're working with. If the data source is a Word document, you'll see a table like this. Word will also display the Database toolbar. Click the Data Form button to display the Data Form dialog box again to continue working with your data source.

- Click the Record buttons at the bottom of the Data Form dialog box to see your records: the four buttons call up the first record, previous record, next record, and last record, respectively, and the Record box lets you type in the record number that you want to move to.

Click the OK button when you've finished adding records to your data source. Word will close the Data Form dialog box and take you to your main document with the Mail Merge toolbar displayed. Skip ahead to "Adding Merge Fields to the Main Document," later in this skill.

Using an Existing Data File

To use an existing data file for your mail merge, click the Get Data button in the Mail Merge Helper dialog box and choose Open Data Source. Word will display the Open Data Source dialog box (shown in Figure 13.5), which you'll recognize as the Open dialog box in disguise. Navigate to the data source document in the usual way, select it, and open it by clicking the Open button.

FIGURE 13.5: Open your existing data source from the Open Data Source dialog box.

Word will now check your purported data source for fields. If it doesn't contain any fields that Word can recognize, Word will display the Header Record Delimiters dialog box for you to indicate how the fields and records are divided (delimited), as shown in Figure 13.6. Pick the delimiter characters in the Field Delimiter and Record Delimiter drop-down lists (you get to choose from paragraphs, tabs, commas, periods, exclamation points, and anything else Word thinks might be a delimiter character in this document) and then click the OK button. (If you opened the wrong file, click the Cancel button to close the Header Record Delimiters dialog box and then click the Get Data button again to reopen the Open Data Source dialog box.)

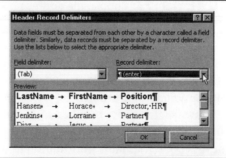

FIGURE 13.6: If Word displays the Header Record Delimiters dialog box, you may have picked the wrong file by mistake. If not, indicate to Word how the fields and records are divided.

Once Word has established that your data source contains fields, it will check your main document for merge fields. If it finds none—which is likely if you're creating a new main document for the merge—it will display a message box inviting you to insert them.

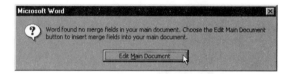

Click the Edit Main Document button, and Word will return you to your main document. Now it's time to add merge fields to it. Skip ahead to "Adding Merge Fields to the Main Document."

Using Your Address Book

To run a mail merge from the data in your electronic address book, click the Get Data button in the Mail Merge Helper dialog box and choose Use Address Book. Word will display the Use Address Book dialog box (see Figure 13.7). From the Choose Address Book list, choose the address book to use and click the OK button.

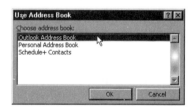

FIGURE 13.7: Choose the address book you want to use in the Use Address Book dialog box.

Depending on which address book you select, the next few actions will vary. For example, if you choose your Personal Address Book, Word may invite you to choose a profile for the merge. Play along, and shortly after interrogating you about your social security number and your mother's maiden name, Word will announce in its status bar that it's converting the address book. It will then scan the address book for viable information to use for the merge. Once Word is satisfied that you've picked a suitable address book, it will display a message box telling you that it found no merge fields in your main document and inviting you to add some. Click the Edit Main Document button to do so.

Adding Merge Fields to the Main Document

Back in the main document, you'll see that Word has opened a Mail Merge toolbar that provides buttons for inserting merge fields and Word fields into the main document.

If you're starting a main document from scratch, add the merge fields as you write it. If you started off with the basis of your merge document already written, you just need to add the merge fields to it.

Insert Merge Field ▾

To insert a merge field, click the Insert Merge Field button and choose the merge field from the drop-down list of merge fields in the data source you created or chose. For example, to enter an address, choose the Title field; Word will insert a field saying <<Title>> in the document. Follow that with a space, insert the FirstName field and another space, and then insert the LastName field. Press Enter and start entering the address fields. Remember the spaces and punctuation that the words will need—they're easy to forget when you're faced with a large number of fields.

```
«Title» «FirstName» «LastName»
«JobTitle»
«Company»
«Address1», «Address2»
«City», «State», «Country» «PostalCode»
```

TIP TIP TIP TIP TIP TIP TIP TIP TIP TIP TIP TIP TIP TIP TIP TIP TIP TIP TIP TIP TIP TIP TIP TIP

The Insert Word Fields button produces a drop-down list of special fields for use in complex merges, such as Ask, If. . . Then. . . Else. . ., and Fill-in. These fields, which provide you with a way to customize your merge documents so that they prompt the user for keyboard input, act in different ways depending on what kind of data they find in merge fields, and so on. They're beyond the scope of this book, but if you do a lot of complex mail merges, you'll no doubt want to learn how to use them.

At this point, you've got the components of the merge in place—a data source with records and a main document with field codes that match the header names in the data source. Next, you can specify options for the merge—filtering and sorting, error checking, and more—or just damn the torpedoes and merge the documents.

If you need to make adjustments to your data source, click the Edit Data Source button on the Mail Merge toolbar—the rightmost button on the toolbar.

If you suddenly realize you've selected the wrong data source, click the Mail Merge Helper button on the Mail Merge toolbar, click the Get Data button in the Mail Merge Helper dialog box, and choose the right data source.

Setting Merge Options

In this section, we'll look quickly at how you can sort and filter merge documents so you can perform a merge without producing documents for every single record in your database. If you don't want to try sorting or filtering, go straight on to the section titled "Merging Your Data."

Sorting the Records to Be Merged

By filtering your records, you can restrict the scope of your mail merges to just the appropriate part of your data source rather than creating a label, catalog entry, or form letter for every single record. For example, you can filter your records so that you print labels of only your customers in California and Arizona, or so that you send a letter extolling your pine-colored leatherette goblins only to people called Green (first name or last).

You can use sorting to restrict mail merges too. By default, Word creates or prints the merge documents in the same order as the records are listed in the data source. (If you haven't sorted your data source, this will be the order in which you entered the records into the data source.) Often, you'll want to sort your records before merging the documents—for example, you might want to sort the records by state and then by city to keep the mail clerk in a reasonable temper.

To sort your records:

1. Click the Mail Merge Helper button to display the Mail Merge Helper dialog box.

2. Click the Query Options button to open the Query Options dialog box (see Figure 13.8). Click the Sort Records tab to bring it to the front if it isn't already there.

   - You can also get to the Query Options dialog box by clicking the Query Options button in the Merge dialog box.

FIGURE 13.8: On the Sort Records tab of the Query Options dialog box, choose how to sort your records.

3. In the Sort By box, choose the first field you want to sort by from the drop-down list and then choose an Ascending or Descending sort order.

4. To sort more precisely, choose the second field in the first Then By box. (For example, to sort by city within state, choose State in the Sort By box and City in the first Then By box.) Again, choose Ascending or Descending order.

5. Specify another sort field in the second Then By box if necessary, and choose the order.

6. Click the OK button to close the Query Options dialog box.

    - If you want to filter your sorted data, click the Filter Records tab instead and skip to step 3 in the next section.

    - If you choose the wrong sort fields, click the Clear All button to reset the drop-down lists to no field.

Filtering the Records to Be Merged

To filter the records you'll be merging:

1. Click the Mail Merge Helper button to display the Mail Merge Helper dialog box.

2. Click the Query Options button to open the Query Options dialog box (see Figure 13.9). Click the Filter Records tab to bring it to the front if it isn't already displayed.

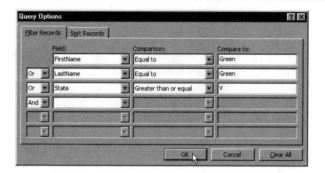

FIGURE 13.9: On the Filter Records tab of the Query Options dialog box, choose how to filter the records you'll be merging.

3. In the Field drop-down list in the top row, choose the field you want to use as the first filter.

4. In the Comparison drop-down list in the top row, choose the filtering operator to specify how the contents of the field must relate to the contents of the Compare To box:

> Equal To (match)
>
> Not Equal To (not match)
>
> Less Than
>
> Greater Than
>
> Less Than Or Equal
>
> Greater Than Or Equal
>
> Is Blank (the merge field must be empty)
>
> Is Not Blank (the merge field must not be empty)

TIP TIP TIP TIP TIP TIP TIP TIP TIP TIP TIP TIP TIP TIP TIP TIP TIP TIP TIP TIP TIP TIP TIP TIP

For these mathematically inclined comparisons, Word evaluates numbers using the conventional manner (1 is less than 11 and so on) and text using the American National Standards Institute (ANSI) sort order: *ax* comes before *blade* alphabetically, so *ax* is "less than" *blade*. You could also use State Is Greater Than Or Equal To V to filter records for Vermont, Virginia, Washington, and Wyoming. For fields that mix text and numbers, Word treats the numbers as text characters, which means that 11 will be sorted between 1 and 2 (and so on).

5. In the second and subsequent rows, choose And or Or in the unnamed first column before the Field column to add a finer filter to the filter in the previous row or to apply another filter. For example, you could choose And Last-Name Is Equal To Green to restrict your merge to Greens in Vermont. Click the Clear All button if you need to reset all the filtering fields.

6. Click the OK button when you've finished defining your filtering criteria. Word will return to the Mail Merge Helper dialog box (unless you got to the Query Options dialog box by clicking the Query Options button in the Merge dialog box, in which case Word will take you there).

Merging Your Data

Now you're all set to merge your data source with your main document. In the Mail Merge Helper dialog box, click the Merge button. Word will display the Merge dialog box (see Figure 13.10).

FIGURE 13.10: In the Merge dialog box, choose whether to merge to a new document, to a printer, or to e-mail.

To merge your data:

1. Choose whether to merge to a new document, to your printer, or to e-mail (if you have Exchange or Outlook installed and correctly configured):

    • If you merge to a new document, Word will divide the resulting documents as it thinks best. For example, it will put page breaks between form letters so that they're ready for printing, whereas mailing labels will share a page with each other.

TIP TIP TIP TIP TIP TIP TIP TIP TIP TIP TIP TIP TIP TIP TIP TIP TIP TIP TIP TIP TIP TIP TIP TIP

By merging to a new document, you give yourself a chance to check the merged documents for errors—and, if you want, to add a personalized note to particular documents that you didn't want to put into your data source.

- If you merge to your printer, Word simply prints all the documents and doesn't produce an on-screen copy.

- If you merge to e-mail, click the Setup button to display the strangely named Merge To Setup dialog box (see Figure 13.11). Specify the field that contains the e-mail address in the Data Field With Mail/Fax Address drop-down box, add a subject line for the message in the Mail Message Subject Line text box, and select the Send Document As An Attachment check box if the document contains formatting that will not survive transmission as an e-mail message. (This depends on the sophistication of your e-mail package and of the service provider you're using: With basic, text-only e-mail, not even bold or italic will make it through unscathed.) Then click the OK button to close the Merge To Setup dialog box and return to the Merge dialog box.

FIGURE 13.11:   In the Merge To Setup dialog box, specify the merge field that contains the e-mail address and add a subject line for the message.

2. If need be, choose which records to merge in the Records To Be Merged group box. Either accept the default setting of All, or enter record numbers in the From and To boxes.

    - If you're using sorting or filtering, the records will be in a different order from that in which they were entered in the data source.

    - To merge from a specific record to the end of the record set, enter the starting number in the From box and leave the To box blank.

3. In the When Merging Records group box, select the Print Blank Lines When Data Fields Are Empty option button if you need to track gaps in your data. Usually, though, you'll want to leave the Don't Print Blank Lines When Data Fields Are Empty option button selected to produce a better-looking result.

4. Click the Check Errors button and verify which option button has been selected in the Checking And Reporting Errors dialog box (shown below). The default choice is Complete The Merge, Pausing To Report Each Error As It Occurs; you can also choose Simulate The Merge And Report Errors In A New Document if you consider the merge potentially problematic; or you can choose "Complete The Merge Without Pausing. Report Errors in a New Document." Click the OK button when you've made your choice.

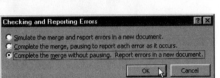

5. Click the Merge button to run the mail merge.

   • If you're merging to a new document, Word will display it on screen. You can then check the merged document for errors before printing, and you can save it if you want to keep it for future use.

   • If you're merging to a printer, Word will display the Print dialog box. Choose the page range and number of copies, if necessary, and then click the OK button to print the documents. When Word has finished printing, it will return you to your main document. Word doesn't create the merged document on disk, so you can't save it.

   • If you're merging to e-mail, Word will check your MAPI profile settings, and then mail the messages and documents (if you're currently online or connected to the network that handles your e-mail) or place them in your Outbox (if you're not currently online or connected to the network).

Merging Labels and Envelopes

In Skill 3, we looked at how you can print labels and envelopes with Word. In this section, we won't grind through *all* that information again—we'll just look at the parts that are different when you're running a mail merge to print labels and envelopes.

Merge-Printing Labels

To create labels for a merge-print:

1. Choose Tools ➤ Mail Merge, select Mailing Labels from the Create drop-down list, and then follow the procedures described earlier in this skill until you've created or selected your data source. Then Word will display a message box telling you it needs to set up your main document; accept by clicking the Set Up Main Document button.

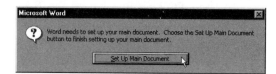

2. Word will then display the Label Options dialog box. Choose your labels as discussed in Skill 3 and click the OK button.

3. Word will then display the Create Labels dialog box (see Figure 13.12) so that you can set up a label format. Click the Insert Merge Field button and choose the fields for the labels from the drop-down list. Word will insert them in the Sample Label box. Include punctuation and spaces, and start new lines as appropriate.

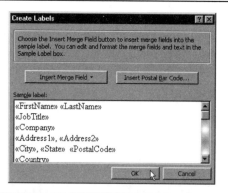

FIGURE 13.12:   In the Create Labels dialog box, set up your labels for merge-printing.

TIP TIP TIP TIP TIP TIP TIP TIP TIP TIP TIP TIP TIP TIP TIP TIP TIP TIP TIP TIP TIP TIP TIP TIP

You can apply formatting to the merge field codes by selecting them and either using keyboard shortcuts (such as Ctrl+B for boldface and Ctrl+I for italic) or right-clicking and choosing Font from the context menu to display the Font dialog box. You can adjust the paragraph layout by right-clicking and choosing Paragraph from the context menu.

4. If you want to include a postal bar code for the address, click the Insert Postal Bar Code button and select the fields from the Merge Field With ZIP Code and Merge Field With Street Address drop-down lists.

5. Click the OK button to close the Insert Postal Bar Code dialog box. Word will insert a boldfaced line saying **Delivery point bar code will print here!** at the top of the Sample Label box in the Create Labels dialog box.

6. Click the OK button to close the Create Labels dialog box.

Word will create the main document for the labels from the contents of the Sample Label box and will return you to the Mail Merge Helper dialog box. From there, follow the instructions in the section titled "Merging Your Data" to complete the merge.

Merge-Printing Envelopes

To set up envelopes for a merge-print:

1. Choose Tools ➢ Mail Merge, select Envelopes from the Create drop-down list, and then follow the procedures described earlier in this skill (in "Creating the Main Document and Specifying the Data Source") until you've created or selected your data source. As with labels, Word will display a message box asking you to click the Set Up Main Document button to finish setting up your main document.

2. Click the Set Up Main Document button and Word will display the Envelope Options dialog box that we investigated in Skill 3.

3. Make your choices in the Envelope Options dialog box, then click the OK button to display the Envelope Address dialog box.

4. Click the Insert Merge Field button and choose the fields for the envelopes from the drop-down list. Word will insert them in the Sample Envelope Address box.

    - Include punctuation and spaces, start new paragraphs where you want them to be, and add any text that you want on each envelope.

    - You can apply formatting to the merge field codes by either using keyboard shortcuts or by right-clicking and choosing Font from the context menu to display the Font dialog box.

    - You can change the paragraph layout by right-clicking and choosing Paragraph from the context menu.

5. To include a postal bar code for the address, click the Insert Postal Bar Code button and select the fields from the Merge Field With ZIP Code and the Merge Field With Street Address drop-down lists.

TIP TIP TIP TIP TIP TIP TIP TIP TIP TIP TIP TIP TIP TIP TIP TIP TIP TIP TIP TIP TIP TIP TIP TIP

You'll see that in the Insert Postal Bar Code dialog box for envelopes, there's also an FIM-A Courtesy Reply Mail check box that you can select if you want to print a Facing Identification Mark on courtesy reply envelopes.

6. Click the OK button to close the Insert Postal Bar Code dialog box. Word will insert a boldfaced line saying **Delivery point bar code will print here!** at the top of the Sample Envelope Address box.

7. Click the OK button to close the Envelope Address dialog box.

Word will create the main document for the envelopes from the contents of the Sample Envelope Address box and will return you to the Mail Merge Helper dialog box. From there, follow the instructions in the section titled "Merging Your Data" to complete the merge. If you choose to merge to a printer, line up the envelopes so they are ready for printing.

Using a Data Source Other Than a Word Document

To use a data source other than a Word document for a mail merge, you hardly need to do anything different from the procedures described earlier in this skill. Word just requires that you specify exactly where the information is coming from; and even that is very straightforward.

Click the Get Data button in the Mail Merge Helper dialog box and choose Open Data Source. In the Open Data Source dialog box, choose the type of file you want to use from the Files Of Type drop-down list; navigate to the file and open it in the usual way.

Unless the application that the file was created in is already open, Word will launch a copy of it in the background (you'll still see Word on screen) and will open the file in question. What follows next depends on the data source you're opening; if it's an Excel spreadsheet, Word will display a dialog box in which you select the range of cells to use for the merge (see Figure 13.13).

FIGURE 13.13: When using an Excel spreadsheet as a data source, select a named range or cell range from the Named Or Cell Range box to use for the merge.

Once you've done that, Word will put you back into the regular mail merge loop of editing your main document. When the merge is finished, Word will close the other application (unless it was already open, in which case Word will close only the file it opened).

Restoring a Main Document to a Regular Document

If you know you won't need to use your main document again for a mail merge, be reassured that it isn't merged forever—you can easily restore it to a regular Word document.

To restore a main document to a regular document:

1. Open the main document.

2. Choose Tools ➢ Mail Merge to display the Mail Merge Helper dialog box.

3. Click the Create button and choose Restore To Normal Word Document from the drop-down list. Word will break the main document's attachment to its data file and restore it to normal document status.

Are You Experienced?

Now you can...

- ☑ create a main document for a mail merge
- ☑ create a mail merge data source
- ☑ use an existing data file in a mail merge, including your address book
- ☑ filter and sort records to be merged
- ☑ merge your data
- ☑ merge envelopes and labels
- ☑ use non-Word documents as mail merge data sources
- ☑ restore a main document to a normal document

SKILL 14

Outlines and Master Documents

- → **Using outlines in Word**
- → **Creating an outline**
- → **Working in the outline**
- → **Creating outline numbered lists**
- → **Creating master documents and subdocuments**
- → **Working with master documents and subdocuments**

In this skill, we'll look at three features that Word provides for working with long documents: Outline view, outline numbered lists, and master documents. Even if the longest documents you create are only a half-dozen pages or so, you can benefit from the first two of these features; if you create long books or reports, you'd do well to investigate master documents as well.

Using Outline view and Word's Heading styles, you can collapse a document to an outline showing any number of Heading levels from one to nine. For example, you can collapse a document to show three levels of Headings, hiding any sub-Headings and body text between the Headings. You can then zero in on a crucial Heading and expand the text underneath it so that you can make a strategic addition or two and then collapse that text again to move quickly to another Heading. You can also move blocks of text around in your document quickly or promote or demote a whole series of Headings in one move.

Outline numbered lists offer capabilities similar to those offered in Outline view. We'll look at how to create and use outline numbered lists at the end of this skill.

Related to Outline view in the way they work, but different in purpose and execution, are Word's master documents and subdocuments. In essence, a master document is a document that combines multiple other documents, letting you work with a project as a whole while keeping it in manageable-sized documents that can be opened separately (for instance, for editing by several different people).

Working with Outlines

Outlines work by using Word's nine Heading styles, Heading 1 through Heading 9. These styles are predefined, so you can't delete them, though you can format them however you like. (These styles are also used for tables of contents, which are closely related to outlines. We'll look at tables of contents in Skill 17.)

TIP TIP TIP TIP TIP TIP TIP TIP TIP TIP TIP TIP TIP TIP TIP TIP TIP TIP TIP TIP TIP TIP TIP

Even if you're creating a short document, Outline view can save you time. As discussed in the section titled "Creating a New Style" in Skill 5, most Heading styles are typically followed by a different paragraph style. This is based on the assumption that you won't want to type several Headings in a row—for example, you might want a Heading 1 paragraph to be followed by Body Text or by some special graphical element that would offset the Heading and draw the reader's attention. In Outline view, however, pressing Enter creates another paragraph with the same paragraph style, so you can quickly create a full chapter's worth of Heading 1 paragraphs, Heading 2 paragraphs, or whatever.

Creating an Outline

Creating an outline in Word could hardly be simpler. You can start with either the blank slate of a new document and build an outline from scratch, or you can start with an existing document.

Creating a New Outline

To create an outline in a new document:

1. Start a new document by choosing File ➢ New and choosing the template you want in the New dialog box, as discussed in the section titled "Creating a New Document" in Skill 2.

2. Choose View ➢ Outline to switch to Outline view. Word will display the Outlining toolbar (see Figure 14.1).

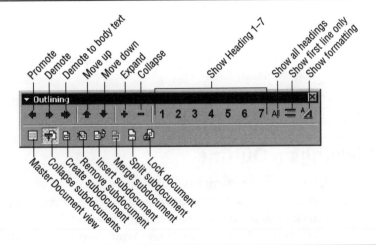

FIGURE 14.1: The Outlining toolbar provides both quick access to the main features of Outline view and tools for working with master documents and subdocuments.

3. Make sure that the paragraph style in the Style drop-down list on the Formatting toolbar is set to Heading 1 style. (Word will usually start the new document with a paragraph in Heading 1 style, depending on which template you chose in step 1.)

4. Enter the first-level Headings, pressing Enter after each one. Word will start each new paragraph in Heading 1 style, no matter what the Style For Following Paragraph for the Heading 1 style is set to.

5. To enter a second-level Heading, press Tab to switch to Heading 2 style. Type the text for the Heading and press Enter; Word will start a new paragraph also based on the Heading 2 style.

   • To enter third-level Headings, fourth-level Headings, and so on, press Tab to move down through the Heading styles.

   • To move back up through the Heading styles, press Shift+Tab.

6. Save the document as usual.

Outlining an Existing Document

To outline an existing document:

1. Open the document.

2. If the document isn't already formatted with styles, apply Heading styles to the Headings by using the Formatting toolbar or the Format Style command.

3. Switch the document to Outline view as described in the next section, "Viewing an Outline."

Viewing an Outline

To switch a document to Outline view, choose View ➢ Outline or click the Outline View button on the horizontal scroll bar (if you have it displayed). Word will shuffle your document into Outline view and display the Outlining toolbar.

When you choose Outline view, Word displays the Outlining toolbar and an outline symbol to the left of the first line in each paragraph, as shown in Figure 14.2. A fat plus sign appearing next to a Heading indicates that the Heading has subheadings or text (or both) underneath it; a fat minus sign means that the Heading has nothing between it and the next Heading. A small, empty square indicates a paragraph of non-heading text. A gray line under a Heading (or under part of a Heading, or extending beyond a Heading) indicates that there is more text collapsed under that Heading.

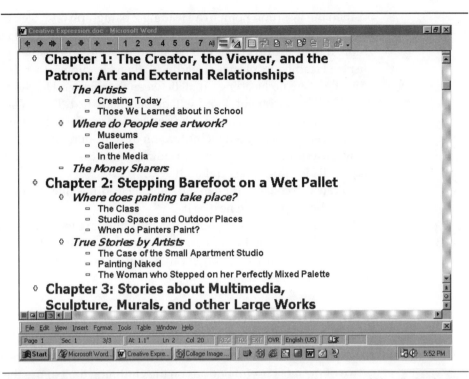

FIGURE 14.2: In Outline view, Word displays a hierarchy of Headings that you can collapse to different levels.

TIP TIP TIP TIP TIP TIP TIP TIP TIP TIP TIP TIP TIP TIP TIP TIP TIP TIP TIP TIP TIP TIP TIP TIP TIP

If you've defined Word's Heading styles with large font sizes, you won't be able to see many Headings on screen at once in Outline view with formatting displayed. Either zoom the view to a smaller percentage—perhaps 75% or 50%—to display more Headings on screen or click the Show Formatting button to toggle off the formatting.

NOTE NOTE NOTE NOTE NOTE NOTE NOTE NOTE NOTE NOTE NOTE NOTE NOTE NOTE NOTE

You'll notice some similarities between Outline view and the Document Map, which provides a navigation pane in all views but Print Preview. Because there's so much overlap between Outline view and the Document Map, you probably won't find the Document Map useful when you're using Outline view.

To collapse or expand the outline to different levels, use the Expand and Collapse buttons and the seven numbered buttons on the Outlining toolbar. The Expand button reveals the subtext for the selected Heading—for example, if you

position the insertion point in a Heading 2 paragraph and click the Expand button, Word will display any Heading 3 paragraphs beneath the Heading 2 paragraph. If there are no Heading 3 paragraphs, Word will display paragraphs with the next Heading level style (Heading 4, then Heading 5, then Heading 6, and so on); if there are no Headings at all between the selected Heading paragraph and the end of the document, Word will display body text. The Collapse button reverses the process, collapsing the outline one available level at a time.

The seven Show Heading *n* buttons on the Outlining toolbar expand or collapse the whole outline to that level of Heading, while the All button toggles the display of all Heading levels and body text.

You can also collapse (or expand) all the Headings under a Heading by double-clicking the fat plus sign next to it.

The Show First Line Only button on the Outlining toolbar toggles the display between only the first line of non-Heading paragraphs and all lines of non-heading paragraphs. This option can be a great help in getting an overview of a large part of your document.

Promoting and Demoting Items

So much for expanding and collapsing your outline so that you can see the appropriate parts of it. Now let's look at how to deal with the resulting outline itself.

Two of the most useful buttons on the Outlining toolbar are the Promote and Demote buttons, which you can use to reorganize the Headings in a document quickly. Click these once to promote or demote the current Heading or selected Headings one level of Heading at a time.

When you select a Heading using its outline symbol (the fat plus sign or fat minus sign that appears to the left of a paragraph, as described in the previous section), you select all of its subHeadings as well (whether or not they're displayed). When you promote or demote a Heading with its subHeadings selected, you promote or demote the subHeadings as well. For example, if I demote the Part 2 Heading shown here from Heading 1 to Heading 2, the Heading 2 paragraphs will be demoted to Heading 3, the Heading 3 paragraphs to Heading 4, and so on.

To promote (or demote) a Heading without promoting (or demoting) all of its subHeadings, first expand the outline to display the subHeadings. Then click in the Heading and click the Promote (or Demote) button until the Heading has reached the level you want it to be.

TIP TIP TIP TIP TIP TIP TIP TIP TIP TIP TIP TIP TIP TIP TIP TIP TIP TIP TIP TIP TIP TIP

To select a Heading without selecting its subHeadings, click in the selection bar next to the Heading. To select several Headings, click and drag in the selection bar.

To demote a Heading to text, click the Demote To Body Text button. Word will apply Normal style to it.

TIP TIP TIP TIP TIP TIP TIP TIP TIP TIP TIP TIP TIP TIP TIP TIP TIP TIP TIP TIP TIP TIP

You can also demote the paragraph you're working in by pressing Tab and promote it by pressing Shift+Tab. To type a real tab in Outline view (without promoting or demoting anything), press Ctrl+Tab.

SKILL
14

Moving Items Up and Down the Outline

Outline view makes reordering the items in an outline speedy and simple. To move a Heading up and down the outline, simply expand or collapse the outline so that the Heading is displayed, then click the symbol next to the Heading and drag it up or down the outline. You'll see a line move up or down the screen with the mouse-pointer arrow indicating where the paragraph will end up when you let go of it.

```
□  The Case of the Small Apartment Studio
↕  Painting Naked
■  The Woman who Stepped on her Perfectly Mixed Palette
```

Alternatively, select the Heading (and any subHeadings you want to move with it) and click the Move Up or Move Down button to move it up or down the outline one displayed paragraph at a time.

Using Heading Numbering

Heading numbering can be a great asset in Outline view. Instead of renumbering your chapters as you drag them about the outline, you can let Word take care of the numbering automatically.

To apply Heading numbering to a document:

1. Right-click in a Heading and choose Bullets And Numbering from the context menu, or choose Format ➤ Bullets And Numbering, to display the Bullets And Numbering dialog box.

2. If the Outline Numbered tab is not displayed, click it to bring it to the front of the dialog box (see Figure 14.3).

FIGURE 14.3: Choose Heading numbering on the Outline Numbered tab of the Bullets And Numbering dialog box.

3. Choose one of the numbering styles that includes the word "Heading," then click the Customize button to display the Customize Outline Numbered List dialog box (see Figure 14.4). If you see a Customize Outline Numbered List dialog box that is smaller than this one, click the More button to display the bottom section.

4. In the Level list box, choose the Heading level on which to work.

5. In the Number Format box, choose how you want the numbering for the Heading to appear. For example, you could enter a word in front of the number to produce numbering such as **Part 1**, or you could enter a colon or other separator character after the number. The Preview box will show the effects of the change.

6. In the Number Style drop-down list, choose the style of numbering: 1, 2, 3; I, II, III; A, B, C; and so on.

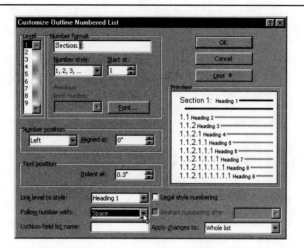

FIGURE 14.4: In the Customize Outline Numbered List dialog box, choose how you want the Heading numbering to appear.

7. In the Start At box, adjust the starting number (or letter) if necessary.

8. In the Previous Level number drop-down list, choose the number for the previous level if you want to produce a multipart number (e.g., **3.2.4**). This works only for levels below Level 1.

9. To change the font formatting of the numbering, click the Font button to display the Font dialog box. Choose font formatting as usual, then click OK to apply the formatting and close the Font dialog box.

10. In the Number Position group box, change the alignment and positioning of the number as necessary.

11. In the Text Position box, adjust the indent of the text as necessary.

12. In the Link Level To Style drop-down list, make sure that the level is associated with the appropriate paragraph style.

13. In the Follow Number With drop-down list, choose whether to follow the number with a tab, a space, or nothing.

14. If you want to use legal-style numbering, select the Legal Style Renumbering check box.

SKILL
14

15. If you want numbering to restart after a certain level, select the Restart Numbering After check box and choose the level in the drop-down list.

16. Repeat steps 4 through 15 as necessary for other Heading levels.

17. In the Apply Changes To drop-down list, make sure that Whole List is selected.

18. Click the OK button to apply the outline numbering to the document.

Formatting in Outline View

As we saw in "Viewing an Outline" earlier in the skill, you can click the Show Formatting button on the Outlining toolbar to stop Word from displaying character formatting in Outline view. This feature can help you get more Headings on screen in a readable format.

You can apply character formatting and style formatting as usual in Outline view, but you can't apply paragraph formatting. Bear in mind when applying style formatting to Headings that you may not see the effect of the changes you're making. Consider splitting the window (by double-clicking or dragging the Split bar at the top of the vertical scroll bar) and switching one of the resulting panes to Normal view or Print Layout view—or simply switch to another view altogether when you need to apply formatting.

Printing an Outline

When you print from Outline view, Word prints only the information displayed on screen. For example, to print only the first three levels of Headings, click the Show Heading 3 button and choose File ➤ Print.

Creating an Outline Numbered List

You can also create an outline numbered list using styles other than the Heading styles. For example, you might want to create an outline numbered list as part of a document without disturbing the Headings.

To create an outline numbered list:

1. Right-click and choose Bullets And Numbering from the context menu, or choose Format ➤ Bullets And Numbering, to display the Bullets And Numbering dialog box.

2. If the Outline Numbered tab is not displayed, click it to bring it to the front of the dialog box.

3. Choose a style with appropriate numbering, then click the OK button.

TIP TIP TIP TIP TIP TIP TIP TIP TIP TIP TIP TIP TIP TIP TIP TIP TIP TIP TIP TIP TIP TIP TIP TIP

You can customize the style by selecting it on the Outline Numbered tab, then clicking the Customize button to display the Customize Outline Numbered List dialog box. Customize the style as described in steps 4 through 15 of the previous section, but leave the Link Level To Style drop-down list set to (No Style).

4. Enter the text for the list:

- Press Enter to create another paragraph at the same numbering level as the previous one.

- To demote the current paragraph by one level, click the Increase Indent button (if you're using Outline view) or press Tab with the insertion point at the beginning of the paragraph.

- To promote the current paragraph by one level, click the Decrease Indent button (if you're using Outline view) or press Shift+Tab with the insertion point at the beginning of the paragraph.

To remove outline numbering from a list, click the Numbering button.

Master Documents

Word's master documents and subdocuments can make large projects easier to handle. A *master document* is essentially a regular document made up of a number of *subdocuments*, which are regular Word documents linked to the master document. Once you've created a master document and subdocuments, different people can work in the subdocuments, and when they're done, you can switch to the master document to see how the whole project is shaping up.

You can decide to use master documents and subdocuments at almost any stage of a project: You can create a master document at the beginning of a long work, or you can convert an existing document to a master document once you realize that it will be too big or unwieldy in a single file, or that multiple people will need to work on it at the same time.

SKILL
14

For simplicity, use master documents and subdocuments only when you really need to. For many projects, you'll find it easier to have everything in a single document, without the complications that subdocuments can cause. (If your computer has enough horsepower and memory to run Word under Windows 95, 98, or NT at a respectable speed, it should be able to handle Word documents as long as several hundred pages without perceptible problems.) For other projects—particularly for long documents that contain many graphics files (which make for large Word files) and for documents in which you need to have different people review different sections simultaneously—master documents and subdocuments can be a great boon.

Creating a Master Document

The first step is to create a master document. You can create one either from scratch or from an existing document. There's essentially no difference between the processes—you can open an existing document and make sure it has the appropriate Headings or you can create a new document and type in the Headings. Both get you to the same stage.

Here's how to create a master document:

1. Start a new document (File ➤ New) or open the existing document you want to turn into a master document.

2. Choose View ➤ Outline. Word will switch the document to Outline view and will display the Outlining toolbar.

3. Adapt the existing outline or create a new outline for the document using the outlining techniques earlier in this skill. You can use any number of Heading levels, but use the same Heading style for the Heading that each subdocument will start with. For medium-sized projects, you'll usually find it easiest to use Heading 1 for the titles of the subdocuments.

4. Select the text that you want to turn into subdocuments, making sure that the first Heading in the selected text is the level of Heading at which you want Word to divide the selected text into subdocuments. For example, if you used Heading 1 style for the chapters, make sure that the first Heading in the selected text is Heading 1 style.

    -   If you're creating a master document from scratch, you can enter text in the master document and then select it.

5. Click the Create Subdocument button on the Master Document toolbar. Word will turn the selected text into subdocuments, dividing it at each occurrence of the selected Heading level it finds. (For example, if the first Heading in the selected text is Heading 2, each Heading 2 section will become a separate subdocument.) The start of each subdocument will be indicated by a subdocument icon in the selection bar at the left side of the screen, as shown in Figure 14.5, and each subdocument will be separated from the others by section breaks.

- If you're creating a master document from scratch and want to enter text directly into the subdocuments, select the subdocument Heading and then click the Create Subdocument button. You can then enter text into the subdocument as you wish.

SKILL
14

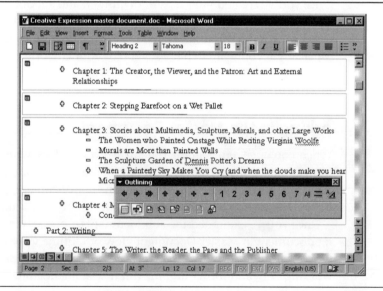

FIGURE 14.5: In Master Document view, Word displays each subdocument in a different section with a subdocument icon to mark the beginning of a new subdocument.

6. Choose File ➤ Save to save the master document; if it's a new document, choose the folder and enter a document name as usual in the Save As dialog box and then click the Save button. Word will save the master document in the regular way and will automatically save all the subdocuments in the

same folder, naming them by the Headings with which they start. If any subdocument filename (including its path) will be more than 255 characters long, Word will truncate the filename at 255 characters.

TIP TIP TIP TIP TIP TIP TIP TIP TIP TIP TIP TIP TIP TIP TIP TIP TIP TIP TIP TIP TIP

Because Word automatically saves the subdocuments in the same folder as the master document, make sure you save the master document to an appropriate folder before creating the subdocuments.

Working with Master Documents and Subdocuments

Once you've created your master document and subdocuments, you can work either in the master document or in the subdocuments. Usually, you'll find it easier to work in the subdocuments when creating and formatting the text—especially if you want to have several of your coworkers work on different subdocuments at the same time. For arranging and managing the project, you'll need to work in the master document.

Working in the Master Document

When you open a master document, Word will display its contents in a collapsed form as a list of hyperlinks to the subdocuments included in the master document (see Figure 14.6). To work in the master document, click the Expand Subdocuments button to display the contents of the subdocuments.

Once you've expanded the subdocuments, you can work with the whole master document in Master Document view or Outline view for rearranging the document's outline, or in Normal view, Print Layout view, or Web Layout view for working with and formatting the full text of the document.

TIP TIP TIP TIP TIP TIP TIP TIP TIP TIP TIP TIP TIP TIP TIP TIP TIP TIP TIP TIP TIP

To switch quickly between Master Document view and Outline view, click the Master Document View button at the right-hand end of the Outlining toolbar.

Word separates the subdocuments in the master document into different sections with an extra section between each subdocument, so section breaks are already in place that you can use for setting up different headers (or footers) in the subdocuments.

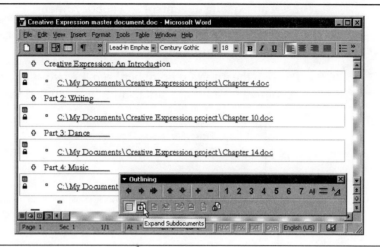

FIGURE 14.6: Word opens a master document in a collapsed form. To work in it, click the Expand Subdocuments button.

Master documents give you several possibilities for printing:

- To get a complete view of your project, choose File ➤ Print Preview in your master document.

- To print the whole of your project, open the Master Document, click the Expand Subdocuments button to expand it, switch to Normal view (View ➤ Normal), and choose File ➤ Print.

- To print an outline of the master document, switch to Master Document view or Outline view and collapse or expand the outline to the level of detail you want. Then choose File ➤ Print.

Inserting a Subdocument in the Master Document

Once you've created your master document, you can easily insert existing documents as subdocuments. As we saw in "Creating a Master Document" earlier in this skill, Word automatically saves subdocuments that you create from a master document in the same folder as the master document; but you can manually insert subdocuments from any available drive and folder into an existing master document. (To keep a project tightly coordinated, however, you may want to move documents to the same folder as the master document before inserting them as subdocuments.)

SKILL
14

To insert an existing document as a subdocument:

1. Expand the master document to show all levels of text by clicking the All button on the Outlining toolbar.

2. Position the insertion point between the two subdocuments in the master document where you want to add the existing document as a subdocument.

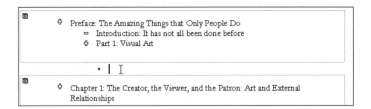

3. Click the Insert Subdocument button on the Master Document toolbar. Word will display an Insert Subdocument dialog box that looks suspiciously like the Open dialog box in disguise.

4. Choose the document to insert and click the Open button. Word will insert it in the master document.

    *   If the subdocument is based on a different template from the master document, it will inherit the master document's settings while the master document is open. (If you open the subdocument later without the master document open, it will appear in its original template.)

Removing a Subdocument from Its Master Document

To remove a subdocument from a master document, select the subdocument icon in the master document and click the Remove Subdocument button. Word will remove the link between the subdocument and the master document, but the subdocument text will remain in the master document and the subdocument file will remain in its previous location on disk. You can then delete the text or move it into another subdocument if necessary—or you can change it without worrying about changing the text in the subdocument at the same time.

Merging Subdocuments

You may occasionally need to combine two or more subdocuments into one subdocument—for example, if you realize that material planned as two sections really should be one section.

To merge subdocuments:

1. Open the master document and click the Expand Subdocuments button to view the subdocuments (rather than the list of hyperlinks).

2. If the subdocuments aren't next to each other, drag them so that they are. Click the subdocument icon for the subdocument you want to move, then drag it to where you want it to appear.

3. Select the first subdocument to merge by clicking its subdocument icon.

4. Select the second subdocument by holding down Shift and clicking its subdocument icon. Repeat this if you want to merge more than two sub-documents.

5. Click the Merge Subdocument button to merge the subdocuments. Word will remove the subdocument icon from the second and subsequent subdoc-uments, and when you save the master document, Word will save the merged subdocuments under the first subdocument's filename.

Splitting a Subdocument

If you realize that, for example, you need to divide one of your chapters into two chapters, you can split the subdocument in question. In Master Document view, enter another Heading of the same level as those that start the other subdocu-ments at the point where you want to split the subdocument, then select the Heading and click the Split Subdocument button.

Renaming a Subdocument

If you need to rename a subdocument, you *must* do it from the master document in Master Document view so that Word can track the change. *Never* rename a subdocument with the Windows Explorer or another file management program; if you do, Word will lose track of the subdocument.

> **WARNING WARNING WARNING WARNING WARNING WARNING WARNING WARNING**
>
> **As mentioned in "Creating a Master Document" earlier in this skill, subdocu-ments that you insert into a master document remain in their original folders; if you rename a subdocument without letting the master document handle the process, the master document will no longer know where the subdocument is.**

In Master Document view, click the hyperlink for the subdocument in order to open the subdocument, choose File ➤ Save As to display the Save As dialog box, enter the new filename or folder for the subdocument, and click the Save button.

If you create subdocuments from a master document, Word automatically saves them in the same folder. If you insert them from other folders, they remain in those folders. Once you've saved the subdocument, choose File ➤ Close to close the subdocument and return to the master document.

Working in Subdocuments

Working in subdocuments is quite straightforward, as they're regular Word documents connected to their master document. You can either open a subdocument in the regular way (via the Open dialog box) or from a master document (by clicking on its hyperlink if the subdocuments are collapsed, or by double-clicking its subdocument icon if the subdocuments are collapsed or expanded).

When you've finished working in a subdocument, save and close it as usual. If you accessed it from the master document, Word will return you to the master document.

WARNING WARNING WARNING WARNING WARNING WARNING WARNING WARNING

The main thing to remember when working with master documents and subdocuments is that only one person can make changes to any one subdocument at a time. Anyone who opens another copy of a subdocument won't be able to save changes to it. And if one person has a master document open, no one else will be able to save changes to it or any of its subdocuments.

Locking and Unlocking Master Documents and Subdocuments

As we saw in the previous section, one way to protect your master document and subdocuments against changes is to keep the master document open all the time. There is a more practical choice, though: You can *lock* them against changes. This can be particularly valuable when you're sharing documents on a network.

To lock a master document or subdocument:

1. Open the master document and click the Expand Subdocuments button to expand the subdocuments.

2. Click in the subdocument you want to lock. If you want to lock the master document, click anywhere in it (i.e., *not* in any of its subdocuments).

3.   Click the Lock Document button on the Master Document toolbar to lock the subdocument or master document.

- If the master document or subdocument contains unsaved changes, Word will prompt you to save them.

- When you lock a master document, Word displays the words **(Read-Only)** in the title bar.

- When you lock a subdocument, Word displays a padlock icon beneath the subdocument icon in Master Document view.

Chapter 4: Master or Dilettante? Does it matter to you?

To unlock a locked master document or subdocument, click in it and then click the Lock Document button. Word will remove the **(Read-Only)** or padlock icon from the master document or subdocument respectively.

> **WARNING WARNING WARNING WARNING WARNING WARNING WARNING WARNING**
> **Locking subdocuments works only while the master document is open—once the master document has been closed, you can open any of its supposedly locked subdocuments without encountering any security. To learn more about tighter security for your documents, turn to Skill 18.**

Are You Experienced?

Now you can...

- ☑ outline an existing document
- ☑ create a new document in Outline view
- ☑ rearrange an outline
- ☑ promote and demote items in an outline
- ☑ create outline numbered lists
- ☑ create master documents and subdocuments
- ☑ work with master documents and subdocuments

Creating Complex Documents

- ⊙ **Creating newspaper-style columns**
- ⊙ **Creating a table of contents**
- ⊙ **Changing the styles of a table of contents**
- ⊙ **Creating a table of figures**
- ⊙ **Creating a table of authorities**
- ⊙ **Creating and building an index**

In this skill, we'll look at several features that Word provides for working with long documents and complex documents. We'll start with newspaper-style snaking columns, which are useful for creating newsletters and multi-column reports. From there we'll move on to generating tables of contents, tables of figures, and tables of authorities, which provide key reference information for long documents. Finally, we'll look at the features that Word provides for marking index entries and creating indexes.

Columns

To create columns in a document, you can either convert existing text to columns or create columns and then enter the text in them.

Word uses sections (discussed in Skill 5) to separate text formatted in different numbers of columns from the rest of the document. If the whole of a document contains the same number of columns, Word doesn't need section breaks, but if the document contains one-column and two-column text, Word will divide the text with section breaks; likewise, two-column text will be separated from three-column text, three-column text from four-column text from two-column text, and so on.

NOTE NOTE NOTE NOTE NOTE NOTE NOTE NOTE NOTE NOTE NOTE NOTE NOTE NOTE NOTE

Word displays column layouts only in Print Layout view and in Print Preview. In Normal view, Online Layout view, and Outline view, Word won't indicate how the columns in your document will look.

Creating Columns Quickly with the Columns Button

To create columns quickly, without worrying about formatting details:

1. To create columns from existing text, select it. To create columns in only one part of your document, select that part.

2. Click the Columns button on the Standard toolbar and drag down and to the right over the grid that appears to indicate how many columns you

want. Release the mouse button. Word will create the columns, will switch the page to Print Layout view, and will display the Document Map.

You can adjust the width of the columns, and the space between them, by dragging the margin markers in the ruler.

Creating Columns with the Columns Dialog Box

For more control over the columns you create, use the Columns dialog box instead of the Columns button:

1. To create columns from existing text, first select the text. To create columns in only one part of your document, select that part.

2. Choose Format ➤ Columns to display the Columns dialog box (see Figure 15.1).

SKILL
▼ 15

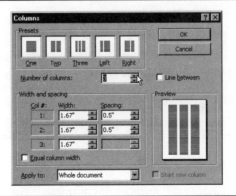

FIGURE 15.1: The Columns dialog box gives you fine control over the number of and formatting of columns.

3. Choose the number of columns you want to create, either by clicking one of the buttons in the Presets list or by entering a number in the Number Of Columns box. (These settings affect each other.) Watch the Preview box as you choose the settings for your columns.

4. If need be, adjust the column width and spacing in the Width And Spacing group box.

   • If you chose two or more columns and want to produce columns of varying widths, clear the Equal Column Width check box.

   • In the Width box for each column, enter the column width you want. In the Spacing box, enter the amount of space you want between this column and the column to its right.

5. To add a line between each column on your page, select the Line Between check box.

6. Click the OK button to close the Columns dialog box and create the columns with the settings you chose.

Changing the Number of Columns

Once you've created columns in a document, you can change the number of columns by selecting the relevant text and using either the Columns button or the Columns dialog box:

• Click the Columns button on the Standard toolbar and drag the grid that appears until you've selected the number of columns you want.

• Choose Format ➤ Columns to make adjustments to the columns as described in the previous section.

Starting a New Column

To start a new column at the top of the page:

1. Place the insertion point at the beginning of the text that will start the new column.

2. Choose Format ➤ Columns to display the Columns dialog box.

3. Choose the number of columns, their layout, and their width.

4. In the Apply To drop-down list, choose This Point Forward.

5. Select the Start New Column check box.

6. Click the OK button to close the Columns dialog box. Word will create the new column or columns from the insertion point forward, inserting a section break between the old columns and the new.

Removing Columns from Text

The way Word thinks, you don't so much remove columns from text as adjust the number of columns. For example, to "remove" two-column formatting from text, you change the text to a single-column layout.

The easiest way to switch back to a single-column layout is to click the Columns button on the Formatting toolbar and drag through the resulting grid to select the one-column bar, then release the mouse button. Alternatively, choose Format ➢ Columns to display the Columns dialog box, choose One from the Presets group box, and then click the OK button.

TIP TIP TIP TIP TIP TIP TIP TIP TIP TIP TIP TIP TIP TIP TIP TIP TIP TIP TIP TIP TIP TIP TIP TIP TIP

To switch only part of a document back to a single-column format, select that part before clicking the Columns button or choosing One in the Presets group box of the Columns dialog box. To switch an entire section, place the insertion point anywhere within that section.

Creating a Table of Contents

SKILL
15

Tables of contents are an area in which word processing programs beat human intervention hands-down. You can create a table of contents for a document with just a few commands and then have Word update it at a moment's notice. This is especially useful for a Web page in which you're often changing the content and you need the table of contents always to be up to date.

Word uses paragraph styles to create tables of contents, so make sure you've applied styles to your document before starting. Typically, Word will use the Heading 1 to Heading 9 styles to create the table of contents (assigning the styles TOC 1 through TOC 9 to the resulting entries), but you can also use other styles for the table of contents if you've arranged your document that way. (You can also use table of contents fields, which work much more slowly.)

Creating a Table of Contents from Heading Styles

To create a table of contents from the Heading styles in a document:

1. Position the insertion point where you want the table of contents to appear in your document.

2. Choose Insert ➢ Index And Tables to display the Index And Tables dialog box.

3. If the Table Of Contents tab (see Figure 15.2) isn't at the front of the dialog box, click it to bring it there.

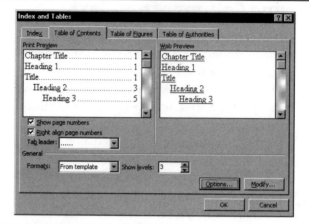

FIGURE 15.2: Choose options for your table of contents on the Table Of Contents tab of the Index And Tables dialog box.

4. Pick a format for the table of contents from the Formats box. (Watch the Print Preview box and the Web Preview box to see what looks best—often From Template is a good choice if you're working with a template that has table of contents styles defined.)

5. In the Show Levels box, choose the number of heading levels you want to include (from one to nine).

6. Choose options for page numbers in the bottom-left corner of the dialog box—whether to include page numbers and (if you do) whether to right-align them or have each appear directly after the heading title it refers to. Right-alignment is not available if the format involves centered text.

7. If you chose to include page numbers, check the Tab Leader setting (it may be set to [none], periods, hyphens, underscores, or raised dots), and, if need be, choose a better tab leader character than the one Word suggests.

8. Click the OK button to insert the table of contents.

Word inserts the table of contents as a huge field containing hyperlinks to the headings. To move to a heading, click it in the table of contents.

Creating a Table of Contents from Different Styles

If you want to create a table of contents from styles other than Heading 1 through Heading 9, click the Options button on the Table Of Contents tab in the Index And Tables dialog box. Word will display the Table Of Contents Options dialog box (see Figure 15.3).

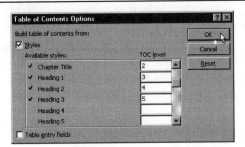

FIGURE 15.3: In the Table Of Contents Options dialog box, choose the styles you want to include in your table of contents by entering the level you want to assign to each heading in the corresponding TOC Level box.

Scroll through the list of styles to the ones you want. Type the TOC entry level you want to assign it in the box next to the heading level style. Remove the level assignments from boxes next to the Heading styles that you don't want to use.

TIP TIP TIP TIP TIP TIP TIP TIP TIP TIP TIP TIP TIP TIP TIP TIP TIP TIP TIP TIP TIP TIP TIP

You can create a table of contents that omits certain Heading styles and assigns higher priority than usual to the other styles. For example, by deleting the *2* Word typically puts next to Heading 2 and the *3* next to Heading 3, and by entering 2 next to Heading 3 and 3 next to Heading 9, you can create a table of contents in which the order of importance is Heading 1, Heading 3, and then Heading 9; the other Heading levels will not appear. You can also create a table of contents that doesn't use any of the Heading styles, should your documents be laid out in such a way as to make this necessary (for example, without headings, or with headings used for elements that you don't want in the table of contents).

Click the OK button to close the Table Of Contents Options dialog box and return to the Index And Tables dialog box, where the Preview box will reflect your changes. Click the OK button to create and insert the table of contents.

Changing the TOC Styles

If the TOC styles in the current document's template are too fancy or plain for your liking, you can change them easily from the Index And Tables dialog box. However, this works only for the From Template format—you can't change Word's own TOC formats, such as Classic or Distinctive.

Click the Modify button to display a stripped-down edition of the Style dialog box we met in Skill 5. Choose the TOC style to change in the Styles list box and then click the Modify button. Modify the style as described in "Modifying a Style" in Skill 2.

When you've finished changing the styles, click the Apply button to return to the Index And Tables dialog box.

Updating Your Table of Contents

To update a table of contents, right-click in it and choose Update Field from the context menu. Word will display the Update Table Of Contents dialog box; choose Update Page Numbers Only if you haven't added any headings to the table of contents or if you've applied formatting to it that you don't want to lose; otherwise, choose Update Entire Table to update the headings and the page numbers.

TIP TIP TIP TIP TIP TIP TIP TIP TIP TIP TIP TIP TIP TIP TIP TIP TIP TIP TIP TIP TIP TIP TIP

You can also update a table of contents by choosing Insert ➤ Index And Tables again. Word will ask if you want to overwrite the current table of contents; click the OK button if you do. This way, you can also modify the table of contents if you want to.

Table of Figures

Word's tables of figures are specialized tables of contents produced from the automatic captions we discussed in Skill 8.

To insert a table of figures:

1. Place the insertion point where you want the table of figures to appear in your document.

2. Choose Insert ➤ Index And Tables to display the Index And Tables dialog box. Click the Table Of Figures tab to bring it to the front (see Figure 15.4).

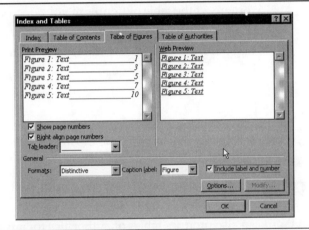

FIGURE 15.4: Choose options for the table of figures on the Table Of Figures tab in the Index And Tables dialog box.

3. In the Formats box, choose a format for the table of figures. You'll notice that this is a different list from that for tables of contents, but you can still choose From Template if you have custom styles defined.

4. Choose options for page numbers and tab leaders as appropriate.

5. Clear the Include Label And Number check box if you don't want *Figure 44.1* or whatever appearing in the list of figures. Watch the Print Preview box and the Preview box for the effect this will produce.

6. If you want to build a table of figures from table entry fields rather than captions, or as well as captions, click the Options button and make your choices in the Table Of Figures Options dialog box. You can also choose to

produce the table of figures from a style other than Caption (for example, you could use Heading 8—or any other style that you had chosen to use to identify your figures). Click the OK button after you've made your choices.

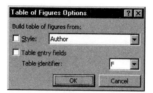

7. Click the OK button to close the Index And Tables dialog box and have Word insert the table of figures in your document.

> Figure 1: Monet at work in Robespierre's boudoir (Fred Shakespeare) ·············· 1
> Figure 2: Miller visiting the Atomic Energy Research Bureau (Andy Zloty) ·········· 8
> Figure 3: Everything Reminds Me of Croydon (Rikki Nadir) ······················· 28

TIP TIP TIP TIP TIP TIP TIP TIP TIP TIP TIP TIP TIP TIP TIP TIP TIP TIP TIP TIP TIP TIP TIP TIP

You can quickly modify the Table Of Figures style by clicking the Modify button.

Table of Authorities

Word can also produce tables of authorities for any case, statute, or treatise you happen to be working on. (Tables of authorities are specialized tables citing the sources referenced in legal or scholarly works. You probably won't want to use them unless you're producing legal documents, theses, or the like.)

Before you can create a table of authorities, you need to mark the citations to be included in it.

To mark citations for a table of authorities:

1   Select the first citation (a long citation—one with all the details) and press Alt+Shift+I to display the Mark Citation dialog box (see Figure 15.5) with the citation displayed in the Selected Text and Short Citation boxes.

2. Use shortcut keys (such as Ctrl+B for boldface and Ctrl+I for italic) to format the citation in the Selected Text box.

3. Edit the Short Citation box to match the other citations of this authority in the document.

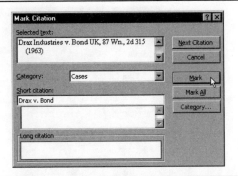

FIGURE 15.5: Coordinate your citations in the Mark Citation dialog box.

4. Choose a category from the Category drop-down list: Cases, Statutes, Other Authorities, Rules, Treatises, Regulations, Constitutional Provisions, or a category that you've defined by using the Category button.

5. Click the Mark button to mark each citation for this authority in turn or Mark All to mark them all at once. Word will perform the marking and will add the citation to the list in the Short Citation list box, with its full text appearing in the Long Citation box.

6. Click the Next Citation button to have Word look for the next citation; when it finds it, repeat the marking process.

7. Click the Close button when you've finished marking all the citations.

Compared to marking the citations, creating the table of authorities is easy. To create the table of authorities:

1. Place the insertion point where you want the table of authorities to appear within the document.

2. Choose Insert ➤ Index And Tables to display the Index And Tables dialog box, then click the Table Of Authorities tab to bring it to the front (see Figure 15.6).

3. Choose a format for the table of authorities from the Formats list box.

4. In the Category drop-down list, choose whether to include all authorities or only those for Cases or Statutes, etc.

SKILL 15

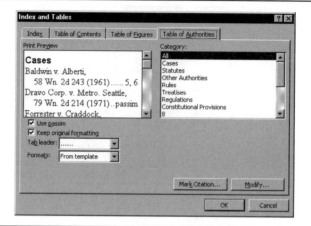

FIGURE 15.6: Choose options for your table of authorities on the Table Of Authorities tab in the Index And Tables dialog box.

5. Make sure the Use Passim check box has been selected if you want authorities with five or more references to be marked with *passim* (throughout the document) rather than with page references.

6. Click the OK button to have Word compile the table of authorities.

> **Cases**
> Baldwin v. Alberti, 58 Wn. 2d 243 (1961)...29
> Drax Industries v. Bond UK, 87 Wn., 2d 315 (1963)...passim
> John Matrix v. Rikki Nadir Industries 89 Wn. 2d. 386 (1998)....................................4, 11

TIP TIP TIP TIP TIP TIP TIP TIP TIP TIP TIP TIP TIP TIP TIP TIP TIP TIP TIP TIP TIP TIP

To update a table of authorities, right-click in it and choose Update Field. To modify the styles in a table of authorities, click the Modify button on the Table Of Authorities tab in the Index And Tables dialog box.

Creating an Index

If you've ever used a good index or been frustrated by an inadequate one, you know that good indexes simply *must* be harder to put together than tables of contents. And indeed they are—though Word gives you as much help as it can in automating the procedure. You don't even have to wait until the end of your project before starting to put the codes for the index entries in. You can add them as you go along, which helps make sure you don't forget to index vital elements in the mad rush to complete a project. Generally speaking, though, waiting until the end of the project lets you benefit most from Word's indexing features.

Creating an index in Word consists of marking index entries throughout your document and then telling Word to create the index. Once the index has been created, you can rearrange your document at will and easily update the index to make sure it includes the latest page numbers.

Marking Index Entries

To mark index entries:

1. Select a word or phrase you want to make into an index entry.

2. Press Alt+Shift+X to open the Mark Index Entry dialog box (see Figure 15.7) with the selected word or phrase in it. (You can also choose Insert ➤ Index And Tables and click the Mark Entry button on the Index tab of the Index And Tables dialog box.)

SKILL
15

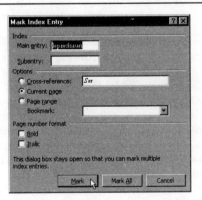

FIGURE 15.7: Set up your index entry in the Mark Index Entry dialog box.

3. Click the Mark button to mark this particular instance of the selected word or phrase as an index entry, or click the Mark All button to mark every instance of the selected word or phrase.

    • To create a subentry, verify the selected entry in the Main Entry box and enter the subentry in the Subentry box.

    • To create a cross-reference, click the Cross-Reference option button in the Options box and enter the name of the entry to see after the word *See* (which you could change to *See also* if you wanted to).

    • To enter ranges of pages (e.g., 10–12), which are a little trickier, mark the range with a bookmark before inserting the index entry (see "Using Bookmarks" in Skill 8 for a discussion of how bookmarks work). Once you've placed the bookmark, choose the Page Range option button in the Options group box and select the name of the bookmark from the Bookmark drop-down list.

4. The Mark Index Entry dialog box stays open until you close it so you can add cross-references or subentries to your original entry. (Once you've marked an entry, the Cancel button changes to a Close button.)

5. Repeat steps 1 through 4 for the remaining entries in your document.

TIP TIP TIP TIP TIP TIP TIP TIP TIP TIP TIP TIP TIP TIP TIP TIP TIP TIP TIP TIP TIP TIP TIP TIP

There's a quicker way to mark index entries, but it requires a good deal of preparation. You create a *concordance file* consisting of a two-column table (Table ➢ Insert Table) that contains, in the left-hand column, all the words you want indexed (one per cell), and in the right-hand column, the entries for those words. For example, in the left-hand column you might enter **John Smith** as the name for Word to find, and in the right-hand column **Smith, John** for the entry. When you've created the concordance file, save it and close it. Then, with the document to be indexed open, click the AutoMark button on the Index tab of the Index And Tables dialog box and choose the concordance file in the Open Index AutoMark File dialog box. When you click the Open button, Word marks all the entries at once.

Inserting the Index

To create and insert the index:

1. Place the insertion point at the end of your document (or wherever you want the index to appear).

2. Choose Insert ➤ Index And Tables to display the Index And Tables dialog box. Click the Index tab to bring it to the front of the dialog box (see Figure 15.8).

3. Choose the type of index in the Type box: Indented usually is easier to read, but Run-in can save you a lot of space if your index is long.

4. Choose a style for the index from the Formats list box. Watch the Print Preview box to get a rough idea of how it will look.

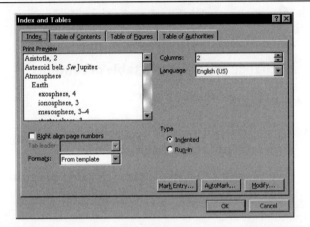

FIGURE 15.8: Choose index options on the Index tab of the Index And Tables dialog box.

5. Choose the number of columns in which to lay out the index in the Columns box. A two-column index is normal, but three columns sometimes work well on $8\frac{1}{2}" \times 11"$ paper (or when you're desperate for space).

6. Click the OK button to insert the index. Word will repaginate your document and build the index.

   To update an index, right-click anywhere in it and choose Update Field from the context menu.

SKILL
15

Are You Experienced?

Now you can...

- ☑ create newspaper-style columns
- ☑ resize columns
- ☑ remove multiple columns for a document
- ☑ create a table of contents
- ☑ change the styles of a table of contents
- ☑ create a table of figures
- ☑ create a table of authorities
- ☑ create and build an index
- ☑ update a table of contents, a table of figures, a table of authorities, or an index

Customizing Word to Suit You

- ⊕ **Customizing toolbars**
- ⊕ **Customizing menus and context menus**
- ⊕ **Customizing keyboard shortcuts**
- ⊕ **Creating your own toolbars and menus**
- ⊕ **Setting Word options**

One of Word's most appealing features is that you can customize the *user interface* to the *n*th degree. The user interface is the face that the application presents to the user—the screen, the menus, the toolbars, the keyboard shortcuts, and so on.

In the first part of this skill, we'll look at how you can create your own toolbars and menus and how you can strip down—or even remove completely—the menus that Word provides. In the second half of the skill, we'll look at the environment options that Word provides—such as the Edit and File Locations options—and see how you can optimize Word for your work.

Customizing Toolbars and the Menu Bar

As we saw in Skill 1, not only can you display any number of Word's toolbars on screen at one time, but you can also float them (and the menu bar) in the middle of the screen and reshape them at will. In this section, I'll discuss how you can create new toolbars, modify your own toolbars or Word's existing ones, and delete your own toolbars.

Creating a New Toolbar

To create a new toolbar:

1. Right-click on the menu bar or on any displayed toolbar to display the context menu of toolbars, then choose Customize.

2. On the Toolbars tab, click the New button to display the New Toolbar dialog box.

3. Enter a name for the new toolbar in the Toolbar Name text box.

4. If you want to make the toolbar available only to the current template, choose the template's name in the Make Toolbar Available To drop-down list. Otherwise, make sure Normal (or Normal.dot) is selected in the Make Toolbar Available To drop-down list.

5.   Click the OK button to create the toolbar. Word will display the new toolbar (with space for just one button, and most of its name truncated) somewhere within easy commuting distance of the Customize dialog box (see Figure 16.1).

FIGURE 16.1: Drag buttons from the Customize dialog box to the new toolbar.

6.   Click the Commands tab to display it, then add the buttons you want to the new toolbar:

- In the Categories list box, select the type of command you're looking for. The Categories list includes all the regular menus (from File through Window and Help), together with Web, Drawing, AutoShapes, Borders, Mail Merge, Forms, Control Toolbox, All Commands, Macros, Fonts, AutoText, Styles, Built-in Menus, and New Menu.

- When you choose the category, the available items for it appear in the Commands list box. Click the item you want and drag it to the toolbar. To see a description of the selected item (for example, to make sure you've gotten hold of the command you thought you had and not one of its close relatives), click the Description button to display a pop-up description of the command.

- If the item you dragged to the toolbar has a button associated with it, Word will add that button to the toolbar. (You'll see any button associated with an item beside the listing of the item in the Commands list box.) If the item doesn't have a button associated with it, Word will create a text button containing a description of the button you dragged.

For example, if you drag the Heading 1 style to the toolbar, Word will create a button named *Heading 1 Style*. You can now rename the button by right-clicking it (or by clicking the Modify Selection button in the Customize dialog box) and entering another name in the Name box. You can also choose an image for the button by right-clicking and choosing Change Button Image from the context menu.

- To rearrange the buttons on the new toolbar, drag and drop each button while the Customize dialog box is open. To remove a button from the toolbar, drag it off and drop it somewhere in the document or in the Customize dialog box. To create a separator line between one button and the button to its left, drag the button a little farther to the right, and Word will automatically add a separator bar.

7. Click the Close button in the Customize dialog box when you've finished creating your toolbar.

Modifying a Toolbar

Word 2000 provides two ways of modifying a toolbar. The first way works only for built-in toolbars and the buttons that Word associates with each toolbar; you cannot use it to modify custom toolbars, and you cannot use it to add to a built-in toolbar any buttons other than those Word associates with the toolbar. The more traditional way of customizing toolbars works for any toolbar (built-in or custom, in both Word 97 and Word 2000) and provides access to the full range of buttons.

To modify a built-in toolbar in Word 2000:

1. Click the More Buttons button at the right-hand end of the toolbar (or at the bottom end of a vertically oriented toolbar) to display a panel containing any undisplayed buttons and the Add Or Remove Buttons button.

2. Move the mouse pointer over the Add Or Remove Buttons button, or click it, to display a context menu of buttons that can be displayed quickly on the toolbar (see Figure 16.2). This set of buttons contains those that Word considers to be related to the toolbar. Buttons that have a check mark next to

them will be displayed; buttons that have a blank square next to them will be hidden.

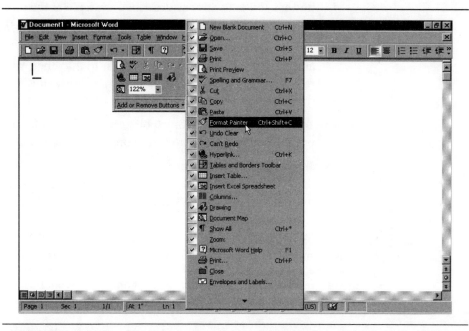

FIGURE 16.2: Use the context menu of buttons to quickly choose which buttons appear on a toolbar.

3. Click to place check marks next to the buttons you want to display; clear the boxes for those buttons that you do not want to display.

4. When you've finished customizing the toolbar, click the More Buttons button again to collapse the context menu and the pop-up panel. (Alternatively, click anywhere in the document.)

To modify a toolbar using the more traditional method that works for any toolbar and for both Word 97 and Word 2000:

1. Display the toolbar on screen by right-clicking the menu bar or any displayed toolbar, then selecting that toolbar in the context menu of toolbars. Alternatively, choose View ➤ Toolbars and select the toolbar from the Toolbars submenu.

2. Add, move, copy, or remove buttons as appropriate:

  - To add buttons to a toolbar, choose Tools ➤ Customize and add the buttons to the toolbar as described in step 6 of the previous section. Close the Customize dialog box when you've finished.

  - To move a button from one toolbar to another, hold down the Alt key and drag the button from one toolbar to the other. You can also rearrange the buttons on a toolbar by holding down the Alt key and dragging the buttons.

  - To copy a button from one toolbar to another, hold down Ctrl+Alt while dragging the button from one toolbar to the other.

  - To remove a button from the toolbar, hold down the Alt key and drag the button off the toolbar and into an open space in a document. Drop the button there and it'll disappear.

WARNING WARNING WARNING WARNING WARNING WARNING WARNING WARNING

If you remove a custom button (one that you've created) from a toolbar as described above, Word will delete the details of the button, so you'll have to re-create it from scratch if you want to use it again. To avoid this, you may want to create a storage toolbar and use it to safely store buttons for future use.

Deleting a Toolbar

To delete a toolbar you've created, right-click in the menu bar or any displayed toolbar and choose Customize from the context menu to display the Customize dialog box. On the Toolbars tab, select the toolbar you want to delete and then click the Delete button. Word will display a message box asking if you want to delete the toolbar; choose OK. Click the Close button to exit the Customize dialog box.

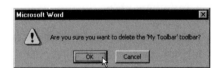

NOTE NOTE NOTE NOTE NOTE NOTE NOTE NOTE NOTE NOTE NOTE NOTE NOTE NOTE NOTE

Word won't let you delete any of its toolbars—you can delete only toolbars you've created.

Renaming a Toolbar

To rename a toolbar you've created, right-click in either the menu bar or any displayed toolbar and choose Customize from the context menu to display the Customize dialog box. Highlight the toolbar to rename in the Toolbars list box on the Toolbars tab. Click the Rename button to display the Rename Toolbar dialog box and specify the new name for the toolbar in the Toolbar Name text box, as shown here. Click the OK button to rename the toolbar and then click the Close button to close the Customize dialog box.

Copying a Toolbar from One Template to Another

To copy a toolbar you've created from one template to another, open the Organizer dialog box by choosing Tools ➢ Templates And Add-Ins and clicking the Organizer button in the Templates And Add-ins dialog box. Click the Toolbars tab to bring it to the front of the Organizer dialog box (see Figure 16.3), displaying the toolbars in Normal (the global template) in one panel and the toolbars in the current document in the other panel.

SKILL 16

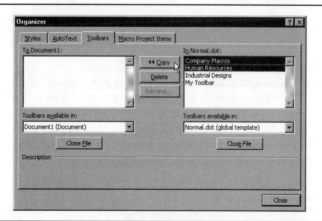

FIGURE 16.3: The Organizer box lets you copy toolbars from one template to another.

To work with the template for the current document, select it from the Toolbars Available In drop-down list in the panel listing the current document. Otherwise, open the templates you want: Click the Close File button on either side of the dialog box to close the currently open file, then click the Open File button (into which the Close File button will have metamorphosed) and choose the template you want from the Open dialog box that Word then displays.

Copy the toolbar by selecting it from the left-hand or right-hand box and clicking the Copy button. When you click the Close button to exit the Organizer dialog box, Word will invite you to save any changes to affected templates; choose Yes. If you copy a toolbar to an open document, Word will not prompt you to save changes.

Customizing Menus

You can customize menus by adding the extra items that you need, from extra Word commands to macros you create (as discussed in Bonus Online Skill 1). You can also remove from menus any items that you don't use—or that you don't want other people to use. Better yet, you can remove entire menus and add menus of your own.

You can customize both the menus that appear on the menu bar at the top of the Word window and the context menus that appear when you right-click in Word.

Adding Items to Menus

By strategically adding items to menus, you can have all the commands, styles, macros, and fonts that you need right on hand.

To add an item to a menu:

1. Right-click the menu bar or any displayed toolbar and choose Customize from the context menu, or choose Tools ➤ Customize, to open the Customize dialog box.

2. If you want to add items to the context menus, select the Shortcut Menus check box on the Toolbars tab.

3. Click the Commands tab to bring it to the front (see Figure 16.4).

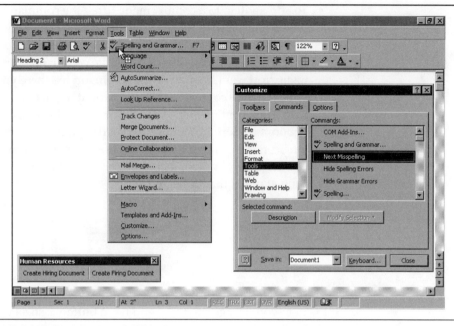

FIGURE 16.4: Adding items to menus from the Commands tab of the Customize dialog box

SKILL
16

NOTE NOTE NOTE NOTE NOTE NOTE NOTE NOTE NOTE NOTE NOTE NOTE NOTE NOTE NOTE

To make changes in a template other than Normal (the global template), open a document based on that template—before starting these steps—and choose the template in the Save In drop-down list in the Customize dialog box. To make changes to an open document, select the document in the Save In drop-down list.

4.   In the Categories list box, select the category of item to add.

5.   In the Commands list box, click the command and drag it to the name of the menu to which you want to add it. Keep holding the mouse button down as Word displays the menu, then drag the command down the menu (and across to any submenu if necessary) to where you want it to appear. Word will indicate with a black bar where the command will land. Drop it when it's in the right place. Alternatively, click the menu to display it before selecting and dragging the command to it.

- To add an item to a context menu, drag the command over the button on the Shortcut Menus toolbar that describes the type of context menu you want: Text, Table, or Draw. Word will display a context menu of the context menus available. Drag the command over the entry for the menu you want, then drag the command to where you want it to appear on the context menu, and drop it. For example, to add an item to the Text context menu, you would drag the item over the Text button on the Shortcut Menus toolbar, drag it down to the bottom of the long context menu of text context menus that appeared until the mouse pointer was over Text, then drag the item to a suitable position on the context menu that appeared.

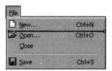

5. If the item you dragged to the menu has a button associated with it, Word will add that button along with the name of the command to the menu. (You'll see any button associated with an item beside the listing of the item in the Commands list box.) You can now rename the menu item by right-clicking it and entering another name in the Name box, or you can choose an image by right-clicking and choosing Change Button Image from the context menu (to add an existing button) or Edit Button Image (to create a new button in the Button Editor).

TIP TIP TIP TIP TIP TIP TIP TIP TIP TIP TIP TIP TIP TIP TIP TIP TIP TIP TIP TIP TIP TIP TIP TIP TIP

You can add an *access key* (also known as a "hotkey" or—bizarrely—a "mnemonic") for the item by putting an ampersand (&) before the access key letter. For best results, make sure the letter you choose isn't already an access key for another item on the menu.

6. Add more items to any of the menus or click the Close button to close the Customize dialog box.

Modifying Menus and Removing Items

To remove one item quickly from a menu, press Ctrl+Alt+– (that's the hyphen key, but think of it as the minus key). The mouse pointer will change to a short, thick horizontal line. With this mouse pointer showing, pull down a menu and click the item you want to remove.

TIP TIP TIP TIP TIP TIP TIP TIP TIP TIP TIP TIP TIP TIP TIP TIP TIP TIP TIP TIP TIP TIP

If you decide not to remove an item, press Esc to restore the mouse pointer to normal.

To remove a number of items from a menu, display the Customize dialog box by right-clicking and choosing Customize from the context menu or by choosing Tools ➤ Customize. Then:

- Reposition a menu item by clicking it and dragging it to a different position on that menu, on a different menu, or on a toolbar.

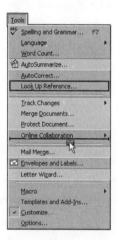

- Remove a menu item by dragging it and dropping it in blank space in the document (or anywhere in the Customize dialog box). Word will display an X next to the mouse pointer as you drag the item to indicate that it will be removed.

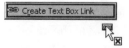

Restoring Word's Menus to their Defaults

You can restore any of Word's predefined menus in any given template to its default state—and at once wipe out any and all changes you've made to it—by opening the Customize dialog box, right-clicking the name of the menu you want to restore, and then choosing Reset from the context menu.

Customizing the Menu Bar

You can customize Word's menu bar by adding menus, removing menus, and renaming menus. To do so, first display the Customize dialog box by right-clicking either the menu bar or any displayed toolbar and choosing Customize from the context menu or by choosing Tools ➤ Customize. Then click the Commands tab to display it and verify the setting in the Save Changes In drop-down list to make sure you're working in the right template.

Adding Menus

To add a menu to the menu bar or to a toolbar:

1. Display the Commands tab of the Customize dialog box.

2. In the Categories list box, select New Menu.

3. Drag the New Menu item from the Commands list box and drop it where you want it to appear—either on the menu bar or on a toolbar (see Figure 16.5). Word will name the new menu *New Menu*, which you'll probably want to change.

4. Right-click the menu name (or click the Modify Selection button) to display the context menu, then drag through the Name box to select its contents. Enter a suitable name for the new menu. Put an ampersand (&) before the letter you want to use as an access key. Make sure this access key letter isn't already assigned to another menu.

5. Repeat steps 3 and 4 if you need to add another menu. Otherwise, you can now add items to the menu as described in the section titled "Adding Items to Menus" earlier in the skill.

6. When you're finished, click the Close button to close the Customize dialog box.

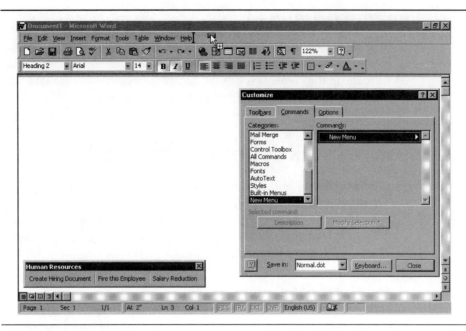

FIGURE 16.5: To add a new menu, drag the New Menu item to the menu bar or to a toolbar.

Removing Menus

You can remove a menu from the menu bar or from a toolbar in either of two ways:

- If you have the Customize dialog box open, click on the menu name, drag it off the menu bar or toolbar, and drop it either in open space in the Word window or in the Customize dialog box.

- If you do not have the Customize dialog box open, hold down the Alt key, click on the menu name, drag it off the menu bar or toolbar, and drop it in open space in the Word window.

Renaming Menus

To rename a menu, first display the Customize dialog box (Tools ➤ Customize). Then right-click the menu name to display the context menu, edit the menu's name in the Name text box (putting an ampersand before the letter you want to use as an access key), and press Enter. You can then perform further customization or click the Close button to close the Customize dialog box.

Customizing Keyboard Shortcuts

Even if you're not a die-hard WordStar user who's finally upgraded to Word, you can speed and simplify your work by customizing the keyboard to suit your needs. While Word comes with an impressive array of preprogrammed keyboard shortcuts, you're likely to find other items that you need to have on hand instead. (If you *are* a former WordStar user, you can remap most of the keyboard so that you don't need to change your habits.)

Most of the keyboard shortcuts in Word perform a particular command available from the menus or the toolbars. For example, the Ctrl+P keyboard shortcut is the equivalent of choosing File ➤ Print, and the Ctrl+B shortcut is the equivalent of clicking the Bold button on the Formatting toolbar. There are also keyboard shortcuts for inserting symbols (such as ®) and special characters (such as —, an em dash).

Assigning a Keyboard Shortcut

To set a keyboard shortcut:

1. Choose Tools ➤ Customize to display the Customize dialog box.

2. Click the Keyboard button to display the Customize Keyboard dialog box (see Figure 16.6).

NOTE NOTE NOTE NOTE NOTE NOTE NOTE NOTE NOTE NOTE NOTE NOTE NOTE NOTE NOTE

To customize a keyboard shortcut for a symbol or special character, you can display the Customize Keyboard dialog box by selecting the Shortcut Key button on either the Symbols tab or the Special Characters tab of the Symbol dialog box (Insert ➤ Symbol). This displays the Customize Keyboard dialog box with only the Common Symbols category available in the Categories list box.

3. Specify the template to change in the Save Changes In drop-down list, if necessary. (Leave Normal selected if you want the changes to apply to all templates that do not have this keyboard combination set to another command.)

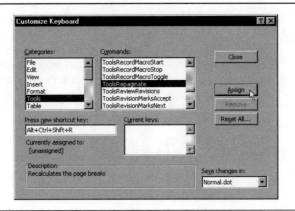

FIGURE 16.6: Setting keyboard shortcuts in the Customize Keyboard dialog box

4. In the Categories list, select the category of item for the new keyboard shortcut.

5. Choose the item to add in the Commands list box. (If you chose Macros, Fonts, AutoText, Styles, or Common Symbols in the Categories list, the list box will change its name to suit your choice—Macros, Fonts, and so on.)

6. Click in the Press New Shortcut Key box and press the key combination you want; Word will display the combination you choose in the Press New Shortcut Key box. A key combination can be any of the following:

- Alt plus a regular key not used for a menu access key
- Alt plus a function key
- Ctrl plus a regular key or function key
- Ctrl+Alt plus a regular key or function key
- Shift plus a function key
- Ctrl+Shift plus a regular key or function key
- Alt+Shift plus a regular key or function key
- Ctrl+Alt+Shift plus a regular key or function key

Because this last option involves using four fingers (or thumbs), you may want to reserve this for seldom-used commands—or for pianists.

SKILL 16

NOTE NOTE NOTE NOTE NOTE NOTE NOTE NOTE NOTE NOTE NOTE NOTE NOTE NOTE NOTE

You can set up shortcut keys that have two steps—for example, Ctrl+Alt+F, 1 and Ctrl+Alt+F, 2—by pressing the second key (in this case, the 1 or the 2, though you can use any key) after pressing the key combination. These tend to be more trouble than they're worth unless you're assigning literally hundreds of extra shortcut keys.

7. Check the Currently Assigned To area under the Press New Shortcut Key box to see if that key combination is already assigned. (If it is and you don't want to overwrite it, press Backspace to clear the Press New Shortcut Key box and then choose another combination.)

8. Click the Assign button to assign the shortcut.

9. Either assign more keyboard shortcuts or click the Close button to close the Customize Keyboard dialog box.

10. Click the Close button to close the Customize dialog box.

You can now press the shortcut key combination to invoke the command or to insert the character or symbol.

Removing a Keyboard Shortcut

Usually you remove a keyboard shortcut by assigning that shortcut to another item—for example, if you assign Ctrl+P to a Photograph style you've created, Word will overwrite Ctrl+P as the shortcut for the Print command. But sometimes you may need to remove a shortcut without assigning it to another item—for example, if you want to prevent the user from performing certain actions.

To remove a keyboard shortcut, display the Customize Keyboard dialog box and specify the template as described in the previous section. Then select the category containing the command associated with the shortcut, select the command, choose the key combination you want to remove, and click the Remove button.

Resetting All Keyboard Shortcuts

You can quickly reset all keyboard shortcuts for the template specified in the Save Changes In drop-down list by clicking the Reset All button in the Customize Keyboard dialog box. Word will display a confirmation message box to make sure you want to take this drastic step.

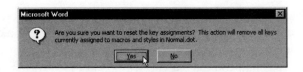

Choose Yes to reset the keyboard shortcuts, click the Close button to exit the Customize Keyboard dialog box, and then click the next Close button to close the Customize dialog box.

Choosing Environment Options

As we've seen in earlier skills, Word offers any number of options for editing, printing, spelling and grammar, and the like, all stored on the ten tabs of the Options dialog box (Tools ➤ Options). In this section, we'll look at the different categories of options and discuss those not touched on in other sections of this book. I won't grind through all the details for every single option, but I'll try to indicate the most useful options for conventional uses of Word. I'll recommend settings based on my experience working with Word. These are suggestions only: You may find that different settings work better for you.

TIP TIP TIP TIP TIP TIP TIP TIP TIP TIP TIP TIP TIP TIP TIP TIP TIP TIP TIP TIP TIP TIP TIP TIP

For more detail on the options not discussed in depth in this section, consult Word's Help files by clicking the Help button (the ? button) in the Options dialog box and selecting an element in the dialog box or by choosing Help ➤ Microsoft Word Help.

SKILL
16

View Options

The options on the View tab of the Options dialog box let you specify which tools and elements you see on screen.

Show Options

The Highlight check box controls whether Word displays highlighting when it is used in a document. You'll usually want to keep this check box selected.

The Bookmarks check box controls whether Word displays bookmark markers on screen. The default setting is not to display bookmark markers. I suggest turning this option on only when working with multiple bookmarks in a document.

Keep the Status Bar check box and the Vertical Scroll Bar check box selected so that the status bar and the vertical scroll bar appear on screen. Clear the Horizontal Scroll Bar check box to remove the horizontal scroll bar from the screen and reclaim a little space unless you find yourself using the horizontal scroll bar to scroll from side to side in your documents. Under most circumstances, you'll do best to work in Normal view and select the Wrap To Window check box (in the Outline And Normal Options area of the View tab).

The ScreenTips check box controls the display of ScreenTips when you move the mouse pointer over a button on a toolbar. Usually this feature is helpful.

Animated Text controls whether Word displays the animation effects you can set on the Animation tab of the Font dialog box. Unless you work with animated text (for example, in Web pages), I suggest turning this feature off.

You can select the Picture Placeholders check box to have Word display empty boxes instead of graphics. This will let you scroll through your documents faster, particularly when using a slower computer or working on a document with many graphics.

Select the Field Codes check box to have field codes rather than results displayed in text. This is useful only when troubleshooting fields, so you'll want to select this check box only intermittently.

In the Field Shading drop-down list, choose when you want to have field codes or results shaded. The default setting is When Selected, which enables you to see fields when they are in selected text. You can also choose Always (which is useful when you need to identify all the fields in a document quickly) or Never, which is useful for when you want to treat the field codes as normal text (for example, when formatting a document).

Formatting Marks Options

Choose which characters and items you want to see on screen: tabs, spaces, paragraph marks, optional hyphens, hidden text, or all of the above. Which settings you choose depend on your work habits: If you find it useful to see where each nonprinting character is, you may want to select the All check box. If, like me, you find the display of these characters distracting, you'll probably want to leave the check boxes cleared, as they are by default, and use the Show/Hide¶ button to display all the nonprinting characters on the rare occasions that you need to view them.

Print and Web Layout Options

The Print And Web Layout Options area of the View tab of the Options dialog box contains options that apply only to Print Layout view and Web Layout view:

- The Drawings check box controls whether Word displays drawing objects. This check box is selected by default, but if you have a slow computer, a slow graphics board, or large drawing objects, you can improve performance by clearing this check box.

- The Object Anchors check box controls the display of the anchors used to denote the paragraphs to which objects such as graphics and text boxes are anchored. You'll probably want to select this check box only when you need to see the precise location an object is anchored to.

- The Text Boundaries check box controls whether Word displays lines marking the area that text can occupy on a page or in a text box, with the current margin settings. Select this check box when you need to place text and other elements exactly on a page.

- The Vertical Ruler (Print View Only) check box controls whether Word displays the vertical ruler at the left-hand side of the screen in Print Layout view. For precise placement, you may want to use the ruler; if you're short of space on screen, you can gain a little by turning the ruler off.

SKILL
16

Outline and Normal Options

The Outline And Normal Options area of the View tab of the Options dialog box contains options that are available only in Outline view and Normal view:

- The Wrap To Window check box controls whether Word rewraps (or *rebreaks*) lines of text to fit the size of the Word window rather than displaying each line as it will break on the page. I recommend turning this feature on (it's off by default) so that you can see the maximum amount possible of the current page on screen without either wasting space (if the margins are narrower than your window is wide) or having to scroll from side to side (if the page is wider than your window).

- The Draft Font check box controls whether Word displays the entire document in the same font (typically a Courier font), ignoring the formatting. This feature is occasionally useful in speeding up the display of large and complexly formatted documents on slow computers. You may also want to try it if one of your colleagues has run amok with character formatting and you need a quick way to get past the boldface, italic, and triple underlining. Otherwise, Draft Font is pretty much useless.

- The Style Area Width box controls the size of the style area, a pane on the left side of the Word window that displays the style for each paragraph (as shown here). To display the style area, enter a measurement greater than 0 (zero); to hide the style area, either reduce the measurement to 0 in the Style Area Width box or drag the divider line between the style area and the document to the left so that the style area disappears.

Inside Address	Marksdale, IL 00000-3323
Salutation	Dear Mr. Thomas,
Body Text	We at Art Through the

General Options

The options on the General tab of the Options dialog box offer a mishmash of choices:

- The Background Repagination check box controls whether Word repaginates your documents in the background as you work. On long documents, background repagination may slow down your computer. Background Repagination isn't available in Print Layout view, which of necessity is always up-to-date with its pagination.

- The Blue Background, White Text check box changes the display to white text on a blue background, which can be visually restful. If you also choose View ➢ Full Screen, you can pretend you're using WordPerfect 5.1 for DOS.

- The Provide Feedback With Sound check box controls whether Word plays sounds when something goes wrong or when Word completes an action (such as saving a file). If an irregular stream of cutesy sounds annoys you, clear this check box.

- The Provide Feedback With Animation check box controls whether Word animates the mouse cursor when Word is performing an action and animates Word actions such as closing dialog boxes and displaying menus. This check box is another candidate for clearing.

- The Confirm Conversion At Open check box controls whether Word displays a Convert File dialog box when you open a file in a format other than

Word. Select this check box if Word is misconverting your files and you want to try a different conversion.

- The Update Automatic Links At Open check box controls whether Word updates any links set for automatic updating in a document when you open that document. (See Skill 17 for information on linking.)

- The Mail As Attachment check box lets you e-mail a document as an attachment rather than inserting the contents directly into the e-mail message (see Skill 18).

- The Recently Used File List check box controls the number of latest-used files that appear at the foot of the File menu. Increase or decrease the number in the Entries box to list more or fewer files (from one to nine); clear the check box to have none appear (for example, for security reasons). Decreasing the number in the Entries box below 1 will clear the Entries box and the Recently Used File List check box.

- The Help for WordPerfect Users check box makes Word perform equivalent Word commands when you press a WordPerfect key combination. For example, if you press Home Home ➤ with Help for WordPerfect Users on, Word will move to the beginning of the document; if you press Home Home ➤ without Help for WordPerfect Users on, Word will move to the beginning of the line, beep, and then move up one line.

- The Navigation Keys For WordPerfect Users check box makes the Page-Up, PageDown, Home, End, and Esc keys behave in Word as they do in WordPerfect.

- The Measurement Units drop-down list box controls the units in which the rulers, Paragraph dialog box, and so on, display measurement: Choose Inches, Centimeters, Millimeters, Points, or Picas, as suits you.

- The Show Pixels For HTML Features check box controls whether Word displays measurements in pixels (picture elements—the dots that make up the picture on a computer monitor) rather than your chosen measurement units when you are working on a Web page. For example, with this feature selected, the Format Picture dialog box will display measurements in pixels. Working with pixels allows you more precise control of the elements in Web pages.

- The Web Options button displays the Web Options dialog box, in which you set options for creating, editing, and viewing Web pages. We discussed these options in Skill 12.

**SKILL
16**

- The E-mail Options button displays the E-mail Options dialog box, which you use to set options for using Word as your e-mail editor. These options are discussed in the Web component for this book on the Sybex Web site.

Edit Options

The options on the Edit tab of the Options dialog box (see Figure 16.7) can make a great deal of difference to your daily maneuverings, so you may well want to change the settings.

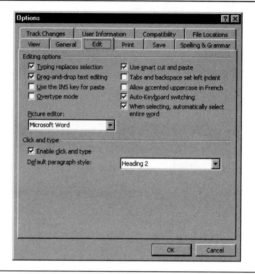

FIGURE 16.7: Make sure the options on the Edit tab of the Options dialog box are set to suit your preferences.

These settings are in the Editing Options area of the Edit tab:

- The Typing Replaces Selection check box causes Word to overwrite selected text when you start typing. If this disconcerts you, clear the check box, and Word will move the insertion point to the beginning of a selection when you start typing.

- The Drag-and-Drop Text Editing check box controls whether you can use drag-and-drop. If you don't use drag-and-drop, turning this off may speed up Word a bit.

- The Use The INS Key For Paste check box makes the Insert key (often labeled Ins) key perform the Paste command. I find this awkward, but your mileage may vary.

- The Overtype Mode check box turns on Overtype mode, discussed in "Insert and Overtype Modes" in Skill 2.

- The Use Smart Cut And Paste check box adds and removes spaces as necessary when you cut, paste, and drag-and-drop text. Keep this check box selected for efficient editing.

- The Tabs And Backspace Set Left Indent check box controls whether you can indent and outdent the left margin by pressing Tab and Backspace, respectively. If you're used to being able to backspace from one paragraph to the one before it, or if you use tabs at the start of paragraphs for whatever reason, clear this check box.

- The Allow Accented Uppercase In French check box does just that.

- The Auto-Keyboard Switching check box automatically changes the keyboard language to that of the text in which the insertion point is currently residing. If you work extensively with polyglot documents, you may find this feature useful.

- The When Selecting, Automatically Select Entire Word check box lets you quickly select multiple words. (See "Selecting Text with the Mouse" in Skill 2 for details.)

- The Picture Editor drop-down list lets you choose which picture editor Word launches when you double-click a graphical object in a Word document. The default setting is Microsoft Word, which uses Word's own drawing tools. If you have a better alternative that Word knows about, select it in the drop-down list.

The Click And Type area of the Edit tab offers the following options:

- The Enable Click And Type check box controls whether the Click and Type feature is active. If you don't find Click and Type useful, or if you want to control exactly which paragraphs are entered in your documents, clear this check box.

- The Default Paragraph Style drop-down list lets you specify the default style for paragraphs that Word creates when you use the Click and Type feature. For example, if you use Click and Type to create second-level heading paragraphs, you might choose Heading 2 in the drop-down list. For you to set and use a style, it must be in use in the current document.

Print Options

The Print tab of the Options dialog box lets you select the default tray of paper for the printer and specify whether to print just the data when printing a form. There are also seven Printing Options and five Include With Document options.

Printing Options

The Draft Output check box lets you print a stripped-down version of your document on some printers.

The Update Fields check box controls whether Word updates all unlocked fields whenever you print. This is usually a good idea, particularly if your document contains, say, date fields that need to be current whenever the document is printed.

The Update Links check box updates all unlocked links whenever you print. If you include linked information in your documents, you'll probably want to select this check box.

The Allow A4/Letter Paper Resizing check box allows Word to resize documents formatted for A4 to print them on letter-size paper (which is proportioned a little differently), and vice versa. Word adjusts the printout, not the formatting of the document. If you work with documents from, say, a British firm, this capability can be a lifesaver.

The Background Printing check box lets you keep working (albeit a bit more slowly) while Word is printing your documents. If you print long, complex documents, you may want to select this check box. Otherwise, most modern printers print documents quickly enough that the wait isn't much of an issue.

The Print PostScript Over Text feature is primarily useful if you need to print a document created in Word for the Macintosh containing PostScript code for special printing effects.

The Reverse Print Order check box prints documents from last page to first. This is useful for printers that deliver the pages face up (i.e., in reverse order) or for certain photocopying tasks.

Include with Document

Choose whether to print document properties, field codes, comments, hidden text, and drawing objects (objects created in Word, including lines) when printing your document. Document properties and comments will each print on a separate page at the end of the document; field codes, hidden text, and drawing objects will print where they occur in the document. The Drawing Objects check box is selected by default, on the assumption that you'll want to include any drawings in the printed document. The other check boxes are deselected by default.

WARNING WARNING WARNING WARNING WARNING WARNING WARNING WARNING

Printing hidden text will alter the layout of your pages. Use Print Preview to check the effect that including hidden text will have before actually printing.

Save Options

The options on the Save tab of the Options dialog box can help keep your work safe when all around you people are losing theirs (and blaming it on you).

Save Options

The Always Create Backup Copy check box controls whether Word creates a backup copy each time you save a document by renaming the previously saved version of that document to **Backup of** *filename* and giving it the extension .wbk. This is a valuable option—with two caveats: First, it will slow down your save operations a little, though usually not enough to worry about; and second, you need to understand that the backup is *not* the same as the currently saved version of the file—if you destroy the latest saved version, the backup will provide you with the previous version.

TIP TIP TIP TIP TIP TIP TIP TIP TIP TIP TIP TIP TIP TIP TIP TIP TIP TIP TIP TIP TIP TIP

To make the backups of your documents virtually identical to the currently saved copies, always save twice in immediate succession.

The Allow Fast Saves check box lets you speed up save operations by saving only the changes to a file, not actually saving the file itself. This option can create bizarre results—if you delete most of a large file (or most of a file containing graphics) and then fast-save it, the file size will still be large; and fast-saved documents will always be somewhat larger than regularly saved documents. Bear this in mind if disk space is at a premium or you're often transferring documents by modem.

TIP TIP TIP TIP TIP TIP TIP TIP TIP TIP TIP TIP TIP TIP TIP TIP TIP TIP TIP TIP TIP TIP

You can't choose both Always Create Backup Copy and Allow Fast Saves at the same time—it's one or the other. Allow Fast Saves saves you only a little time unless you have a very slow computer or you're working with huge documents (or both).

SKILL
16

The Prompt For Document Properties check box governs whether Word displays the Properties dialog box automatically the first time you save a document. This is useful if you use the document properties information to identify your documents; if you don't, it rapidly proves tedious.

The Prompt To Save Normal Template check box makes Word check with you before it saves changes to Normal.dot, the global template. Select this option if you spend time mucking about with Normal.dot and want to be able to escape any embarrassing changes you make by mistake. Otherwise, leave this check box selected to have Word save changes to Normal.dot automatically.

The Embed TrueType Fonts check box lets you save the fonts used in a document with the document so that the fonts will appear in the document even on a computer that doesn't have those particular fonts installed. This option can greatly increase the size of document files, so use it only if you're sharing files and need to ensure they look exactly the same on the other computers. When you do use it, you can select the Embed Characters In Use Only check box to restrict the number of embedded characters to those used in the document. This keeps the document size down a bit, but it may prevent the recipient of the file from using certain characters if they edit the file.

The Save Data Only For Forms check box controls whether Word saves only the data from a form or the entire form.. Forms are discussed in Bonus Online Skill 2

The Allow Background Saves check box notionally allows you to keep working while Word saves a file to disk. In my experience, it seems to help neither on fast computers nor on slow ones.

The Save AutoRecover Info Every *nn* Minutes check box and text box control whether Word saves an automatic backup of documents at a specified interval (from one minute to 120 minutes). You can use these AutoRecover files to recover documents if Word crashes or your computer crashes. When you exit Word successfully, it deletes any AutoRecover files made in that session. These backups are stored in the AutoRecover Files location specified on the File Locations tab of the Options dialog box (which I'll discuss in "File Locations Options" in a page or two). When you restart Word after a crash, it should open any AutoRecovered files that haven't been deleted and display them to you as **(Recovered)**. Check the files carefully and save them under new names if they're still viable.

WARNING WARNING WARNING WARNING WARNING WARNING WARNING WARNING

Never rely on AutoRecover files to save your work for you. Always save your files manually after making changes to them that you would not want to have to make again. Reserve your use of AutoRecover files for the direst of emergencies.

The Save Word Files As drop-down list lets you choose the default format in which to save Word documents you create. The default setting is Word Document, but you might want to choose Web Page if you normally create Web pages, or Word 6.0/95 if you need to make sure the documents you create can be read by people with Word 6 or Word 95.

The Disable Features Not Supported By Word 97 check box prevents you from using features that Word 2000 has but which Word 97 (the previous version of Word) does not support. Use this feature if you need to make sure that colleagues who use Word 97 can see everything you include in your Word 2000 documents.

File-Sharing Options

These options—for protecting your documents from intrusion, alteration, and damage—are discussed in Skill 18.

Spelling & Grammar Options

The options on the Spelling & Grammar tab of the Options dialog box—for controlling Word's automatic spell-checking and grammar-checking, working with dictionaries, and so on—are discussed in Skill 7.

Track Changes Options

Track Changes options let you specify the colors and marks to use with revision marks. See the "Tracking Changes" section in Skill 18 for a full discussion of these options.

User Information Options

Make sure your name, initials, and mailing address are entered correctly on the User Information tab of the Options dialog box. Among other things, Word uses the name for document properties information, the initials for comments, and the mailing address for envelopes.

Compatibility Options

The options on the Compatibility tab of the Options dialog box are for fine-tuning the way in which Word converts files created in other word processors or in other versions of Word. We won't get into these options in detail here. Briefly, the Font Substitution button allows you to specify which fonts to use when a document contains fonts that are not installed on your computer. The Recommended

Options For drop-down list lets you pick the format in which a file was created, and the Options list box contains options for tweaking the conversion of that file format to Word. If you work with many documents created in another word-processing format, you may want to investigate these options to make sure that files convert as nearly perfectly as possible. If you open the occasional document in another format, you probably won't want to bother with these options.

File Locations Options

The options on the File Locations tab of the Options dialog box let you specify where Word should locate documents, clip-art pictures, templates, AutoRecover files, and other files it maintains.

Documents is the category that can save you the most time: If you want Word to suggest saving documents somewhere other than where it's decided is most appropriate (probably the My Documents folder or the Personal folder), change Documents straight away.

To change a file location:

1. Choose the item to change in the File Types list box.

2. Click the Modify button to display the Modify Location dialog box.

3. Choose the folder for the new location by using standard Windows techniques.

4. Click the OK button to close the Modify Location dialog box.

If you use workgroup templates that are located on a network, you'll want to set the Workgroup Templates setting to that location by using the technique described above.

Are You Experienced?

Now you can...

- ☑ customize toolbars, menus, and context menus to contain the commands you need
- ☑ assign keyboard shortcuts to provide quick access to commands
- ☑ create your own toolbars and menus
- ☑ understand and set Word options

SKILL 17

Linking and Embedding Objects

- ⊖ Linking objects to your documents
- ⊖ Updating a link
- ⊖ Breaking a link

As we've seen so far in this book, Word's many features give you all types of text, from regular text to complex tables. But sooner or later, you'll find yourself needing to include in your Word documents information created in other applications—part of a spreadsheet created in Excel, perhaps, or a couple of slides from a PowerPoint presentation. Beyond that, however, you may find you need to group several Word documents together with that spreadsheet and presentation to form a complex document.

In Skill 10, we looked quickly at how you can insert pictures created in other applications into your documents. In this skill, we'll look at how you can use Automation (formerly known as Object Linking and Embedding, or OLE for short) to enhance your Word documents.

TIP TIP TIP TIP TIP TIP TIP TIP TIP TIP TIP TIP TIP TIP TIP TIP TIP TIP TIP TIP TIP TIP TIP TIP TIP

When Automation falls short of your needs, you can use Office binders, discussed in the online component for this skill, to pull disparate elements together into a super-document.

What is Automation?

Automation (which used to be known as Object Linking and Embedding or OLE) gives you two ways to include information from other applications in Word documents:

- By *linking* information from another application to a Word document, you can have the information automatically updated whenever you open or print the document (or when you choose to update the information manually).

- By *embedding* information from another application in a Word document, you can make that information part of the document, so you can change that information even when you don't have access to the original data source— for example, you can include data from an Excel spreadsheet in a Word document, transfer the document to your laptop, and then hit the road.

NOTE NOTE NOTE NOTE NOTE NOTE NOTE NOTE NOTE NOTE NOTE NOTE NOTE NOTE NOTE

Object **is one of those great computer terms whose meaning people can never quite agree on. For the moment, think of an object as being a chunk of information (data) that knows which application it was created in—for example, a group of spreadsheet cells that knows it was created in Excel.**

Linking

Linking connects information from another application to a Word document. The information appears in the Word document but stays connected to its source in the other application, so that if you change the information in the source, you can have Word automatically update the information in the document as well. For example, by linking the sales figures in an Excel spreadsheet to a Word document, you can make sure the Word document always has the latest sales figures in it.

NOTE NOTE NOTE NOTE NOTE NOTE NOTE NOTE NOTE NOTE NOTE NOTE NOTE NOTE NOTE
Word includes linked information as a field. Fields are discussed in Skill 8.

To link information from another application to a Word document:

1. Start the source application for the object you want to link to a Word document.

2. Open the file containing the object.

TIP TIP TIP TIP TIP TIP TIP TIP TIP TIP TIP TIP TIP TIP TIP TIP TIP TIP TIP TIP TIP TIP TIP
Linking objects to your documents enlarges the document files only a little—not nearly as much as embedding. To keep your documents as small as possible, choose linking over embedding when you have the choice.

SKILL
▼ 17

3. Select the object to insert. For example, if you're inserting a group of cells from a spreadsheet, select those cells.

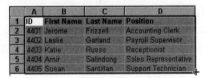

4. Choose Edit ➤ Copy (or click the Copy button in that application or choose Ctrl+C) to copy the object to the Clipboard.

5. Start Word if it isn't already running, or switch back to Word by clicking the Microsoft Word icon on the Taskbar or by pressing Alt+Tab until the Word icon is selected in the task-switching list.

6. Position the insertion point where you want the linked item to appear.

7. Choose Edit ➤ Paste Special to display the Paste Special dialog box (see Figure 17.1).

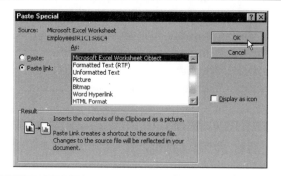

FIGURE 17.1: To link information, select the Paste Link option in the Paste Special dialog box and choose the option from the As list box that describes the item as "Object"—here it's Microsoft Excel Worksheet Object.

8. Select the Paste Link option on the left side of the dialog box.

9. In the As list box, choose the option that describes the item you're linking as "Object." (Here it's Microsoft Excel Worksheet Object because Excel is the source application; with other source applications, you'll see different descriptions.)

10. To have the item display as an icon rather than at its full size, select the Display As Icon check box. To change the icon, click the Change Icon button and select a different icon in the Change Icon dialog box; then click OK. (The Change Icon button appears when you select the Display As Icon check box.)

TIP TIP TIP TIP TIP TIP TIP TIP TIP TIP TIP TIP TIP TIP TIP TIP TIP TIP TIP TIP TIP TIP TIP
When using the Paste Special command with documents that will become Web pages, select the HTML Format item in the As list box.

11. Click the OK button to insert the object in your document (see Figure 17.2).

You can now format the linked object, for example, by adding borders and shading or by placing it in a text box.

FIGURE 17.2: The cells from the Excel spreadsheet inserted in the document

TIP TIP TIP TIP TIP TIP TIP TIP TIP TIP TIP TIP TIP TIP TIP TIP TIP TIP TIP TIP TIP TIP

To open the source file for the linked object in the application that created it, double-click the linked object (or the icon for it) in your document.

Updating Links

You can update links either manually or automatically so that a link is updated every time you open the document that contains it or every time the source file is updated (when the document containing the link is open). You can also lock a link so that it cannot be updated.

To set updating for links:

1. Open the document containing the links in Word.

2. Choose Edit ➤ Links to display the Links dialog box (see Figure 17.3).

SKILL
17

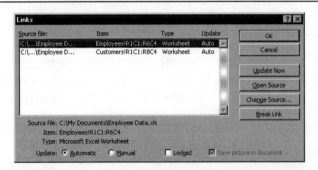

FIGURE 17.3: Choose how to update your links in the Links dialog box.

3. In the Source File list box, select the link or links on which to work. (Use Shift+click to select several adjacent links or Ctrl+click to select nonadjacent links.)

4. Choose how the link or links should be updated by selecting the Automatic option button or the Manual option button.

   - To update a link or links manually, click the Update Now button.

   - To lock the link or links, click the Locked check box. Word will then dim the Automatic option button and the Manual option button to indicate that the choices are not available. To unlock a link, select it in the list box and clear the Locked check box.

5. Click the OK button to close the Links dialog box.

Breaking Links

If you no longer need to be able to update a link or if you're planning to share a document with someone who won't have the linked information available, you can break the link. Essentially, breaking the link turns the linked information into embedded information.

To break a link:

1. Choose Edit ➤ Links to display the Links dialog box.

2. Select the link or links in the list box.

3. Click the Break Link button. Word will display a message box to make sure that you want to break the link.

4. Click the Yes button to break the link.

5. Click OK to close the Links dialog box.

WARNING WARNING WARNING WARNING WARNING WARNING WARNING WARNING
Once you've broken a link, you cannot restore it (except by reinserting the linked information, thus creating the link again).

Deleting Linked Objects

To delete a linked object, click it to select it, then press the Delete key or choose Edit ➤ Clear.

Embedding

To embed an object in a document, you follow a similar procedure to linking, but the result is completely different: Instead of creating a connection from the object in the document to its source file in the application that created it, Word saves all the information needed to edit the object in the Word document. Because the object is not connected to the file that it comes from, you cannot update the object in the Word document; but you can edit the object in the Word document to your heart's content without worrying about changing the source file.

TIP TIP TIP TIP TIP TIP TIP TIP TIP TIP TIP TIP TIP TIP TIP TIP TIP TIP TIP TIP TIP TIP TIP TIP

The advantage of embedding as compared to linking is that you can edit the embedded information in place, independent of the original data file. The disadvantage is that embedding objects in your documents makes the documents much larger than linking objects does because all the data contained in the object is stored in the Word document (instead of just the information pointing to the source file and source application).

Embedding an Existing Object

To embed an existing object in a document:

1. Start the source application for the object you want to embed in the Word document.

2. Open the file containing the object.

3. Select the object to embed.

4. Choose Edit ➢ Copy (or click the Copy button in the application or choose Ctrl+C) to copy the object to the Clipboard.

5. Switch back to Word by clicking the Microsoft Word icon on the Taskbar or by pressing Alt+Tab until the Word icon is selected in the task-switching list.

6. Position the insertion point where you want to embed the object.

7. Choose Edit ➢ Paste Special to display the Paste Special dialog box.

8. Select the Paste option.

9. In the As list box, choose the option that describes the item you're embedding as "Object."

SKILL
17

10. To have the item display as an icon rather than at its full size, check the Display As Icon box. To change the icon, click the Change Icon button (which will materialize when you select the Display As Icon check box) and select a different icon in the Change Icon dialog box; click OK to return to the Object dialog box.

11. Click the OK button to insert the object in your document.

So far this all seems singularly similar to linking. But you'll notice the difference when you double-click the embedded object—it displays a border from its source application, and the toolbars and menus change to those of the source application, so you can edit the object within Word as if you were working in the source application. Figure 17.4 shows a PowerPoint slide open for editing within a Word document.

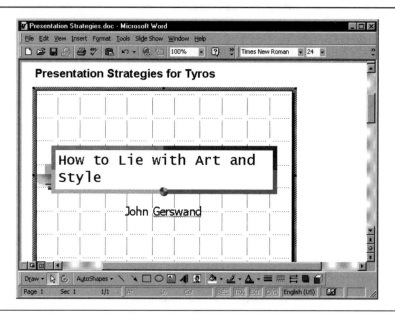

FIGURE 17.4: Double-click an embedded object to edit it in place. Word will display the menus and toolbars from the source application (in this case, PowerPoint).

TIP TIP TIP TIP TIP TIP TIP TIP TIP TIP TIP TIP TIP TIP TIP TIP TIP TIP TIP TIP TIP TIP TIP

To edit a sound clip or video clip, right-click the object, choose the Object submenu (e.g. Media Clip Object), and then choose the Edit option. Double-click an embedded sound or video clip to run it.

Embedding a New Object

You can also create a new object and embed it at the same time. For example, you could insert a sound clip in your document as follows:

1. Choose Insert ➤ Object to display the Object dialog box (see Figure 17.5).

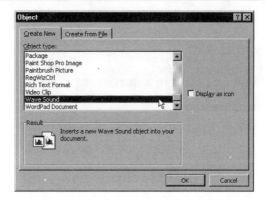

FIGURE 17.5: On the Create New tab in the Object dialog box, choose the type of object to create, then click the OK button.

2. Click the Create New tab to bring it to the front of the dialog box (unless it's already there).

3. From the Object Type list, choose the type of object you want to insert. (Here I've chosen Wave Sound.)

4. Select the Display As Icon check box if you want the object to display as an icon in the document. To change the icon for the object, click the Change Icon button (which will appear when you select the Display As Icon check box) and select a different icon in the Change Icon dialog box; click the OK button to return to the Object dialog box.

5. Click the OK button. Word will start the application you chose.

6. Create the object as usual in that application.

7. Choose File ➤ Exit And Return To *Document Name* to close the application and return to the Word document. Word will insert the object, which you can then position and format as necessary.

Skill
17

Deleting an Embedded Object

To delete an embedded object, select it by clicking it, then press the Delete key or choose Edit ➤ Clear.

Are You Experienced?

Now you can...

- ☑ link an object to a document
- ☑ update a link
- ☑ break a link
- ☑ embed an object in a document
- ☑ edit an embedded object

SKILL 18

Using Word's Workgroup Features

- → **Using comments**
- → **Working with change marks**
- → **Working with versions**
- → **Locking and protecting documents**
- → **Mailing documents around the office**

Now that many computers are networked, more and more people are working together on documents they create. Word provides a minor host of features to make workgroup computing faster and easier. Comments let you speak directly to others who are working on a document (literally so if you use sound comments). Change marks help track who made which change to a document when, and document versions provide a way of tracking the different stages of a document's evolution. When change marks aren't enough, you can lock your documents to protect them from your coworkers. Office's online collaboration tools let you and your coworkers work on a document together at the same time, either via a local area network or via the Internet. Finally, Word's built-in mail features make it easier to propagate your documents among those who need them.

Comments

Word's comments are most useful for making notes to yourself and your colleagues when creating a complex document. Word automatically marks each comment with the identity of the current user (as drawn from the User Information tab of the Options dialog box), so you can easily track who made which suggestions. Text with comments attached is highlighted, and when you move the mouse pointer over the commented text, Word displays a ScreenTip containing the text of the comment.

TIP TIP TIP TIP TIP TIP TIP TIP TIP TIP TIP TIP TIP TIP TIP TIP TIP TIP TIP TIP TIP TIP
You can lock documents so that users who don't know the password can add comments but cannot change the text of the document itself. We'll look at locking and protecting documents later in this skill.

Word's tools for working with comments are grouped on the Reviewing toolbar (see Figure 18.1), which you can display at any time by right-clicking the menu bar or any displayed toolbar and choosing Reviewing from the context menu of toolbars.

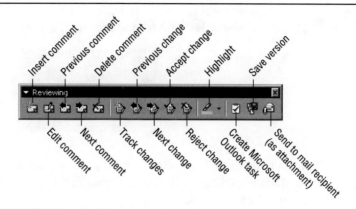

FIGURE 18.1: Use the Reviewing toolbar to work with comments.

Inserting a Comment

To insert a comment at the insertion point:

1. Click the Insert Comment button on the Reviewing toolbar or choose Insert Comment. The current user's initials and a comment number will be inserted as hidden text in the document; Word will temporarily display this hidden text and will highlight the current word and the initials and comment number. Word will also open the Comments pane, again inserting the user's initials and a comment number.

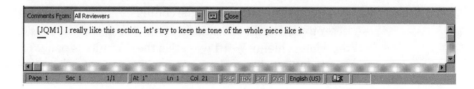

SKILL
18

2. Type the comment in the Comment pane.

    • To insert an audio comment, click the Insert Sound Object button on the Comments pane. Word will display your currently configured sound recorder. Record the comment (by clicking the Record button of the sound recorder) and close the sound recorder. Word will display a loudspeaker icon for the comment in the Comments pane.

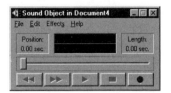

2. Click the Close button to close the pane and return to the body text of your document. Word will faintly highlight the word to which the comment is attached.

TIP TIP TIP TIP TIP TIP TIP TIP TIP TIP TIP TIP TIP TIP TIP TIP TIP TIP TIP TIP TIP TIP TIP TIP TIP

To see highlighting and ScreenTips on comments, you need to have the Screen-Tips check box selected on the View tab of the Options dialog box (Tools ➢ Options). If you don't, you'll see only the initials and comment number as you enter the comment; once you close the Comment pane, you'll see no visible indication of the comment's presence.

Viewing Comments

You can review the comments in a document in several ways:

- To view a comment on-the-fly, move the mouse pointer over a faintly high-lighted word. Word will intensify the highlighting and will display a Screen-Tip with the text of the comment, as shown here. (For an audio comment, you'll see only the name of the commentator and the word **[empty]**, which is deceptive.) To edit the comment, right-click and choose Edit Comment from the context menu; Word will open the Comments pane. To delete the comment, right-click and choose Delete Comment from the context menu.

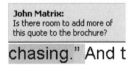

- Alternatively, click the Next Comment or Previous Comment button to move to the next comment or previous comment. Keep the mouse pointer over the Next Comment or Previous Comment button, and Word will display the full highlight and the ScreenTip for the comment. Click the Edit Comment button to edit the comment in the Comments pane or the Delete Comment button to delete the comment.

- Once you start reviewing comments, Word will set the Object Browser to browse by comments and will replace the Next Page and Previous Page buttons below the vertical scroll bar with Next Comment and Previous Comment buttons. Click these buttons to move from comment to comment in the document. To reset the Object Browser to browse by page, click the Select Browse Object button (the button between the Next and Previous buttons) and choose Browse By Page from the pop-up panel, as shown here. (You can also manually set the Object Browser to browse by comments by clicking the Select Browse Object button and choosing Browse By Comment from the pop-up panel.)

- To view comments in the comments pane, click the Edit Comment button or choose View ➤ Comments. Word will display the Comments pane at the bottom of the screen. Scroll through the comments using the scroll bar, or click a comment in the Comments pane, to move the highlight in the main document window to the commented text to which the comment refers.

 TIP TIP TIP TIP TIP TIP TIP TIP TIP TIP TIP TIP TIP TIP TIP TIP TIP TIP TIP TIP TIP TIP TIP TIP TIP
If you have hidden text displayed in your document, you can double-click in a comment marker to display the Comments pane.

To play a sound comment, double-click its icon in the Comments pane, or right-click the icon and choose Play from the Wave Sound Object submenu of the context menu.

By default, you'll see all the comments in the document displayed in the Comments pane in the order in which they appear in the text. To see only the comments entered by one author, choose the author's name from the Comments From drop-down list.

Reviewing Comments

To review comments, display them by choosing View ➤ Comments. You can then edit and delete comments, move them by dragging the comment marks about the document, and copy and paste (or drag and drop) comment text into the main document.

You can also either print just the comments from a document (by choosing File ➤ Print and choosing Comments in the Print What drop-down list in the Print dialog box) or print the comments along with the document (by choosing Tools ➤ Options to display the Options dialog box and selecting the Comments check box in the Include With Document area on the Print tab).

Editing and Deleting Comments

You can edit the comments in the comments pane using regular editing methods, but you can't delete an entire comment.

To delete a comment, right-click in the commented text in the main window and choose Delete from the context menu.

Track Changes

Word's Track Changes feature—known as *revision marking* in Word versions up to Word 95—lets you track both the edits (additions, deletions, and some formatting changes) a team of users make in a document and which user made which edits. You can then review the edits one by one and either accept or reject them with due consideration or you can go ahead and blithely accept (or reject) all the edits in one fell swoop.

By default, Word marks additions with a single underline and deletions with a strikethrough, but you can customize these settings to make them easier to distinguish from your regular text. Each user gets (by default) a different color of change mark, so you can quickly identify which user made which marks; again, this is customizable.

WARNING WARNING WARNING WARNING WARNING WARNING WARNING WARNING
Track Changes tracks only where text or another object (such as a graphic) is either added to or deleted from a document, and where attributes such as bold or italic are applied to or removed from the text—it doesn't track changes in style for whole paragraphs or changes in capitalization using Format ➤ Change Case.

You can turn Track Changes on and off at will. You can also turn the display of change marks on screen on and off while change marking is on. This can be helpful for seeing the text that remains during heavy editing.

TIP TIP TIP TIP TIP TIP TIP TIP TIP TIP TIP TIP TIP TIP TIP TIP TIP TIP TIP TIP TIP TIP TIP TIP

You can protect a document so that other users have to use change marks when they make changes to it. We'll look at protecting documents later in this skill.

Turning Track Changes On and Off

To turn Track Changes on and off, either click the Track Changes button on the Reviewing toolbar or double-click the TRK indicator on the status bar. Alternatively, right-click the TRK indicator on the status bar and choose Highlight Changes, or choose Tools ➣ Track Changes ➣ Highlight Changes, to display the Highlight Changes dialog box. Then select the Track Changes While Editing check box and click the OK button.

Choosing Track Changes Options

To choose different options for Track Changes:

1. Choose Tools ➣ Options to display the Options dialog box, then click the Track Changes tab (see Figure 18.2).

    - You can also move quickly to the Track Changes dialog box (which contains the Track Changes tab from the Options dialog box) either by clicking the Options button in the Highlight Changes dialog box or by right-clicking the TRK indicator on the status bar and choosing Options from the context menu.

SKILL
18

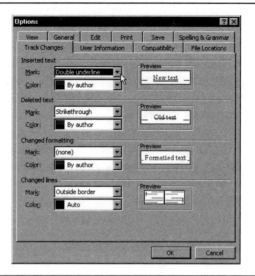

FIGURE 18.2: Choose options for change marks on the Track Changes tab of the Options dialog box or in the Track Changes dialog box. Use the Preview boxes to see the effect your changes will have.

2. In the Inserted Text area, choose a means of marking new text and a color for that text: From the Mark drop-down list, choose None, Bold, Italic, Underline, or Double Underline, and from the Color drop-down list, choose By Author, Auto (which matches the default font color), or one of the sixteen text colors Word offers.

    •   By Author assigns different colors to the first eight authors who use change marks on a document (for the ninth and subsequent authors, Word recycles the colors, starting from the top). Word identifies authors by the contents of the Name box on the User Information tab of the Options dialog box, so if you change your Name setting (from, say, Joseph Takagi to Joseph Y. Takagi), Word will mark subsequent changes in a different color.

TIP TIP TIP TIP TIP TIP TIP TIP TIP TIP TIP TIP TIP TIP TIP TIP TIP TIP TIP TIP TIP TIP TIP
By Author is the most convenient setting for tracking changes made by different authors, but you may sometimes want changes by two or more authors to appear in the same color—for example, if they are members of the same team or fulfilling the same role. In that case, choose an appropriate color manually.

3. In the Deleted Text area, choose how to mark deleted text (with Strikethrough or Hidden formatting or a caret [^] or pound sign [#]) and a color for that text (again, By Author, Auto, or a color of your choice).

4. In the Changed Formatting area, choose a means of marking text whose formatting has changed and a color for the marking. Word will use this marking for changes such as the application or removal of bold and italic.

5. In the Changed Lines area, choose a position for the vertical bars Word puts in the margin next to lines containing changes (None, Left Border, Right Border, Outside Border) and a color for them (Auto or your choice of color). Left Border and Right Border are useful for standard manuscript, while Outside Border is good for bound manuscript, where the marking might otherwise get lost in the binding.

6. Click the OK button to close the Options dialog box or Track Changes dialog box. (If you opened the Track Changes dialog box by clicking the Options button in the Highlight Changes dialog box, Word will return you to the Highlight Changes dialog box.)

Displaying Change Marks

Once you've turned Track Changes on, you can turn the display of on-screen change marks on and off by selecting and clearing the Highlight Changes On Screen check box in the Highlight Changes dialog box. Turning off the display of change marks on screen can make heavily edited documents much easier to read and can make minor errors, such as extra spaces or missing spaces resulting from cutting and pasting, easier to find. But it can make it hard to tell that you're still using change marks for the edits you're making.

You can also turn the display of change marks in your printed documents on and off from the Highlight Changes dialog box: Simply select or clear the Highlight Changes In Printed Document check box. This way, you can print out drafts without showing all the editing going on in the background.

Reviewing Changes

Once you've had someone else—or half the office—go through your prized document and make their edits, you can quickly review the changes. If you chose to have change marks color-coded by user, you'll easily be able to see who made which changes.

SKILL
18

To review individual changes, move the mouse pointer over a changed word. Word will display a ScreenTip showing who made the change and the nature of the change they made: *Inserted* for added text, *Deleted* for deleted text, and *Property Change* for a change to an attribute such as boldface or italic.

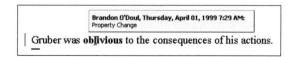

To accept or reject a change, click in it and click the Accept Change button or Reject Change button on the Reviewing toolbar. Alternatively, right-click in the change and choose Accept Change or Reject Change from the context menu.

To review a number of changes and either accept or reject them:

1. Right-click the TRK indicator in the status bar and choose Accept Or Reject Changes from the context menu to display the Accept Or Reject Changes dialog box.

2. If necessary, adjust the setting in the View group box:

    - Changes With Highlighting shows the changes in the document marked with change marks.

    - Changes Without Highlighting shows the document without change marks (i.e., as if all the changes had been accepted).

    - Original displays the document without the changes (i.e., as if all the changes had been rejected).

2. Click the ← Find button or the Find → button to find either the previous or the next change in the document. Word will indicate the type of change (Deleted, Inserted, Property Change) in the Changes box (see Figure 18.3).

4. Click the Accept button to accept the change or the Reject button to reject it.

5. Use the Find buttons to review the rest of the changes.

6. Click the Close button to close the Accept Or Reject Changes dialog box.

TIP TIP TIP TIP TIP TIP TIP TIP TIP TIP TIP TIP TIP TIP TIP TIP TIP TIP TIP TIP TIP TIP TIP

To accept or reject all changes in the document quickly, right-click the TRK indicator, choose Accept Or Reject Changes, and click the Accept All button or the Reject All button in the Accept Or Reject Changes dialog box. Word will display a confirmation message box; choose Yes. Then click the Close button to exit the Accept Or Reject Changes dialog box.

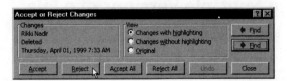

FIGURE 18.3: Use the Accept Or Reject Changes dialog box to review multiple changes.

Merging Revisions by Using Compare Documents

You can also route multiple copies of your document around the office and have a number of people review it at the same time, either using Track Changes or not, as suits you. When you get back several copies of the document with different people's revisions, you can merge the changes into your original document so that you can deal with them all at once.

To merge revisions:

1.   Open the document containing the changes.

2.   Choose Tools ➤ Track Changes ➤ Compare Documents to display the Select File To Compare With Current Document dialog box. (This dialog box is a variation on the Open dialog box.)

3.   Select the original document and choose Open. Word will compare the current document with the original and will identify with revision marks how the current document differs from the original.

4.   To merge revisions from other documents, repeat steps 2 and 3.

Versions

Word's versioning features let you save multiple versions of a document within the same file. Instead of containing only the information in the document from when it was last saved, the file contains snapshots from whenever a version was saved. For example, if several people review a document of yours, each person can save a version of the document when they're finished. When the document returns to you, you can review each version of the document and revert to an earlier version than the last if you want—which can prove handy if one of your colleagues has made ill-advised changes that could otherwise have ruined the document.

SKILL
18

Saving Multiple Versions of a File

To save a version of a file:

1. Choose File ➢ Versions. Word will display the Versions dialog box (see Figure 18.4).

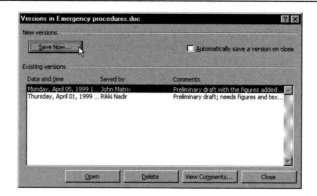

FIGURE 18.4: To save a version, click the Save Now button in the Versions dialog box.

2. Click the Save Now button. Word will display the Save Version dialog box (see Figure 18.5).

3. Enter any comments about this version in the Comments On Version text box, then click the OK button.

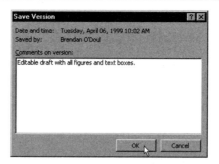

FIGURE 18.5: Enter any comments on the version in the Save Version dialog box.

Saving Versions Automatically

If you need to keep a record of changes to the documents your company creates, you can try saving a version of the file automatically each time anyone closes it. This can help you track who has opened a file (even if they make no changes).

To have Word automatically save a version of the file whenever it is closed, choose File ➤ Versions and select the Automatically Save A Version On Close check box. Word will now automatically save a version of the file and will add the comment *Automatic version* to it.

Saving a Version as a Separate File

No matter how happy you are with Word's versioning features, when a document is complete and ready for delivery, you'll probably want to save a fresh copy of it so that it does not contain all the versions that have gone before. To do this, choose the version in the Existing Versions list box and click the Open button, then use File ➤ Save As to save the file under another name.

Deleting a Version

To delete a version, select it in the Existing Versions list box in the Versions dialog box and click the Delete button. (To delete multiple versions, use Shift+click or Ctrl+click to select them.)

Opening a Version

To open a version of the document, select it in the Existing Versions list box and click the Open button. Word will open it in a separate window. You can revert to this version of the document by closing all other versions of the document that you have open and using File ➤ Save As to save the document with the original name of the file (thus overwriting the other file that contains the versions).

To view the comments on the version of a document you're thinking of opening, click the View Comments button to display the View Comments dialog box for the selected version. Click the Close button to close the View Comments dialog box and return to the Versions dialog box.

Locking and Protecting Documents

By using Word's document locking and protection features, you can safely share your documents with fair protection against their getting trashed.

SKILL
18

Word offers four types of protection:

- You can save a document as *read-only recommended*. Whenever a user opens the file, Word displays a message box recommending that they open it as a read-only file, which means that they cannot save changes to the original. The user can choose to bypass this, however, so it isn't effective protection.

- You can password-protect a document so that others can open it but can either only make changes using revisions marks or only insert comments.

- You can password-protect a document so that others can open it but cannot save changes to the original without entering the correct password. They can still save versions of the document under another name by choosing File ➤ Save As.

- You can password-protect a document so nobody can open it without entering the correct password.

Saving Files as Read-Only Recommended

To save the open file as read-only recommended, choose File ➤ Save As to display the Save As dialog box. Click the Tools drop-down menu button and choose General Options to display the Save dialog box, which you'll recognize as the Save tab from the Options dialog box. In the File Sharing Options area, select the Read-Only Recommended check box, then click the OK button. Word will return you to the Save As dialog box; choose the Save button to save the file.

Whenever anyone opens the document, Word will display a message box recommending that they open it as a read-only file.

The user can choose Yes to open the document as a read-only file, No to open the document with full privileges, or Cancel to not open the document. When you open a document as a read-only file, Word displays **(Read-Only)** after the document's title in the title bar.

To remove the read-only recommendation, open the document (not as read-only), clear the Read-Only Recommended check box on the Save tab of the Options dialog box, and save the file again.

Password-Protecting Files

As you can see, a read-only recommendation has no teeth—it's a suggestion that the user can instantly ignore. For files that you value more, you'll need to use password protection.

Word's passwords can be up to 15 characters long (letters, numbers, keyboard symbols, or spaces) and are case sensitive—**02binSF** is different from **02BinSF**, and so on.

Protecting Documents for Tracked Changes and Comments

To protect the open document so that users can only make changes using change marks or only add comments:

1. Choose Tools ➢ Protect Document to display the Protect Document dialog box (see Figure 18.6).

FIGURE 18.6: In the Protect Document dialog box, choose whether to protect the document for tracked changes, comments, or forms, then enter a password.

SKILL
18

2. In the Protect Document For area, choose whether to protect the document for tracked changes or comments.

3. Enter a password in the Password text box.

4. Click the OK button. Word will display a Confirm Password dialog box, as shown here.

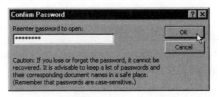

5. Enter the password again, then click the OK button. If you enter the same password, Word will close the Confirm Password dialog box and protect the document; if you get it wrong, Word will return you to the Protect Document dialog box for another try.

6. Save the document to set the protection.

When a user opens the protected document, Word will allow them only to make changes using change marks or only to insert comments (depending on which you chose).

To remove the protection, choose Tools ➣ Unprotect Document and enter the password in the Unprotect Document dialog box, as shown here.

If you get the password right, Word will unprotect the document; if you get it wrong, Word will display a message box to that effect.

Protecting Documents with Password to Modify

The next level of protection is *password to modify*, which means the user can only write changes to a file if they supply the correct password when opening the file. If they can't supply the password, they can open the file as read-only but cannot save changes under the document's original name.

To protect the file using password to modify:

1. Choose File ➣ Save As to display the Save As dialog box, then click the Tools drop-down menu and choose General Options to display the Save dialog box.

2. Enter a password in the Password To Modify text box.

3. Click OK. Word will display the Confirm Password dialog box.

4. Enter the password again (to make sure you didn't misspell it the first time) and click OK. If you get the password right, Word will set the password and

return you to the Save As dialog box. If you get it wrong, Word will let you know the error of your wayward fingers and will return you to the Save dialog box in the hope that you'll redeem yourself.

5.   Click the Save button to save the document. The password to modify protection will apply from when you close the document.

The next time the document is opened, the user will have to enter the password in the Password dialog box to open the file with write access.

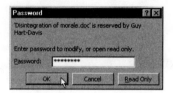

Alternatively, the user can choose the Read Only option to open the document as a read-only file.

TIP TIP TIP TIP TIP TIP TIP TIP TIP TIP TIP TIP TIP TIP TIP TIP TIP TIP TIP TIP TIP TIP TIP TIP

To remove (or change) a password to modify, open the file (using the password), then choose Tools ➤ Options to display the Options dialog box. Click the Save tab to bring it to the front. Delete (or change) the password to modify and click the OK button. Save the file to store the change.

Preventing Others from Opening Word Documents

You can also prevent others from opening your Word documents unless they enter the correct password.

To password-protect a document:

1.   Choose File ➤ Save As to display the Save As dialog box, then click the Tools drop-down menu and choose General Options to display the Save dialog box.

2.   Enter a password in the Password To Open text box.

3.   Click the OK button. Word will display the Confirm Password dialog box.

4.   Enter the password again and click the OK button. If you get the password right, Word will set up the password and return you to the Save As dialog box.

SKILL
18

5. Click the Save button to save the document. The password protection will apply from when you close the document.

The next time the document is opened, the user will have to enter the password in the Password dialog box to open the file at all.

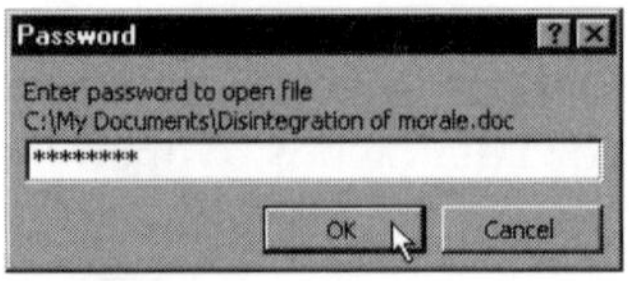

WARNING WARNING WARNING WARNING WARNING WARNING WARNING WARNING

If you forget a password to open, you will never be able to reopen the document without using special password-cracking software.

To remove a password from a document, open the document (by providing the password), choose Tools ➢ Options to display the Options dialog box, and click the Save tab. Delete the password to open and then save the file.

Online Collaboration

In this section, we'll look at the online collaboration features that Word provides. Word piggybacks on Microsoft NetMeeting to let you establish connections over a network or over the Internet (either via a dial-up connection or a permanent connection). Briefly, you can work together with other people on documents: Two or more people can view the same document at the same time, taking turns to edit it. They can also share a chat session and a whiteboard at the same time to help them communicate. If their computers have microphones and speakers (or headphones), they can speak to each other at the same time; if they have video cameras, they can videoconference as well.

NOTE NOTE NOTE NOTE NOTE NOTE NOTE NOTE NOTE NOTE NOTE NOTE NOTE NOTE NOTE

As you probably know from surfing the Web, audio and video need to transfer a large amount of information quickly to work effectively. If you're sharing documents over a modem connection, you'll usually do best to stick with the application, the chat window, and the whiteboard if you need it. Over a local area network, audio and video are much more feasible.

Getting Set Up for Online Collaboration

To use online collaboration, you need to have Microsoft NetMeeting set up and working on your computer. NetMeeting is a component of Internet Explorer that is automatically installed under most installations of Internet Explorer, and you'll usually find it by choosing Start ➢ Programs ➢ Internet Explorer ➢ Microsoft NetMeeting. If NetMeeting is not already set up for use on your computer, when you choose this command, it will walk you through its setup, in which you identify yourself and provide information on which connection server you will use with NetMeeting. (If you're having trouble getting NetMeeting running, consult your network administrator or computer guru.)

TIP TIP TIP TIP TIP TIP TIP TIP TIP TIP TIP TIP TIP TIP TIP TIP TIP TIP TIP TIP TIP TIP TIP

Depending on the type of Internet connection you use, you may need to start a connection manually before using the online collaboration features.

Once you have NetMeeting set up, you're ready to start online collaboration in Word. You can choose either to meet straightaway to work on a document or to schedule a meeting in the future. We'll look at each in turn.

Meeting Straightaway

To start online collaboration straightaway:

1. Choose Tools ➢ Online Collaboration ➢ Meet Now to display the Place A Call dialog box (see Figure 18.7) and the Online Meeting toolbar (see Figure 18.8).

2. Select the directory in the Directory drop-down list. At the top of the Directory list is the Most Recently Called List, which becomes useful after you've made a few calls to regular collaborators. After that is the Speed Dial list, to which you can add people you need to call frequently. (To add them, choose SpeedDial ➢ Add SpeedDial in NetMeeting.) After that is the list of available directory servers.

3. Select the person you want to call in the list box.

**SKILL
18**

FIGURE 18.7: To start online collaboration, choose your victim in the Place A Call dialog box and click the Call button.

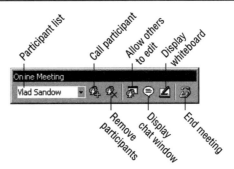

FIGURE 18.8: The Online Meeting toolbar provides commands for creating and conducting online meetings.

4. Click the Call button to place the call. You'll see a Waiting For A Response message box, while the person receiving the call will see the dialog box shown here and will hear a ringing sound (if their computer has audio). If and when the person accepts the call, NetMeeting will establish the

connection, and you can start sharing documents and collaborating, as described in the section after next.

Scheduling a Meeting

Choose Tools ➤ Online Collaboration ➤ Schedule Meeting to schedule a meeting via Outlook. Word will start Outlook and will create a meeting invitation (see Figure 18.9).

Set up the details for the meeting as usual, with the following exceptions:

- Make sure the This Is An Online Meeting Using check box is selected and that Microsoft NetMeeting is selected in the drop-down list.

- Choose the NetMeeting directory server in the Directory Server drop-down list.

- If you want NetMeeting to start automatically in time for the meeting (if NetMeeting isn't running already), select the Automatically Start NetMeeting With Reminder check box.

- Make sure that your address is shown in the Organizer's E-mail text box.

- Enter the name of the document on which to collaborate in the Office Document text box, either by typing it in directly or by clicking the Browse button and selecting the document from the Browse dialog box.

Click the Send button to send the meeting request. When the invitee accepts the request, the meeting will be on.

Conducting an Online Meeting

Once you've connected, you can share Word documents (and other Office documents), communicate via chat (and via audio and video, if you have those capabilities), and share a whiteboard.

**SKILL
▼ 18**

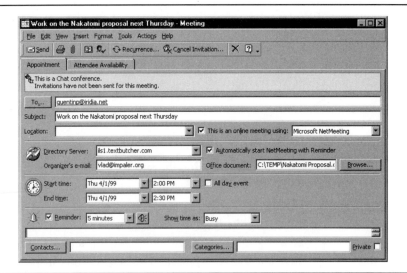

FIGURE 18.9:   Word uses Outlook to schedule an online meeting.

Sharing a Document

To share a document:

1. Open the document you want to share.

2. Click the Allow Others To Edit button on the Online Collaboration toolbar. The document will appear on your collaborator's screen, together with an annotation that it has been shared by you.

TIP TIP TIP TIP TIP TIP TIP TIP TIP TIP TIP TIP TIP TIP TIP TIP TIP TIP TIP TIP TIP TIP

The first time you do this, Word will display an Online Meeting dialog box warning you that there may be a security issue if you leave the document unattended. If this is OK, click the OK button. If you don't want to see this message again, select the Don't Show Me This Message Again check box before clicking the OK button.

3. To start working in the document, your collaborator double-clicks in the window.

TIP TIP TIP TIP TIP TIP TIP TIP TIP TIP TIP TIP TIP TIP TIP TIP TIP TIP TIP TIP TIP TIP TIP TIP

The first time you start collaborating, NetMeeting displays an explanatory message box. Click the OK button to dismiss it. If you don't want to see the message box again, select the Don't Show Me This Message Again check box before clicking the OK button.

4. You can now both work in the document, but only one at a time; as Net-Meeting terms it, one person "has control" of the document. To establish control, click in the document or press any key on your keyboard.

5. Both collaborators will see each change to the document.

6. To regain control of the document even when someone else is editing it, press the Esc button.

NOTE NOTE NOTE NOTE NOTE NOTE NOTE NOTE NOTE NOTE NOTE NOTE NOTE NOTE NOTE

The first time you press Esc, NetMeeting displays a message box asking if you want to stop collaborating. You can select the Don't Show Me This Message Again check box to avoid seeing the message box again.

7. To end the collaboration on this document, click the Stop Others From Editing button on the Online Collaboration toolbar.

Communicating via Chat

While you're working on a document, or in between sessions, you can chat with your collaborators. Click the Display Chat Window button on the Online Collaboration toolbar to display a Chat window (see Figure 18.10).

Enter the text you want to send in the Message box, then press Enter or click the button to the right of the Message box to send it.

By default, your messages go to all the current collaborators. To send to only one, choose them in the Send To drop-down list.

To save the chat session, choose File ➤ Save and specify the filename and location in the Save As dialog box.

To end the chat session, click the Close button on the Chat window or choose File ➤ Exit. If you haven't saved the chat session, Chat will prompt you to do so. Choose Yes or No, as appropriate.

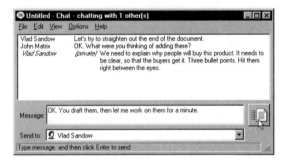

FIGURE 18.10: Use a Chat window to communicate quickly with your collaborators without changing the document.

Sharing a Whiteboard

You can also share a whiteboard while working on a document. The whiteboard in question is essentially a shared Paint window, in which you can draw, add text, and so on. The whiteboard can be useful for illustrating an idea or for brainstorming an approach to a problem—or for doodling, or insulting your colleagues remotely, or whatever you find conducive to furthering the project.

To display the whiteboard, click the Display Whiteboard button on the Online Collaboration toolbar. The whiteboard will appear (see Figure 18.11), and you can use it in much the same way as the familiar Paint application. Some points of difference to note are:

- Use the Insert New Page button to add a new page to the whiteboard.

- Use the First Page, Previous Page, Next Page, and Last Page buttons to navigate among the pages. Use the Page text box to move to a specific page by number.

- To quickly show your collaborators the contents of a window on your screen, choose Tools ➢ Select Window, then click the resulting mouse pointer on the window you want to show. NetMeeting will paste it into the whiteboard.

- To prevent your collaborators from making further changes, choose Tools ➢ Lock Contents.

- To save the contents of the whiteboard, choose File ➢ Save and specify the name and location for the file in the Save As dialog box.

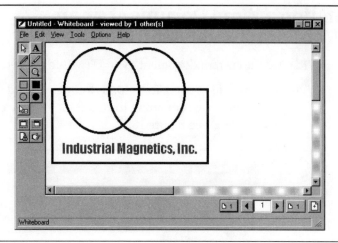

FIGURE 18.11: Use the Whiteboard to brainstorm or to illustrate a point.

To end your whiteboard collaboration, choose File ➢ Exit or click the Close button on the whiteboard window. If your whiteboard has unsaved changes, NetMeeting will prompt you to save them.

Ending Your Online Meeting

To end your online meeting, click the End Meeting button on the Online Collaboration toolbar and select the Yes button in the resulting message box.

Sending Word Documents via E-Mail

Word provides three quick ways of sending a document via e-mail right from a Word document window:

- You can send the document as an e-mail message formatted in HTML.

- You can send the document as an attachment to an Outlook e-mail message.

- You can route the document around your local network using a routing slip. In the following sections, we'll look at each technique in turn.

SKILL
▼ 18

Sending a Word Document as an HTML-Formatted E-Mail Message

To send the current document as an HTML-formatted e-mail message:

1. Choose File ➤ Send To ➤ Mail Recipient. Word will add a panel to the top of the message containing the Outlook toolbar, a To box, a Cc: box, and a Subject box (see Figure 18.12).

FIGURE 18.12: To send the current document as an e-mail message, choose File ➤ Send To ➤ Mail Recipient and fill in the To and Subject fields that Word adds.

2. Type the recipient's name in the To box and any cc:s in the Cc: box; or click the To button or Cc: button and choose the recipient and any cc:s in the Select Names dialog box.

3. To set options for the message, click the Options button and choose them in the Message Options dialog box.

4. Click the Send A Copy button to send a copy of the document as a message.

Sending a Word Document as an Attachment

To send the current document as an attachment:

1. Choose File ➤ Send To ➤ Mail Recipient (As Attachment). Word will start a new Outlook message and will insert the document as an attached file. If the Send To submenu contains a Mail Recipient (As Text) item rather than a Mail Recipient (As Attachment) item, you probably need to select the Mail As Attachment check box on the General tab of the Options dialog box (Tools ➤ Options). If this doesn't work, consult your system administrator.

2. Choose the recipient and any cc:s for the message as usual.

3. Enter the subject for the message in the Subject box and the text for the message in the main text box.

4. Click the OK button to send the message with the file attached to it.

Routing a Word Document with a Routing Slip

To route a document around your local network:

1. Start Word and open the document.

2. Choose File ➢ Send To ➢ Routing Recipient to display the Routing Slip dialog box (see Figure 18.13).

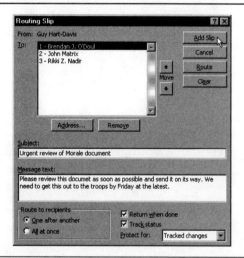

FIGURE 18.13: Choose recipients for the open document, specify a subject, enter message text, and decide how to route the message in the Routing Slip dialog box.

3. Choose the recipients. Click the Address button to display the Address Book dialog box.

4. Select the names of the recipients and click the To button to add them to the list.

   - You can Shift-click to select a range of recipients or Ctrl-click to select a group of recipients one by one.

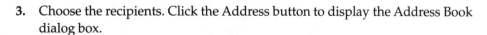

- If need be, choose another address book from the Show Names drop-down list.

5. Click the OK button when you've finished selecting your recipients. Word will return you to the Routing Slip dialog box.

6. Check the Subject line that Word has automatically entered from the title of the file set in File ➤ Properties. Change this line if necessary.

7. Enter any message text in the Message Text box.

8. Choose how messages should be routed to recipients: One After Another, or All At Once.

    - If you choose One After Another, Word will send out only one copy of the document, and it will be passed on from one recipient to the next (we'll look at how the recipients pass the document on in a moment). Each will see their predecessor's comments, so you may want to arrange the To list carefully. (Highlight a name and use the Move buttons to move up or down the To list.)

9. Choose from among the options in the lower-right corner of the Routing Slip dialog box:

    - Leave Return When Done selected if you want the document to come back to you after its routing experience.

    - Check the Track Status box if you want to have an e-mail message sent to you each time one of the recipients in a One After Another routing sends the message on to the next recipient.

    - Choose how to protect the document in the Protect For drop-down list: (none), Tracked Changes, Comments, or Forms.

10. To route the document now, click the Route button.

    - To save your recipient list, subject, and message before routing the document so you can return to it to do more work, choose Add Slip. You can then choose File ➤ Send To ➤ Next Routing Recipient to send the document on its way. Word will display the Send dialog box, in which you can choose whether to send the document with or without the routing slip. Click the OK button when you've made your choice.

Receiving a Mailed Document

Here's what to do when you receive a mailed document:

1. Open the document in Word. If you're using Microsoft Outlook as your e-mail package, you can do so by simply double-clicking the document icon in the message.

2. Review and revise the document as appropriate:

    *   If the document is protected for tracked changes, the change marks will appear automatically whenever you alter the document.

    *   If the document is protected for comments, you will only be able to insert comments.

3. When you're finished, choose File ➤ Send To ➤ Next Routing Recipient to send the document either on to the next recipient or back to the sender (depending on what the originator chose on the routing slip). Word will display the Send dialog box showing you where the document is headed and telling you that it contains a routing slip. Click the OK button to send the document on its way.

Are You Experienced?

Now you can. . .

SKILL
18

- ☑ add comments to a document
- ☑ view comments in sequence or by an individual commentator
- ☑ use change-tracking to mark changes in a document
- ☑ compare edits in different documents
- ☑ save different versions of a document in the same file
- ☑ designate a document as read-only
- ☑ protect a document for tracked changes
- ☑ protect a document with a password
- ☑ send a document as an e-mail message
- ☑ send a document as an e-mail attachment
- ☑ route a document around the office

APPENDIX A

Installing Word and Office

In this Appendix, we'll look at installing Word on your PC. Because it's most likely you'll be installing Word as part of Office, we'll concentrate on the Office installation. Installing the stand-alone version of Word works in a similar way, but the installation is simpler because there are fewer options.

System Requirements

You can install and run Word and Office on any computer capable of running Windows 95 or Windows 98, or Windows NT Workstation 3.51 or higher. That means, in practice, a 486 or higher Intel processor (Pentium, Celleron, Pentium Pro, Pentium II, Pentium III) or equivalent (AMD K6, Cyrix 6x86 or M-II, and so forth) with 8MB or more of RAM for Windows 95, 16MB RAM for Windows 98, 12MB or more of RAM for NT Workstation 3.51, or 16MB of RAM for NT Workstation 4. For decent performance, you'll want at least a mid-range Pentium with 32MB of RAM. For screaming performance, a Pentium III 450 with 256 MB of RAM will do quite nicely.

What Should You Install, and Where?

As you'll see in a moment, Word and Office include a number of optional components that you can install if you want. If you have plenty of hard disk space, my advice is to install Word with all the components—in fact, if you really have plenty of space, install Office with all its components. This way you'll be equipped to use all the features of Word (and Office). If you find that you don't need certain features and you want to reclaim the disk space they're hogging, you can remove selected components of Word (or Office); we'll look at this later in this appendix.

Apart from letting you choose to install certain pieces but not others, Word and Office have the capability to install components in three different ways:

Run From My Computer   Installs the component on your computer's hard drive or on a networked drive to which your computer is regularly connected. This is the "normal" installation procedure for most programs and offers the best performance. The disadvantage is that it also takes up the most disk space.

Run From CD   This option is available for some but not all components and tells Word or Office to run the component from the CD drive rather than installing it on your computer's hard drive. The disadvantages to using Run From CD are that you have to have the CD in the CD drive to run Word or Office successfully, and performance is marginal to middling depending on the access speed and data-transfer speed of your CD drive. The main advantage is that you save hard-disk space. If you install from a network drive rather than from a CD drive, the Installer will offer the choice Run From Network rather than Run From CD. The same restrictions apply: The network drive must be available whenever you run that component and there is a performance hit compared to running the component from a local hard drive.

Installed On First Use   Tells Word or Office not to install the component during the installation, but to install it the first time the user tries to use it. At that point, the Office application launches the Windows Installer and installs the component. This takes anywhere from a few seconds to a couple of minutes. As you might guess, the CD has to be in the CD drive at this point. Again, the main advantage is that you save hard-disk space—at least until you have installed all the features that you didn't initially install.

The Installer also provides a fourth choice: **Not Available**. This option lets whoever installs Word or Office on your computer decide that certain features will be unavailable to you. It is useful for network administrators and IS professionals who need to prevent users from doing certain things in Word or Office. The Not Available choice removes the feature in question from the menus, so that under normal circumstances the user will not be able to try to summon it. The Not Available choice is available only for non-critical features of Word and the other Office applications. For example, you cannot designate the Spell Checker as Not Available, whereas you can choose not to make themes available; and the Microsoft Binder mini-application is designated as Not Available by default.

Installing Word or Office

To install Word or Office:

1. Place the CD-ROM in your CD drive. If AutoPlay is enabled on your computer, the setup program will start automatically. Otherwise, choose Start ➤ Run to display the Run dialog box. Click the Browse button to display the Browse dialog box, then navigate to your CD drive and double-click the file SETUP.EXE to place its name and location in the Run dialog box. Click the OK button to start the Setup program running. You'll see the Microsoft Office Setup dialog box, followed swiftly by the Microsoft Office 2000 Customer Information panel of the Setup dialog box.

2. Enter your name, initials, organization information, and CD key. The CD key is the long and awkward alphanumeric code you'll find on the back of the CD jewel case or sleeve.

3. Click the Next button. The Setup program will display the Microsoft Office 2000 End-User License Agreement panel of the dialog box. Read the agreement, then select the I Accept The Terms In The License Agreement option button if you want to proceed.

4. Click the Next button. The Setup program will display the Microsoft Office Ready To Install panel of the dialog box.

5. If you have a previous installation of Office on your computer, or a competing product that Microsoft offers the Word or Office upgrade for, you'll have the choices of Upgrade Now or Customize. If you're not eligible for an upgrade, your choices will be Install Now or Customize. Select the button that describes your needs.

    • If you want to accept the default installation or upgrade, click the Install Now button or the Upgrade Now button, as appropriate. Then skip to the end of this numbered list, because the Setup program will make all the remaining decisions for you. Be warned that Setup will remove any previous versions of Office that it finds.

    • If you want to install Word or Office anywhere other than the default location the installation program selects (the \Program Files\Microsoft Office\ folder, usually on the C: drive), choose the Customize button. The Setup program will display the Microsoft Office 2000 Installation Location panel of the dialog box.

TIP TIP TIP TIP TIP TIP TIP TIP TIP TIP TIP TIP TIP TIP TIP TIP TIP TIP TIP TIP TIP TIP TIP TIP
Unless you want to accept Office's judgement of your needs, select the Customize button. This way, you can choose which features to install and which not to install, rather than letting Microsoft make bad decisions for you by proxy.

6. Unless you want to accept the default installation location, click the Browse button to display the Select A Destination Location dialog box. Select the folder in which to install Office (use the Create New button to create a new folder if necessary) and then click the OK button to return to the Microsoft Office 2000 Installation Location dialog box. Click the Next button to display the Detect Previous Versions panel of the dialog box (if you're upgrading) or the Updating Windows panel or Web Browsing Support panel of the dialog box.

7. If you have a previous version of Word or one or more of the other Office applications installed, the Setup program will notify you that it has found them and will remove them. To keep the previous version of an application, select Keep These Programs check box. (To keep an application, you need to be installing Office 2000 into a different folder than the previous version is in.) Click the Next button to display the Web Browsing Support panel or Updating Windows panel of the dialog box.

8. For most purposes, Microsoft Internet Explorer 5.0-Standard is the best bet. Your other choices are Microsoft Internet Explorer 5.0-Minimal, which installs less of the Internet Explorer, or either the Do Not Upgrade Microsoft Internet Explorer (if you have an earlier version of Internet Explorer installed) or Windows Web Browsing Component Only (if you do not).

9. Click the Next button to display the Selecting Features panel of the Installer. As you can see in Figure A.1, the Installer presents the features of Office as an expandable (and collapsible) tree.

   - Click the + sign next to an item to expand the list of items under it; click the resulting – sign next to an item to collapse the list again.

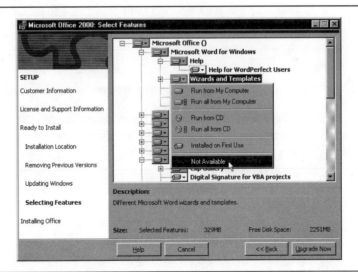

FIGURE A.1: On the Select Features panel of the Installer, choose which features to install on your computer, which to run from the CD network, and which to install the first time they are needed.

- For each item, select Not Available, Run From My Computer, Run From CD (or Run From Network if you're installing from a network drive), or Installed On First Use, as appropriate. The item will display the icon associated with the choice. You can also choose Run All From My Computer to install all the components onto your computer, Run All From CD to run all the components from the CD, or Run All From Network to run all the components from the network. The Run All choices affect the component whose list is currently displayed and any components it contains. To quickly choose the same installation for all components, select the appropriate Run All choice for the Microsoft Office item at the top of the tree.

- Many of the items have sub-items beneath them; be aware that choosing an option such as Run From My Computer or Run From CD for an item does not necessarily apply that same choice to all of its sub-items.

TIP TIP TIP TIP TIP TIP TIP TIP TIP TIP TIP TIP TIP TIP TIP TIP TIP TIP TIP TIP TIP TIP

As I mentioned earlier in the Appendix, you'll usually do best to install all the components of Word (or Office) that you might possibly ever need. Run All From My Computer will provide the best performance and the least hassle—assuming you have enough hard-disk space to install the components.

10. Click the Install Now button or Upgrade Now button to install the components you chose to the destination you specified. The Setup program will display a running meter showing the progress of the installation.

At the end of the installation, you'll see the Installer Information dialog box, which tells you that the installer needs to restart your computer. Click the Yes button to have the Installer go ahead and restart the computer by itself; click the No button if you want to restart the computer yourself (for example, if you need to finish up some work you've been doing in another application while the Installer has been running).

When the computer restarts, and you log yourself in, the Setup program will run automatically and will display the Finishing Microsoft Office 2000 Setup dialog box as it finishes setting up the applications for use with Windows.

Installing Features on First Use

As you saw in the previous section, you can designate Office components to be installed on first use—only when the user actually needs them.

When the user invokes such an item, Word (or the application in question) notifies the user that the component has not been installed yet and invites them to install it (see Figure A.2). If the user chooses to do so, the application launches the Windows Installer to install the item. Provided the CD is in the CD drive or the computer is attached to the network drive from which Office was installed, the process is slick and painless. However, for many people, a full installation (one setting every component to Run From My Computer) is preferable for its simplicity.

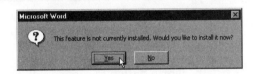

FIGURE A.2: When the user invokes a feature set to Installed On First Use, the application invites the user to install it.

Installing and Uninstalling Items

To change the components of Word or Office that you have installed on your computer:

1. Run the Setup application again. The Windows Installer will display the Microsoft Office 2000 Maintenance Mode panel of the Setup dialog box.

2. Click the Add Or Remove Features button. The Windows Installer will display the Microsoft Office Update Features panel of the dialog box.

3. Choose the items you want, as described in the previous section. Use the Not Available choice to remove an item.

4. Click the Update Now button to have the Installer add or remove the features you selected.

Repairing or Reinstalling Word or Office

If files in your installation of Word or Office get accidentally deleted or become corrupted, you may need to repair the installation or even reinstall Word or Office. To do so:

1. Run the Setup application again. The Windows Installer will display the Microsoft Office Maintenance Mode panel of the Setup dialog box.

2. Click the Repair Office button. The Installer will display the Reinstall/Repair Microsoft Office 2000 panel of the dialog box.

3. Choose the Reinstall Office 2000 option button to reinstall Office. Choose the Repair Errors in My Office 2000 Installation to have the Installer replace files that may have been damaged. If you choose this item, you can select the Restore My Shortcuts check box to have the Installer replace any shortcuts that have been deleted.

4. Click the Finish button to carry out the reinstallation or repair.

Index

Note to the Reader: Page numbers in **bold** indicate the principal discussion of a topic or the definition of a term. Page numbers in *italic* indicate illustrations.

ESSENTIAL SKILLS

for the
ESSENTIAL TOPICS

WINDOWS 98
NO EXPERIENCE REQUIRED

ISBN 0-7821-2128-4
$24.99; 544 pages

OFFICE 2000
NO EXPERIENCE REQUIRED

ISBN 0-7821-2293-0
$24.99; 704 pages

THE INTERNET
NO EXPERIENCE REQUIRED

ISBN: 0-7821-2385-6
$19.99; 496 pages

LOTUS NOTES 5
NO EXPERIENCE REQUIRED

ISBN: 0-7821-2184-5
$24.99; 560 pages

WORD 2000
NO EXPERIENCE REQUIRED

ISBN 0-7821-2400-3
$19.99; 452 pages

OUTLOOK 2000
NO EXPERIENCE REQUIRED

ISBN 0-7821-2483-6
$19.99; 400 pages

ACCESS 2000
NO EXPERIENCE REQUIRED

ISBN 0-7821-2485-2
$24.99; 608 pages

EXCEL 2000
NO EXPERIENCE REQUIRED

ISBN 0-7821-2374-0
$19.99; 432 pages

FRONTPAGE 2000
NO EXPERIENCE REQUIRED

ISBN 0-7821-2482-8
$19.99; 400 pages

SYBEX

www.sybex.com